I0804715

BEING AND ITS SURROUNDINGS

Being and Its Surroundings

Gianni Vattimo

Edited by Giuseppe Iannantuono, Alberto Martinengo, and Santiago Zabala

Translated by Corrado Federici

McGill-Queen's University Press
Montreal & Kingston • London • Chicago

© McGill-Queen's University Press 2021

Originally published in Italian as *Essere e dintorni* © 2018
La nave di Teseo Editore, Milano

ISBN 978-0-2280-0672-5 (cloth)
ISBN 978-0-2280-0784-5 (ePDF)
ISBN 978-0-2280-0785-2 (ePUB)

Legal deposit third quarter 2021
Bibliothèque nationale du Québec

Printed in Canada on acid-free paper that is 100% ancient forest free (100% post-consumer recycled), processed chlorine free

The translation of this work has been funded by SEPS
Segretariato Europeo per le Pubblicazioni Scientifiche

SEPS
SEGRETARIATO EUROPEO PER LE PUBBLICAZIONI SCIENTIFICHE

Via Val d'Aposa 7 – 40123 Bologna – Italy
seps@seps.it – www.seps.it

Funded by the Government of Canada | Financé par le gouvernement du Canada | Canada

Canada Council for the Arts | Conseil des arts du Canada

We acknowledge the support of the Canada Council for the Arts.
Nous remercions le Conseil des arts du Canada de son soutien.

Library and Archives Canada Cataloguing in Publication

Title: Being and its surroundings / Gianni Vattimo ; edited by Giuseppe Iannantuono, Alberto Martinengo, and Santiago Zabala ; translated by Corrado Federici.
Other titles: Essays. Selections English.
Names: Vattimo, Gianni, 1936– author. | Iannantuono, Giuseppe, editor. | Martinengo, Alberto, editor. | Zabala, Santiago, 1975– editor. | Federici, Corrado, 1946– translator.
Description: Translation of: Essere e dintorni. | Includes bibliographical references and index.
Identifiers: Canadiana (print) 20210183306 | Canadiana (ebook) 20210183403 | ISBN 9780228006725 (cloth) | ISBN 9780228007845 (ePDF) | ISBN 9780228007852 (ePUB)
Subjects: LCSH: Philosophy.
Classification: LCC B3654.V382 E5 2021 | DDC 190—dc23

This book was typeset in 10.5/13 Sabon.

Contents

BEING AND ITS SURROUNDINGS

Being and Its Surroundings: A Theological-Philosophical Breviary, Rather than a Treatise

The texts in this book are not "chapters" of a treatise. They are unified by a main idea that is not always obvious or predominant and yet, at least in terms of my intentions, one that is solidly coherent. They constitute variations on a single theme: the theme of a philosophy that is practised by testing perspectives and exploring occasions – we might call it a philosophy of occasions. The essays, whose novelty consists in the very fact that they are recent works – and, therefore, represent provisional endpoints – were composed on specific occasions: conferences, lectures, seminars, congresses, and invited talks. I challenge anyone to argue that philosophy is not done this way today; only a "blind metaphysician" would think so. This is especially true because the kind of philosophy I engage in – I can call it "my thought" (apologies, but this is what it amounts to) – is based more on a conversational, as opposed to a dense and argumentative, logic. We do not "arrive" anywhere, we always wander in the surroundings and remain within a given horizon. After all, this is our relationship with Being itself; we find ourselves at an opening, which is nothing like a systematic structure with a beginning, a middle, and an end. What can we expect, therefore, from such an inconclusive thinking, one that does not intend at all to reach a conclusion but that aims to remain open? You will recall what Richard Rorty said: philosophical systems are like novels. In this sense, at least, he was right: we can certainly arrive at the end of a novel but this reliance on a logic of literary experience is not another step toward another "real" inroad. If I were to recommend that someone read the present book; I would do so for the reason that the reading would make his or her life better, even if only to the extent that it provides material for "enjoyment." More realistically, I contend that it makes life better because it "changes" it; you may recall that, for Gadamer, this was what experiencing the truth of art meant: after – the reading, in this case – you are no longer the same, and, according to Hegel, this is not because you have lost something but because you have added or acquired something. Is this change that occurs in the reader sufficient to respond to the need expressed by the – always relevant – eleventh of Marx's "Theses on Feuerbach," i.e. the need for philosophy to change the world rather than to limit itself to interpreting it? In this sense too the book does not presume to be more than an essay or an attempt to address this issue.

The pages that follow are interconnected by the "diary of a crisis," which makes them something of an introduction. They are reflections and writings produced in the climate of crisis created by Heidegger's *Black Notebooks*, since both the reading itself (which is always partial and, above all, impatient) of the text and the critical response that it generated and continues to generate (see the congress *I "quaderni neri" di Heidegger 1931–1948*, Rome, 23–25 November 2015) seemed to "us Heideggerians" that the day of general reckoning had arrived. And, to put it succinctly, it seemed to signal the end of "Heideggerianism" in all of its iterations. To be read in this light is my contribution to the 2015 congress, as well as the essay on hermeneutics and globalization, and the one on religion and emancipation, which are intended to underscore the sense of global criticism of the widespread "machination" we in a society under complete *Verwaltung* (control) find ourselves thrown into, which only Heidegger allows us to see it in its most radical ontological sense.

I

What Need, What Metaphysics?

This essay essentially asks if there still exists the need (whether old or new) for metaphysics. In a world in which control over the lives of citizens and the politics of security are increasingly oppressive, it indeed seems that the truths of traditional metaphysics are precisely what we no longer need. If anything, we need a critical attitude that avoids the absolutes of the past and all their tragic social implications.

As Martin Heidegger taught us in *Sein und Zeit* (*Being and Time*) in order to answer a philosophical question, we should begin by considering who is asking the question. Hence the provocative meaning of the title I gave my essay, as it is not clear where the new or old need for metaphysics originates. What is immediately evident is that the demand for secure and unquestionable certainties, upon which our social and individual life is presumably grounded, comes from the *auctoritates* (authorities). As an Italian, I cannot avoid mentioning that the call for fixed "structures," that is, nonnegotiable values, is a constant theme of the pope's teachings in Rome. However, through a different authority and meaning, something similar occurs in the case of the claims coming from the laws of economics and, in general, from those values that politics ought to aspire to. We are repeatedly told, for example, that democracy must be imposed on the entire world through wars even if the traditions of other populations are violated. The so-called "international community," which is constantly evoked in these cases, presumes to have the obligation and the right to "take down dictators" (such as Gaddafi and Assad) or to intervene wherever they believe that fundamental human rights have been violated. Although this seems to be an indisputable argument, we must admit that it has been used too often to cover the imposed ideological interests of certain groups. The same goes for the so-called "economic laws," which are often presented as objective, that is, as "natural" as the law of gravity, as though they were the results of "scientific" studies conducted by allegedly neutral subjects.

Perhaps it is precisely in relation to science's claim of neutrality, and especially in relation to economics' claim of neutrality, that we can talk about a "new" need for metaphysics. In this case, the term "metaphysics" should primarily be understood as emphasizing the meta (beyond) in its Greek literal meaning: feeling the need for something "beyond" physics, i.e. beyond scientific certainty.

Once again, the need for metaphysics in this sense can have different origins. If we think of the Church and religious authorities, and their assumption that they are founded on "revealed" and transcendent certainties and/or on the "natural" constitution of the human being and the world (this latter justification applies equally for "human rights"), then the term "beyond" refers to a knowledge that is much more valid than the one provided by scientific reason, and it feels superior to that reason. We are facing here a sort of conflict between two claims of absoluteness: that of the Churches and that of the so-called "scientific community": an antinomy that recalls the clashes between the papacy and the empire in medieval Europe. It is interesting to recall this analogy because it allows us to see how, in modernity, the position occupied by the (secular) reason of the empire was actually taken up by science. Science can, therefore, be regarded as the incarnation of the recent "secular" power that used to confront the "traditional" power of the Church and the *auctoritates*, a power grounded in transcendence. This hypothesis is not extravagant if we think of the way modern science arose side by side with political and economic power: scientists today require very expensive and complicated machines and laboratories that force them to count upon private or public funding, which they must somehow justify – for instance, by directing their research towards a particular field rather than another (weapons instead of medicines, drugs for common diseases of wealthy populations rather than of poor ones).

In this way we are considering a variety of meanings of the need for metaphysics that always have a great deal to do with relations of power. The question that occurs immediately is, is there not also a more "genuine" need for metaphysics that does not have anything to do with metaphysics itself? The first example that comes to mind, probably because it is the most classic and emblematic, is that of the French Revolution, which we all regard as the historical source of modernity. The Enlightenment and the thought of the philosophes, which are the basis of the Declaration of the Rights of Man and of the Citizen that guided the revolution, also aimed to be a metaphysical position; the philosophes presupposed that they were affirming universally valid truths for every human intellect. But even these truths were affirmed for reasons of power or, better, for reasons of "lack of power." The French Revolution and the many revolutions that, throughout the centuries, claimed universal human rights against the demands of monarchs or dominant classes were not enacted out of the love for the universal truth of these principles. In some sense, the groups or entire populations that came to support these principles have "discovered" them because of their own condition of dispossession. As we all know, this is the classical theory (obviously still metaphysical) of Marx, who argued that the proletariat, which is dispossessed of all its goods, has the right to revolt because, not being blinded by property interests, knows and embodies the truth of human essence. What difference is there between the metaphysical need affirmed by the *auctoritates* that regret the loss of civil and religious morality generated by postmodern "nihilism" and by the spread multiculturalism, that is, by an excess of freedom, on one hand, and the need for the metaphysics of the French revolutionaries or of the rebellious American colonies of the British monarchy or of all those revolutionaries who feel legitimized by universal "human rights," on the other hand? The difference, as we can easily see, lies in the fact that some invoke metaphysics in order to preserve the status quo – traditional family values, the sacred power of religious hierarchies, the "objective" validity of official science, or simply the indisputability of the mainstream opinion of the major newspapers and television networks – while others appeal to metaphysics as a truth that critically opposes the status quo and wishes to change it. A statement by Richard Rorty, a great American thinker (and friend) who recently passed away, comes to mind here: "Take care of freedom and truth will take care of itself."[1]

In this sense, the "need for metaphysics" is not something new, since it has the same history that humanity has – or at least of *homo sapiens*, *homo politicus*, who lives in a society and must contend with the relations of power. Obviously, the mythical animal of the primitive woods, if it ever existed, in the age of *bellum omnium contra omnes* (the war of all against all) did not need metaphysics to legitimize its own power claims. If there actually is a new need for metaphysics today, it is because, in a paradoxical way, we are again in the condition that used to be that of mythical primitive man; this idea can be expressed using the aphorism with which Nietzsche begins the first volume of *Human, all too Human*: "Philosophical problems, in almost all their aspects, present themselves in the same interrogative formula now that they did two thousand years ago."[2] But, as Nietzsche indicates in so many other pages of his writings, this occurs because we live in a society characterized by an "Indian wildness" (the capitalist society that was already flourishing in his time), where – and this is the meaning of nihilism to which I refer when I talk about postmodernism – the highest values are devaluated and where a polytheism of values, as Max Weber called it, becomes widespread, one in which nothing functions anymore as a definitive point of reference and in which we must recognize that it is impossible to talk of universal truths from a divine point of view. Even the different meanings, as I have suggested, that the need for metaphysics can assume, express the "polytheism of values" that nihilism as event makes possible.

To sum up: the need for metaphysics characterizes the entire history of the civilized man – who requires legitimation in the community in which he lives both in relation to his fellow citizens and his own moral conscience (which has interiorized the community's expectations and towards which he feels responsible). Today this request is felt in a much more urgent manner because the same conditions of civilization within which we live have directed us towards the polytheism of values or to the so-called (as per Nietzsche) school of suspicion: we no longer trust the universal claims because in the modern world, which is more and more globalized, different cultures and "metaphysics" have emerged. This has also occurred because the universalism of European and Western philosophy has been (practically) put into doubt by the revolts of the so-called primitive populations that have come forward with their own demands. In this situation, the need for metaphysics is felt only in two forms that are not reducible one to the other: either the form of the *auctoritates*, which are interested in preserving the order that also guarantees their power (be it the authority of the popes or that of the scientific communities authorized and financed by governments or corporations), or the form of the dispossessed who wish to change the status quo and try to legitimize their own projects. The meta (beyond) of "metaphysics," therefore, has two meanings: either a truth beyond both the visible world and common knowledge, which is in the hands the *auctoritates*, or a projected "truth" which is not grounded in facts and "data" but rather in the power itself of the project of the marginalized.

I realize that describing such a situation may seem "dangerous" and not "philosophical" enough to be presented in a scientific/academic venue. Nevertheless, even this account may be related to positions of distinguished philosophers of the past: Nietzsche as the theorist of completed nihilism and Heidegger as the critic of metaphysics conceived as the pretension to mirror "reality" (the Aristotelian essences, Plato's ideas, etc.) to the point of constituting a norm for human behaviour. When he writes that God is dead, and has been killed by his own believers, Nietzsche simply means what we intend when we talk about postmodernity: it is the progressive integration of the world under the pressure of the political and technical powers of modernity that determines the end of the values of polytheism in which there is no possible universality. To the announcement that God is dead, Nietzsche also adds an invitation: now we want several gods to flourish. The (imperialistic, colonialist, technical-scientific, and also metaphysical) unity of modernity dies, and with it dies the possibility of peace – which so far was assured by the unity of dominion (empires, transnational powers, churches). Now, that unity can be achieved only by acknowledging the many metaphysics and by creating the conditions under which they can negotiate with one another. Universal truth is not the root and the beginning of everything; it can only be attained, ultimately, through free consensus.

It goes without saying that, in the choice between the metaphysics of the *auctoritates* and the metaphysics of the dispossessed, it is the latter that this essay recognizes and invites everyone to prefer as the good "metaphysics"; not only for a love of the dispossessed, not only for a certain sympathy for the (still metaphysical) thought of Marx, according to which those who are expropriated, and therefore have no ideological veils, can see the real truth. At the basis of my preferred choice, there is an idea of Being and philosophy that comes first and foremost from Heidegger, who in *Sein und Zeit* (at least as I see it) definitively challenged the idea that Being is a given and stable structure that thought should adequately mirror and respect as a norm. It is metaphysics conceived in this way that is, in the end, a metaphysics that excludes freedom, historicity, and the open structure of existence. Heidegger formulated this criticism in the 1920s, not only for theoretical reasons; together with the artistic and intellectual avant-gardes of the time, Heidegger acknowledged that objectivist metaphysics had ultimately produced the universal objectification of the human being and had paved the way for what the Frankfurt School later called the society of total *Verwaltung* of totalitarian rationalistic domination. For him and the existentialist thought of his time, it was a matter of opposing this with a new ontology, that is, a conception of Being that rendered freedom and future imaginable. As for Heidegger at the start of the last century, what appears to us as a new need for metaphysics is not inspired by theoretical reasons; we need metaphysics, a "beyond," because the *Verwaltung* has become even more total – with the difference that today it is also infinitively more visible. Almost no one still believes in "universal" metaphysical truths. With Nietzsche's death of God, the new gods, or simply a new God in which we can hope, can no longer be the God of classical metaphysics, the one that Pascal called "the God of the philosophers." Thus, the metaphysical need we feel can no longer be thought of as a need for a necessary given, a universal truth. The tragic damages produced by the universalistic claims of Western thought (religious persecutions, colonialism, and fundamentalism of every kind) are now there for everyone to see. This is also why traditional forces (churches, states, official science, ethics) invoke metaphysics; they are losing their credibility and wish to control consciences (now faithful to "many gods") once again through unifying and absolute principles. Against these traditional forces, there is a call for a metaphysics that, as Rorty's quotation above suggests, favours freedom over objective "truth," which always needs an absolute power for validation. Even the action required to make possible a society where different metaphysics may freely confront each other, negotiating accords that force none of them to annul itself in the name of an absolute truth, demands a "metaphysical" commitment. May I suggest that a similar commitment has more to do with a (not exclusively Christian) religious precept of charity, rather than with a search for ultimate principles that guarantee peace by forcing all of us to recognize them as the truth?

2

Philosophy and Contradiction

Philosophy never tolerated contradictions. One may say that it was born exactly in order to eliminate them by the recourse to the ultramundane order of Plato's ideas or to the principle of noncontradiction in Aristotle's logic and metaphysics, and so on. One may suggest that even the reversal expressed by Marx's eleventh thesis on Feuerbach is basically directed against this traditional conciliatory essence of philosophy. That is another reason for the "definitive" supremacy of Hegel and, of course, the conservative appearance of his theory. When he opposed a non-Aristotelian, or epic, theatre to the one described and prescribed by Aristotle's *Poetics*, Bertolt Brecht was clearly revindicating the resistance of contradictions to the pretended force of the mediating reason.

Given these presuppositions, it would be strongly self-contradictory (!) to propose the idea of insuperable contradictions for theoretical reasons. A theory, we assume in the ordinary language of philosophy, has to be noncontradictory, so it belongs to its very essence to be an overcoming of contradictions. The general character of philosophy since its birth in Greece is a sort of "pedagogical" vocation to offer a way of salvation to human beings. Very often this offer is presented in terms of the myth of the Platonic Republic, where the one who succeeds in seeing the true things outside the cavern calls on his fellow men to come and share his "vision," with the constant temptation to oblige them for the sake of their happiness to follow him outside. My impression is that also the purpose of promoting a philosophical reflection upon contradiction follows this traditional path: there would be no point in discussing contradictions if it were not in order to create the conditions for a conciliation. (Remember

Spinoza: *Humana actiones non ridere, non lugere, neque fiere eque ridere sed intelligere.*) Of course, we can see from the reference to Spinoza, at the basis of the conciliation there is the view of the "objective" truth, independent from personal interests, which means that it imposes the respect of the given objective truth as the source of moral law.

If one does not want to follow the traditional path of the metaphysical conciliation of contradictions, how would he or she explain the interest in a philosophical reflection on them? Is the pedagogical-metaphysical attitude the sole possible philosophy? What I want to do in these remarks is to propose a reflection on contradictions that does not assume that conciliation is the task of philosophy, but refusing this assumption implies several radical changes in the very notion of philosophy one tries to practise. First of all, the decision to propose a reflection on a topic like contradictions – as on any other topic chosen for a philosophical discussion – cannot be motivated by theoretical reasons. This would require that theory feels by itself the need to discuss – confirm, correct, renew, etc. – its idea of contradiction. As if it were "contradictory" not to do that; as if philosophy needed to complete itself by clarifying this theme. I know that the editors of this book would not accept such a simplification of their decision. Very likely – and this is important especially from a "Hegelian" point of view – they would appeal to a sort of "actuality" of the theme in our present situation. It is exactly this implicit, presupposed actuality of the theme that I would like to challenge, in order to be able to better answer the questions proposed. Are we invited to discuss contradictions because the current situation (a very general term, of course and analogous to the "general condition of the world," which Hegel evokes in a point of his *Aesthetics*) demands from philosophy a special cooperation in order to reduce conflicts, contradictions, etc.? This, I assume, would be more or less the explanation of the theme we are invited to discuss – an explanation that does not seem to need a strong analysis and attention; we all know that the problem of peace, on both the international and domestic level, is urgent. The fact is that the emphasis on the problem of conciliation has always been the favourite topic of philosophy, very often explicitly and many times at least implicitly. I do not remember a philosophy advocating for conflict or for insuperable contradictions. Even Karl Marx's eleventh thesis on Feuerbach as formulated within a perspective dominated by an eschatological hope in the final victory of the general class, the proletariat, entitled to make the revolution because of its capacity to catch the truth beyond the veil of ideology, i.e. without an interest disturbing the objective knowledge of the real meaning of history.

What I mean is that when we accept easily, and as obvious, that philosophy responds to the need for peace and reconciliation, we probably are already prepared for this by the fact that philosophy (love for Sophia, wisdom) has always thought of itself as a factor of pacification. My paper asks, very simply, if it is so obvious that today we need pacification, and therefore the task of philosophy has to be that of reflecting upon contradictions in order to overcome them in a realm of nondistorted truth (Fukuyama's idea of the end of history: philosophy triumphs because and insofar as there are no conflicts). You may recognize at the root of this question the basic opposition between hermeneutics and the epistemological belief in the objectivity of scientific truth. In my view (not only mine but also the view of classical authors of hermeneutics, starting with Heidegger) hermeneutics is not the discipline that studies the method of deciphering what appears *prima facie* nonunderstandable, discovering its hidden meaning. Hermeneutics is basically the philosophy of the irreducible otherness of the other, which does not mean necessarily that it is a philosophy of conflict, but surely it is not a theory of conciliation on the basis of the shared objectivity of (scientific) truth. Paradoxically, Marx's eleventh thesis on Feuerbach is much closer to hermeneutics than to scientific objectivism. And more than that: Marxism cannot believe that changing the world involves overcoming interpretation in favour of objectivism if it does not want to turn into dogmatic Stalinism.

Let me try to show that today's world does not need more conciliation (also) through philosophy, or more catharsis through Aristotelian theatre, but the opposite. Take the rather generally acknowledged crisis of democracy: i.e. the loss of credibility of the representative institutions – something of the kind of problem that was already well known to Winston Churchill – today intensified and magnified by the increasing possibility of social control. In many of our "democracies" people do not believe any longer in their capacity to influence by their vote the policies of government. Participation in elections diminishes constantly; public discussion is more and more limited to gossip or to complaints against politicians, etc. Would anybody describe this situation as a multiplication of conflicts? Or is what we see simply a condition of progressive "neutralization" – to take the term from Carl Schmitt – or, better, of "lack of emergency" to use the expression of Heidegger? More recently, one speaks of *la pensée unique* which, translated into political terms, means roughly the "Washington consensus." The *pensée unique* is a strong enemy of hermeneutics whose relativism it reproaches. The more or less new "realism" of philosophers like John Searle (prized by George W. Bush some years ago) and that sort of mésalliance of the residues of phenomenology with the postanalytic empiricists seems to be substituting for the epistemological metaphysics of the past decades is, as a matter of fact (and sometimes independently from the intentions of the authors), the intellectual support of the neoliberalistic world, still centred in the imperial (military and economic) power of the United States and multinational capitalism. The Searle–Bush ideology wants to purify philosophy from hermeneutic relativism, which appears as a threat to the official, scientific truth; its connections to the social and economic power do not need to be proved, if one thinks of the public (military) and private money involved in the modern scientific enterprise.

I do not want to expand here on the analysis of the current condition of "lack of emergency." In many senses, I could also refer to Fukuyama's famous thesis on the end of history, though I do not share its ideological apologetic implications: democracy and liberal capitalism have triumphed; therefore, no more history, i.e. no more conflict, neither of interpretations nor of weapons (Paul Ricoeur). Apparently, and not only apparently, nothing can happen. The sole emergencies seem to be those of "international terrorism" which has not the character of an enemy (in the Schmittian sense) but only of a criminal: NATO and even the United Nations are more and more involved in operations of international policing; so-called public opinion seems to ask mainly for security, no matter how much it costs in terms of freedom, privacy, the meaning of everyone's lives. Even the general humanitarian respect for "life," which means, by the way, mere biological survival, no matter in which condition (see what happens with euthanasia, prohibited even in the case of pure vegetative state and the free decision of the individual, etc.), seems to belong to this climate of acceptance of low-profile existence, very probably determined by the fear diffused by the media (fear of terrorists, fear of unemployment, fear of immigrants ...). In a word, the triumph, in practice and in theory, of the status quo.

As I said, neither a reflection on contradiction(s) nor a theory advocating conflict corresponds to a theoretical need internal to philosophy. But even if one wants to explain theoretically the choice made by the editors of this book, one has to refer to "the general condition of the world," whatever that means. To admit this elementary observation means already – be cautious – to accept a hermeneutical approach instead of the scientific objectivistic. But this does not mean admitting a realistic attitude, i.e. the idea that if you claim to correspond to a historical need of the "world" you have to "know" that need correctly, therefore its truth, etc. What we call facts is what *we* call facts: a matter of experience more in a Hegelian sense than in empiricist terms.

Do we have good rational, as well as philosophically motivated (obviously not "proved") reasons to advocate for more conflict instead of a more intense pacification? The situation of "lack of emergency," or neutralization, I described above may be considered either as a desirable "end of history" or as the extreme *Gefahr*, or danger, of the forgetting of Being in favour of beings – the existent order taken as the sole possible "reality." As Walter Benjamin wrote in his "Theses on the Philosophy of History," there may well be people who prefer the existent order instead of any change: they are the "victors" in the game of history, for whom the actual world is the best possible one. Why should philosophy stay on the side of the others, the vanquished, and therefore advocate conflict in order to produce change? In other words, is philosophy intrinsically conservative or necessarily revolutionary? Again, from the point of view I am trying to propose, there cannot be any "logical" proof for one or the other alternative. One can only offer "historical" (even psychological) experiences, which are consciously related to a specific historical condition, the lack of emergency, and do not claim to hold forever. Of course, the supporters of a metaphysical and logical order may be in favour of change – if the world is "out of joint" it deserves to be put back in joint (*Hamlet*, Act 1, scene 5) – but always in the name of a given metaphysical structure, which is bound to eliminate conflicts (all wars are presented as the last one, in view of peace …) and reestablish *to ti en einai* or *quod quid erat esse* (the what it was to be), with the already cited risk of Stalinism: the revolution is over; now let us go to work.

I have the justifiable impression that the philosophers engaged in a project on contradictions feel radically unsatisfied with a theory that does not propose, at least in the end, a conciliated ideal of rational life based in the acceptance of a metaphysical (stable, objective, etc.) truth. What can philosophy imagine instead of that? Even revolution – one thinks of Marx – can be inspired only by the ideal of a final elimination of alienation, albeit remote and hard to reach. Hermeneutics accepts the risk of proposing a sort of open dialectics (I do not know whether or not we are facing once more the Freudian duality of Eros and Thanatos), which, considering itself nothing but a historically situated response to the call of the current situation (in theory and in political practice), does not have to offer a "complete" system, not even in terms of an ideal of "good life"; the sole good life (I think this is a suggested by Alasdair McIntyre) is the one in which everybody is in the condition of deciding what good life means to her or him.

Now, on the basis of what I argued for to this point, insuperable contradictions are those that escape logical conciliation, i.e. the claim by an "objective truth" to decide who is right and who is wrong. The simple introduction of interpretation into the picture "corrupts" everything. There is no "metalanguage" capable of guaranteeing a radical translation; therefore one has to introduce the "principle of charity," and there is no absolute neutral point of view independent of interests, and therefore one has to introduce the principle of negotiation or, when this does not work, conflict. Even in order to regulate conflicts by a constitution one very often has to struggle, more or less violently, against the existing (dis)order. Insuperable contradictions may be described in the terms used by Richard Rorty in his (insuperable) book *Philosophy and the Mirror of Nature*: hermeneutics vs. epistemology. Should we really believe that a world in which every contradiction is reducible to an epistemological "puzzle" (Thomas Kuhn) would be better than ours? Should philosophy cooperate to that "end" (which would have the double sense of the term)?

I do not want to call hermeneutics an ontology of revolution, but it is in fact something of this kind. The reduction of every contradiction to an epistemological puzzle involves a Parmenidian ontology of eternal structures – even only in terms of stable laws of becoming, where the only possible changes concern the more or less complete knowledge of truth or the more or less complete development of a given plan. Metaphysics, in the sense criticized by Heidegger from the very beginning of his philosophical career of *Being and Time*, involves the denial of all possible events, all interpretation not purely useful for the correspondence *intellectus* and *res*, and finally the erasure of historicity and freedom. I know very well that all this seems to be a way of blaming too many errors on metaphysics, which on the contrary seems to have made an important contribution to many revolutions, starting with the French Enlightenment of the eighteenth century. If you cannot appeal to truth (natural law, natural human rights, etc.) how can you revolt against the tyrant? Well objected, but let us not forget the dictum of the Gospel: truth will set you free. Relativists and pragmatists like Rorty (and myself, allow me to say) willingly agree with these sacred words. Only they take it very seriously: truth is (only) what sets you free. In order to accomplish this task, truth has to be historically effective. The idea of natural rights connected to the very nature of human beings has often been a useful device for revolutions (e.g. in order to combat the opposite belief in the divine right of the monarch), but in other situations it can become a way of reinforcing oppression: see what happens in Catholic morals where surely absurd authoritarian imperatives (the ban on condoms in a time of AIDS) are always justified in the name of the presumed natural law.

To speak, as I dare to do, of an ontology of revolution in a time in which the dominant new realism of the "Searle–Bush school of thought" tends to reduce ontology to the description of what objects "are," proposing as phenomenology and ontology the everyday meaning of the words with a further apologetic addition, a "supplement d'âme" (in this case, a supplement of presupposed reality), involves many risks. Not only of being considered a potential terrorist (relativism in social disorder) but also the risk of being expelled from the profession of philosopher. I can try to justify myself by recalling that the idea of Being as event (*Ereignis*) proposed by Heidegger – which implies the consequences I tried to describe very briefly in this paper – is still one of the most reasonable alternatives philosophy has been able to imagine to metaphysical submission of theory and practice to the often violent authority of "what there is." Insuperable contradiction is, in many senses, the very place where Being happens (*ereignet sich*, that is, *es*, *das Sein*, *gibt*) and truth sets itself to work. The strong connection among truth, the event of Being, and conflict is a constant of Heidegger's later thinking, which a pacified and irenic version of hermeneutics may have left someone aside in its effort to "urbanize." Let the philosophical meditation on contradiction, albeit inspired by the same purpose of promoting conciliation, serve (contradictorily) to remind us of the ontological necessity of conflict.

3

Wittgenstein and Historicity

I am not a Wittgenstein specialist, merely an interested reader with a different intellectual background. I do, however, deal with his work not just as a curiosity or a tour *in partibus infidelium* (in the lands of the unbeliever). I think that it is important to reflect on the topic of Wittgenstein and historicity because it encapsulates many of the questions that always occur to me whenever I think of Wittgenstein and, I must confess, of analytical philosophy. As I prepared to work on this presentation, I had to take into account, as anyone would I believe, the fact that the topic almost "does not exist" in the secondary literature (only Glock's essay, *A Wittgenstein Dictionary*) and perhaps not even in Wittgenstein's work itself. This fact, this "absence," however relative or absolute, justifies interest in the topic.

My "hermeneutic" background (Heidegger, Nietzsche, Gadamer), however, makes me less incompatible at least with the second Wittgenstein: from the 1970s, Karl-Otto Apel (anticipating many of the themes that were later popularized by Habermas) pointed out the affinity between Heidegger's ontological approach to language and Wittgenstein's language games. It appears to me that today Heidegger's claim that "language is the house of being" has merit (even with its rather divergent meanings, but to what extent?). That the "world is the totality of facts and not of things" (Wittgenstein, *Tractatus* 1.1) can be stated in Heideggerian language as follows: the thing exists as an object only in language (or in logical space, Wittgenstein would say); things come to be only in that they come to be in language (Heidegger) or as parts of a state of affairs (*Sachverhalt*; Wittgenstein). "Just as we cannot think of spatial objects at all apart from space, or temporal objects apart from time, so we cannot think of any object apart from the possibility of its connection with other things" (Wittgenstein, *Tractatus* 2.0121), outside of logical space.[1] More so than in *Being and Time* (1927), where he certainly posits the premises, Heidegger asserts that language is the house of Being in the so-called second phase of his thought, which opens with the essay *The Origin of the Work of Art* (1936) and, prior to that, sadly, with his acceptance of the Nazi rectorate of the University of Freiburg (*Die Selbsthebautung der deutschen Universität*, 1933). The change from *Being and Time* to *Der Ursprung de Kuntswerkes* (*The Origin of the Work of Art*) is not by chance marked by the decision to join the Nazi Party; the *Kehre* or "turn," which, in his *Letter on Humanism* (1946), Heidegger attributes to the "failure of language" that impeded the writing of *Being and Time*, is also above all a "historic" turning point, one that is biographically dense and not at all reducible to a clarification (or obfuscation) of concepts. I emphasize this point because, even for someone who began to study Heidegger more than fifty years ago (which is my case), the connection has become increasingly clear due to the flowering of historical-biographic studies that, mostly with the intent of denying the philosophical value of Heidegger's thought, have forced us to see the historical connection and relations that were previously understated. Here, without going into details, I allude to the fact that, though Heidegger's decision to enrol in the Nazi Party in 1933 is well known, it is only since Victor Farias's study (*Heidegger and Nazism*) and, more recently, Emmanuel Faye's (*Heidegger, The Introduction of Nazism into Philosophy*) that the issue has been explored in all its aspects. What happens with the *Kehre* is well represented by some changes in terminology that we find in the Heideggerian texts of the period. For the first time in *The Origin of the Work of Art*, the term "world" is used in the plural form; it no longer signifies only existence as *in der Welt Sein* or "being in the world." Rather, the author speaks of a world – a determined historical construct characterized by a specific way of accessing truth. Also regarding terminology, after the *Kehre* the emphasis that *Being and Time* placed on authenticity (*Eigentlichkeit*) disappears, and the root *-eigen* remains central to the notion of *Ereignis* or "event." I would like to provide a brief overview of this transformation. The Heidegger of *Being and Time* is interested in expressing the being-there of man in terms of his authenticity and, in doing so, he discovers that the existent is above all, and for the most part, lost in inauthenticity, which is identified with the "metaphysical" forgetting of Being. According to Heidegger, as we know, the metaphysics we inherited from the Greeks identifies Being with the objective facticity of objects, their rational measurability and predictability, but, as such, it also reduces the being of man to objectivity, thereby losing what is particular to him. Thinking of himself as an object among other objects, the being is lost in inauthenticity. To get out of this state, Heidegger says in a rather "auratic" fashion that the being must (or should, but never ethical insistence!) explicitly accept the possibility of his own (absolutely his own, *eigen*) mortality. We are aware of the amount of existentialist literature that has been produced on this theme and how much the critical thinkers of industrialized society (Marcuse had been a student of Heidegger's, for example) have drawn from this aspect of his work. Now, why does the *Kehre* also signal the disappearance of the rhetoric of inauthenticity in Heidegger? The fact is that the decision to join the Nazi Party in 1933 is also explained by a less abstract and literary notion of inauthenticity. As well, the firm expectation of one's own death about which he speaks in *Being and Time*, when we wish to read it in understandable terms, is not so much a predisposition for heroic martyrdom as the acceptance of one's finite historicity, essentially of one's belonging to a historical world. Heidegger the Nazi rector makes this choice because he thinks – it is pointless to underline how erroneously – that loyalty to the world of European civilization, which is threatened by the two industrialist giants, Stalin's USSR and capitalist America, compels him to support Hitler. The being that exists in the historical language of a community is precisely the *Ereignis* to which we must conform in order not to lose ourselves in inauthenticity, forgetting Being. What is more, we must remember here that the inspiration for *Being and Time* (1927), expressed in the quote from the first page of Plato's *Sophist* (244a), namely, the need to recollect Being that has been forgotten for some time, was not only an attempt to complete Husserl's phenomenology with a foundational ontology, but, on a deeper level, his project was to question the metaphysical concept of being-objectivity that made it impossible to think of existence as Being and that, as the philosophical, theological, and artistic avant-gardes of the time (see Ernst Bloch, *The Spirit of Utopia*) saw clearly, was the ideology of the emerging mass civilization, of social rationalization (the total *Verwaltung* of Horkheimer and Adorno). I mean to say that *Being and Time* already responded to a "historical" question and not to an abstract and universal theoretical need as though philosophy were being called upon to answer eternal questions related to the very essence of man, etc. As regards the error committed by Heidegger in considering Hitler as a possible defender of the true European tradition (on which, see also Bouveresse in D. Sparti, *Wittgenstein politico*, 52), he can be criticized also and especially from the internal point of view, that is, in relation to his theoretical intentions: i.e. believing in the possibility of reconstituting a nonmetaphysical society comparable to that of classical Greece, as many preromantic German poets and the Nietzsche of *The Birth of Tragedy* believed, Heidegger betrays the idea of ontological difference. We cannot imagine reconstituting an authentically nonmetaphysical society; that would mean identifying Being with the object at hand.

We can grasp the complexity of the analogy with the Wittgenstein of the language games and "forms of life." A first hypothesis in such an analogy, a very general and perhaps too far-fetched one, is that suggested by the same event, namely, the *Kehre*. Can we imagine that, between the Wittgenstein of the *Tractatus* and the Wittgenstein of the forms of life, there occurs a *Kehre* similar to the one that separates the two periods of Heidegger's thought? Here we need to consider detailed biographical information. What happens to Wittgenstein after the *Tractatus*? What "explains" the shift to *Philosophical Investigations* and the language games? It is a shift that occurs during a not insignificant period in European history. Is it possible that it is all a problem of relations with Rudolf Carnap, the Vienna Circle, the logical syntax of language, etc.?

All the introductions to the *Philosophical Investigations*, and prior to that to the *Blue Book* and the *Brown Book*, seem "internal" to philosophical questions. If there exists a "historical" explanation for Wittgenstein's *Kehre*, assuming we can even speak of such a thing, it is to be sought in the *Verwirrung* (confusion) that Wittgenstein experienced immediately after the First World War, beginning in 1919. The time of despair that Ray Monk describes in rich detail dates from this year and the one following. It seems easy to understand what disturbs Wittgenstein so much in that period; after all, he was a soldier for several years, and a prisoner, in a war that literally destroyed Europe and rattled the European social elite. Wittgenstein's interest in Oswald Spengler and his *The Decline of the West* can also be attributed to theoretical reasons (Goethe, the idea of form applied to history, etc.), but it certainly, and above all, has something to do with the perturbed European consciousness that came to terms with the fact that it had failed in its civilizing mission, to which it felt it had been dedicated for centuries. The spirit of the European avant-garde, which, as I mentioned, can be felt in Heidegger's antimetaphysical project, was also an attempt to free itself from its ties to a culture that had experienced its own failure by sowing corpses and mutilated bodies throughout Europe (see Hermann Broch's novel *The Sleepwalkers*, 1932). If, however, the "decline of the West" can serve as a framework for the crisis endured by Wittgenstein and many intellectuals of his time, it remains truly difficult to cite only this generalized turmoil as the explanation for the decision, which he makes precisely in 1919, to divest himself of all his wealth by transferring his entire estate to his sisters and other members of his family. Nor is it sufficient to consider the fact that his family's wealth came from profits made in the steel industry – therefore, a link with the war that could evoke a legitimate feeling of disgust. I remind the reader here that I am only trying to explain, with some "historical" justification, what I refer to as Wittgenstein's *Kehre* and that, at least from the standpoint of its theoretical content, appears to me as profoundly similar to that of Heidegger. So, even from a careful reading of memoirs and documents, such as Monk's monumental biography *Wittgenstein: The Duty of the Genius* (1920), the reasons for the crisis experienced by Wittgenstein in 1919 and 1920 appear to be basically attributed to the difficulties the author faced in getting the *Tractatus* published, with the subsequent sense of failure that accompanied rejections from publishers. This is ironic because, among other things, the Austrian publishers he contacted expected subvention fees that Wittgenstein could not afford on his salary as an elementary school teacher, after having given away his family wealth. It is also true that he did not want to pay the subvention fees (there are eloquent notes to this effect, even though he could have remembered that one of the authors he read and admired, Nietzsche, always paid for the publication of his works himself). It is, nonetheless, impossible to justify the frequent allusions to the temptation to commit suicide only because of his lack of success in finding a publisher. From this arises the legitimate question of the happiness or unhappiness in his private life. The theory advanced by William W. Bartley in *Wittgenstein* (1973), that Wittgenstein's unhappiness and especially the great sense of guilt over his homosexuality, which at the time was not explicitly acknowledged – and which was acted out, it would appear, occasionally and in Vienna's

Prater public park – does not appear to be absurd even though it is not supported by evidence other than the subsequent sentimental biography of Wittgenstein, which clearly explores the homosexual aspect and which has him publicly linked, for some, with David Pinsent, Francis Skinner, etc. (see Monk).

In the early 1920s, then, Wittgenstein experiences a spiritual crisis that would resolve itself only partly with the publication of the *Tractatus*, which contained an Introduction by Bertrand Russell. But with that Introduction, the publication of the book becomes another decisive aspect of the *Kehre*. Wittgenstein comes to realize that his increasingly numerous readers and commentators misunderstood his intentions – starting with Russell himself, who expresses scepticism with respect to the mystical quality of the work. Therefore – as I believe the most acute Wittgenstein critics contend – the change from the *Tractatus* to the language games is primarily brought about by the need to correct a misunderstanding of the theory he intended to present in his first work.

No references to "external" history, then, i.e., to the "general condition of the world," as Hegel would say in the *Aesthetics*? In 1933, when Heidegger was making the dramatic decision to accept the rectorate at Freiburg, Wittgenstein was planning a trip to Russia together with his friend Skinner. This was not out of sympathy for the communist regime but for the purpose of experiencing manual labour in the spirit of a new–old Russia greatly idealized by Tolstoy. I am not reproaching Wittgenstein for not having been more earnestly leftist, as he essentially considered himself, even with a good deal of nostalgia for the old Austria. The point is that the lack of reference to the history of the period precisely at a time like the twenties, when people were preparing for a second world war, strikes me as a sort of original sin that, in my view, reverberates through the entire subsequent history of analytic philosophy. Obviously, this is not Wittgenstein's fault or a state of affairs for which he is responsible. It is that such an absence perhaps reflects a more remote feature of Anglo-Saxon philosophy – even though it is not so univocal and deeply ingrained; it suffices to think of the political and critical engagement of John Locke or Stuart Mill. But, above all, is it not the case that another consequence of this closure to the history of the world is the conservative aspect of analytical philosophy, especially where the untranscendability of the language games seems to cross over into conformism? As regards my search for history in

Wittgenstein – the history of Wittgenstein and the meaning of history for his theory – what comes to mind is what Dilthey said about the Kantian subject: in his veins runs no real blood. As I speculated a short while ago, I do not even know if the separation of philosophy from social criticism and political discourse is a trait that is deeply rooted in the Anglo-Saxon tradition – as soon as I say this, counterexamples come to mind. Bertrand Russell and his political engagement seem to stand as a serious objection to such a claim, but Russell too always separated his own work as a philosopher of logic and mathematics from his political views. Certainly, this professional distancing of philosophers from politics applies to post-World War II Anglo-American thought, and this can be generally accounted for by the "scientific" or clearly scientistic approach of analytical philosophy, which is perhaps Wittgenstein's approach leading up to the *Tractatus*: philosophy seen as scientific, specialized knowledge that only indirectly relates to the social and political realm, to "historical" events – with the "blood" that even a "professor" like Dilthey felt was missing in the veins of the Kantian subject.

I now return to the analogy between Heidegger's *Kehre* and what increasingly appears to be Wittgenstein's. Whatever the factors may be (more private and "internal" to the development of his theory in the case of Wittgenstein and decidedly more "epochal" in the case of Heidegger), in both instances, what we find to be the consequence of the turn are the forms of life as (perhaps) the untranscendable horizon of therapeutic reflection of philosophy. In both cases, this – real or apparent – untranscendability depends on the antifoundationalism that the two thinkers have in common. Language is the house of Being; we are always "thrown" into a language that is historically determined: Being is not accessible (to us) directly (it would not be Being but rather the presence of an existent object). For Wittgenstein, it is possible for us to experience Being, or the world, only within forms of life that have their own language, their own *Sprachspiel* with its rules. If something does not "work," philosophy helps us to resolve the "mental cramp" by clarifying the rules of the game. What we can and must do in order to "feel better" (or to be happy or less unhappy) is to adapt to the game that we are playing (as we have always been playing). "Is this all?" – we might ask ourselves. The dissatisfaction one might feel in the face of such a result probably does not take into consideration the fact that, for Wittgenstein himself, the theory of language games was already a form of emancipation, a critical revolt against the tendentious dogmatism of the *Tractatus*. Ultimately, it does not account for the fact that this theory helps Wittgenstein to free himself from the neopositivism that had come to dominate his work. In brief, the *Tractatus* thinks it can cure the ills of language – and the ensuing philosophical unhappiness – by leading discourses back to an ideal form of validity (protocol propositions, etc.). The *Investigations* retain this objective except that the "normal" form of language that saves us from quandaries is not the one described "definitively" in the *Tractatus*: "normal" discourses are those that "function" in the contexts in which they are formulated. The question of historicity emerges here in the form of two questions: a) How did Wittgenstein arrive at this theoretical position, which is evidently different (or not?) from the one presented in the *Tractatus*? and b) In the theory of language games is there more or less historicity, more or less real blood, than in the *Tractatus*? Is the "critical" philosophy made possible by the theory more powerful in the first instance or the second?

The two questions are closely connected. To know how and why Wittgenstein arrived at the language games is to understand the historical developments that the theory can have. The questions themselves are exquisitely historical. I want to know if analytical philosophy is intrinsically conservative or – which, however, is the same thing – only "neutral" relative to the historical–political situation within which it operates.

The unease or *Verwirrung* that drove Wittgenstein's thinking in the early twenties, and that revolved around a cluster of personal reasons (including the still unresolved matter of his homosexuality and his religiosity), can provide his readers with the historical horizon I am looking for here in order to answer question b) in some way.

Of course, even looking at the issue from outside the language games leaves more space (relative to the physicalistic rigour of the *Tractatus*) for the persistence of the religious element in Wittgenstein that, in his work from 1918, leads him into a mysticism destined to become silence: the things about which we cannot speak are the only ones worth thinking about, or almost. But the twenties are also the years when Wittgenstein tried to find his place again in the world, as he studied to become an elementary school teacher and participated in the project of renovating the Austrian schools. If, then, we consider both the need for religion and the matter of his *Anständigkeit*, his efforts to be a "decent" man – an issue whose components include his homosexuality (at least it seems so to me) – the reference to the form of life as a horizon within which to clarify oneself and to escape the linguistic traps appears to be quite understandable. I would describe the situation in the following way: (using terms that are more bluntly hypothetical than categorical) despite its logical–ethical rigour, the *Tractatus* is permeated by a religious spirit that is almost identical to a feeling of guilt (I have in mind the secret diaries that date from the war years and the prison experience), whatever may be the concrete manifestations of the sense of sinfulness that torment Wittgenstein (not even Bartley considers the possibility that he had a homosexual experience with his fellow soldiers). His return to civilian life and the difficulties he encountered with the publication of the *Tractatus* and the *Verwirrung* associated with that closes that period in his life "mystically," we might say, with his renunciation of his inheritance. The mysticism, however, remains and the dissatisfaction with Russell's opinion confirms the persistence of this theme (see Monk). The concept of *Anständigkeit* too is already part of the concept of the forms of life and the language games. If he does not want to be reduced to complete silence, the mystic cannot avoid reasoning in relative conformity with what a society that functions according to its own rules expects of him. There is, in this, a sort of Aristotelianism that is not unlike the one we find in such authors as MacIntyre. Who is the virtuous man for Aristotle? It is the man considered so by his fellow citizens. The decency to which Wittgenstein aspires, and that he justifies with the theory of the forms of life and the language games, seems to be precisely describable in these terms. The *Tractatus* remains a "metaphysical" (in the Heideggerian sense) work, basically inspired by a foundationalist spirit, a sort of logical–moral fanaticism. The form of life in which we find ourselves living – consider Heidegger's notion of the being who is thrown into existence – is entirely without foundation; it has no rational justification; it is nothing less than God. I am thinking of notes such as the following one from 1916: "In order to live happily I must be in harmony with the world … Then I am in harmony with that alien will on which I appear dependent (see in an earlier entry: the world is given to me; I am dependent on it. Perhaps I can call the world itself God) … Conscience tells me whether or not I am in harmony with the world) … Therefore … conscience is the voice of God" (*Tractatus*, *Quaderni* [*Notebooks*], 175). And in *On Certainty* we read, "You must not forget that the language game is, so to speak, something unforeseeable. I mean to say: It has no foundation; it is not reasonable (or unreasonable). It is there, like our life" (no. 559, 91).

Here, the form of life is the ultimate fact, with which I must enter into harmony in order to be happy (as well as decent): "If life is problematic, it is a sign that your life is not adapting to the form of life. You must, therefore, change your life; when it adapts to the form, the problematic element will then disappear" (*Pensieri diversi* [*Thoughts*], 58; translated by Corrado Federici).

If we return to the two questions I posed above, it appears that in Wittgenstein's words there is no, or almost no, historical element. It is true that, for everyone, historicity is being thrown into a form of life and perhaps finding ourselves playing different language games (a mathematician can also be religious but heaven help you if you confuse the languages).

4

Initial Paradox

Initial paradox: philosophy, which traditionally has presented itself as the most "essentialist" science (indeed, it was born as such), cannot define itself in essentialist terms, as though it could say, philosophy is ... precisely because one of the terms used quite often in philosophical discussion is philosophy itself – what it is, what it does, what purpose it serves (from Aristotle onward it is said that if you must philosophize, philosophize, and if not, state your reason, philosophically) –; which indicates an excessive self-awareness, a permanent self-critical questioning. If there has always been something of this sort in the other forms of "knowledge" as well, the issue has been left largely to philosophers – *Wissenschaftslehre* (epistemology), etc.

To begin with this paradox is also to start out with the historical situation and at the same time the radicalness that has always been expected from philosophers. Why do we continue to ask what it means to do philosophy? Answer: because we still do not know why. But, then, is the entire history of philosophy we studied a history of nothing? If so, what would be the point of our books, seminars, courses, and congresses?

It is not true that that the history of philosophy is the history of nothing. We have learned, repeated, criticized, and modified something. If we want to be serious, we can and must try to understand the reason why, with everything we know about the philosophies of the past and the present, we still ask this question. The serious answer cannot be: because the essence of philosophy is still hidden from us, like a datum that lies out there somewhere, but that we have not yet managed to "discover." This is not a very serious response since what we know about past and present philosophies more or less leads us to reject the suggestion that we can think of philosophy in these terms, i.e. as an essence that, for some unknown reason, remains hidden from us. The answer is not very serious as well because few, or none, of us are by now ready to accept as valid a discourse that proposes to define the essence of philosophy by finally discovering the datum that until now has supposedly eluded philosophers. Even the most ardent essentialists, analytical philosophers, would frame the discourse in the following terms: what are we saying when we call something philosophy? With a kind of typical blindness to the historical transformations that the term and the concept have undergone, they would end up identifying the essence of philosophy with the meaning of the noun we find in our dictionaries.

But this fact is anything but stable; it is not enough to consult the dictionary; we need to have an encyclopedia, which is a record of the changes the use of the term has undergone through the ages, and which provides reasons for these changes as well as their connections with culture in general and with the events of "external" history. This is how I would more or less sum up the meaning of the term "ontology of actuality," which I borrow from Foucault giving it, however, a Heideggerian spin not found in Foucault. Philosophy understood in this way is the recollection of the history of Being, whose only history is that of the meaning the term has (has acquired) in our language. Language is the house of Being, where Being exists as an "opening" of historical worlds. Being resides there and is its "owner": language is not an instrument available to someone, neither to those who speak it nor to Being itself (which would in this case have to distinguish itself in the same way that someone uses an instrument). This "identification" of Being with language, which Heidegger develops while experiencing difficulties in writing *Being and Time* (on this, see the *Letter on Humanism*), is the real way to go beyond metaphysics as the identification of Being with the object/being. The language that we speak and that speaks to "us" is not a datum, an instrument, or a structure: it is an event that concerns and involves us in a relationship of reciprocal possibilities. This is because at the base of Heidegger's dissatisfaction (or impatience) with the identification of the metaphysics of Being with the object was his need to understand (or experience) freedom (recall the existentialist climate of the early-twentieth-century avant-gardes, Bloch and Expressionism, and the theological studies of the young Heidegger). To think of Being as event that occurs first in language is the (only) way to think of freedom as well. There are existents and they construct history "for we are a conversation," according to a verse from Hölderlin that Heidegger often cites ("Conciliator, you that no longer believed in me"). The person who speaks is also used by language-Being, and all language acts constitute the reception and interpretation of the message that speaks to "us" as speakers. Ontology of actuality means hermeneutic ontology, which is characterized by the comprehension-interpretation circle that Heidegger thematizes in *Being and Time*.

Is this idealism? Or even empirical idealism, in the fashion of Berkeley, as "realist" critics of hermeneutics object? Hermeneutics, instead, claims legitimately to be a radicalized Kantianism: the phenomenal world, the "real datum" becomes accessible to us as such only if it is organized by the *a priori* of reason. But, for hermeneutics, these are not at all eternal structures – like those of mathematics – which are, precisely, already constructed by reason with its *a priori*. It is no coincidence that one of Heidegger's teachers, much more so than Husserl, was Dilthey, who felt the urgency of making the Kantian subject (in whose veins "runs no real blood") a historical existent. It is not enough, however, to ground Kantian reason, that is, place it in the *Dasein* (there-being) of analytical existentialism (I have in mind, basically, a neo-Kantian Heidegger, whom we derive from reading a book like Alphonse De Waelhens, *Chemins et impasses de l'ontologie heideggerienne* (*Paths and Impasses of Heidegger's Ontology*). The *Kehre* or turn that Heidegger explicitly discusses in his *Letter on Humanism* is the effort to take seriously the results of analytical existentialism: if being-there (or there-being) with its precognition of the world is not Kant's immutable reason, it does not suffice to say that it is "always" in history (this is how Derrida responded to my objections to the problem of the historicity of deconstruction). We need to try to understand what becomes of Being in the concrete historical situation into which we are thrown. We encounter this requirement – of taking seriously Dilthey's historicity – in his review of Jaspers in 1919, published only in the last essay of *Wegmarken* (*Milestones*), and it is also, unfortunately, the source of Heidegger's "deviation" into Nazism in 1933.

We do not have an external scientific "description" of Being-event. In the review of Jaspers's *Psychology of Worldviews*, the criticism directed at the author, who stated in the introduction to the work that he wanted to study different worldviews in order to interrogate his own, is that of having indeed forgotten this intention and having ended up writing a sort of purely "aesthetic," contemplative we might say, panorama without taking into account his own concrete historicity. As it appears, then, in some allusions in the last part of the review, this criticism is directed also, or even essentially, at the Husserlian phenomenology of the period, and this probably explains why Heidegger left the text unpublished. His break with Husserl, which came about for these reasons, occurs only later, around the year in which he published *Being and Time*. Naturally, going from a text on Jaspers to the break with Husserl omits some biographical facts that I cannot, nor want to, reconstruct here. But these seem to be understandable as elements of the *Kehre*. This is one aspect of the issue that leftist critics of Heidegger, in particular, failed to see, blinded as they were, I would say, by the scandal of his acceptance of the Nazi rectorate in Freiburg and of the infamous speech he made on that occasion. That decision should have been justifiably censured precisely "from a leftist perspective," but its deep-rooted causes should have been studied and understood: it was a pure and simple case of not waiting at the window of Being, of living hermeneutic ontology as a philosophy of praxis and not as a contemplative, aesthetic gaze on the flow of history. In sum, Heidegger acted like a committed philosopher – in the manner of a Lukács or a Bloch, who chose to support Stalin, or a Giovanni Gentile, who collaborated with Mussolini until the end. There is, of course, no justification for Heidegger's choice; it was a colossal example of self-misunderstanding conditioned by the German tradition as a whole which, from at least the late 1700s (Hölderlin) and then from Nietzsche's tragic, pre-Socratic culture, considered Germany, due to its own political and social backwardness, as the true place for a possible revival of the pre-metaphysical culture, one not infected by the virus of industrialism and capitalist alienation.

As ontology of actuality, that is to say (a philosophy of) praxis, philosophy must incur risks without the guarantee of any first principle to give it legitimacy and to justify the philosopher's historical choices. We are dealing with choices and, therefore, not objective descriptions of the *Weltanschauungen* (worldview), in the manner of Jaspers, or descriptions of the alienated human condition, even in the manner of Sartre, a taking a position either for or against. On the basis of this choice alone – which defines and activates the horizon of our understanding since we are not pure Kantian reason – the being discovers itself as an object as well; if it is not directed by an interest, *Dasein* simply does not see the world. This is an "objective" gaze onto the world since it is opened up by an interpretative disposition; as well, interpretation is the quotidian view of *man*, of the anonymous "one" who, however, is not in a state of *Verfallenheit* or fallen-ness until he accepts and configures himself explicitly for his mortality or (I say) historicity. All this is to say (to have Heidegger say or simply what can be drawn from him) that we cannot do philosophy, and therefore the ontology of actuality, without involving ourselves in the conflicts of concrete historicity. Why is it "that we cannot"? Are we perhaps talking about a "logical" necessity, a performative self-contradiction that we should avoid in order not to be incoherent? No, it is simply what Aristotle already noted: if we ought to philosophize, we certainly philosophize; if we ought not, then we need to philosophize in order to explain why we ought not. So, in what conflicts are we involved?

To choose also means to decide what is for us the "main conflict" – as in the case of Heidegger, who thinks an epoch in relation to some founding word ("what remains is found by the poets," in Heidegger, "Hölderlin and the Essence of Poetry"). What conflict do I recognize as constitutive of my present condition? In other words, how do I "condense" the world in the face of which I must take a position? This is what makes it difficult, or ultimately impossible, to elaborate an "ontology of actuality."

Am I indulging in a sort of "amateur" sociology (Lukács called Simmel's work "sociological impressionism," if I am not mistaken)? Am I trying to describe the "general state of the world" that Hegel speaks of in his *Aesthetics*? Here we again have the "panoramic" need that Jaspers wanted to satisfy in order to interrogate his own *Weltansschauung*. It is as if we posed the problem of choosing a religion on the basis of a complete list of "available" religions. The importance of the case of "Heidegger's Nazism" is also and above all this: it teaches that an ontology of actuality can be constructed only on the basis of an explicit, unavoidably "subjective" stance. We cannot look at the event of Being as though it were a panorama unfurled before our eyes, which we need to "explore" before orienting ourselves within it. But is the being-in-the-world about which *Being and Time* speaks not something similar to this? We already know approximately what the world consists of, what the world is, even if we do not have analytical knowledge of it. But for *Being and Time*, as in the case of the ontology of actuality, we can escape the world of man, and ordinary talk, only by explicitly acknowledging what we are and deciding to change ourselves. What compels us to decide? It is never a generic human need but a specific need: urges in general, such as the sexual urge and hunger, always have a historical and cultural aspect. All the more so in the case of our dissatisfaction with our place in the world and our expectations for the future. Perhaps we can even talk of a "spirit of revenge," to use a Nietzschean phrase; this comes to mind when I read an important passage of Benjamin's "Theses on the Philosophy of History": the actions of revolutionaries are not motivated so much by the image of a radiant future that they want to construct for their children and grandchildren as by their indignation for their enslaved and exploited ancestors (thesis no. 12).

The escape from metaphysics that Heidegger seeks also means acceptance of Being as event; for this reason, Heidegger writes, in *Contributions to Philosophy (of the Event)*, that the real emergency today is the lack of emergency – the fact that nothing happens (I mean on the level of openness of Being: social order, great works of art, etc.) is the triumph of an objectivist metaphysics; the way things are can be the only horizon possible. *Dasein* as thrown projection is not possible in a world where everything is calculated in an increasingly impersonal and, therefore, "disinterested" way. Do we have here a Heideggerian vitalism? Perhaps, although it would be more appropriate to call it existentialism. In Heidegger there is no metaphysics of vitalism; which is to say, Being is life. Identifying Being with event does not mean attributing an "essence" to it. Being gives itself as event; it demands to be thought as event in the specific, concrete, possible state into which we are thrown, which is the culmination of metaphysics in the society of "total organization." We did not "discover" that Being is event. As the Heidegger of *Being and Time* did not "discover" that Being is not the object. He was experiencing existentially the impossibility of thinking his own being (with its past and future, historicity, and freedom) using the objectivist, reified concepts of metaphysics. Even saying that Being is event is an event of Being – a specific historicodestinal (that is to say, dependent on history and destiny) opening. We are not dealing with a metaphysical statement because it is an interpretation of our specific and possible condition. To try to grasp the features of the opening into which we are thrown does not mean to try to see, in Being-event as a category, the specific condition of "our" event. Double genitive? Ontology of actuality in two senses: what Being is in our specific condition and our specific condition characterized by Being only as event. Ontology of actuality, thus, becomes thought's response to Being as event and not (no longer), let us say, as *actus purus* (pure act), eternal structure, Platonic idea, and so forth. This is an ontology of nihilism in the sense that its content is nothing more than the history in which Being as such ultimately is no longer Being. *Es* ("it"), *das Sein* ("Being"), *gibt* ("there is"). The impersonality of *Sein*, which is not the subject that gives but that "is given" or occurs, implies that the *gabe* (gift), the "given-ness" of Being, is never "given" but is the occurrence into which one receiving the gift enters as active collaborator and not as pure, passive addressee.

Ontology of actuality or tautology of actuality? Does not claiming that our actuality is defined by the fact that Being is (no longer) given to us as structure, objectivity, Platonic idea, but rather as event, entail some content that is not pure tautology? But the fact that today we can experience Being (only) as event is not the individual's pure volition; it is the history that Nietzsche describes as the history of nihilism and that Heidegger rereads and "recovers" (*Denken* [thinking] and *An-denken* [memories]) as the history of metaphysics. The account of (the history of) metaphysics as nihilism is certainly not "objective" history; it too is interpretation, not the presentation of "facts." We can deduce the nihilistic outcome of metaphysics by interpreting history, that is to say, soliciting the consensus of the interlocutors for the same reasons that Heidegger offers in *Being and Time*. Do you also sense that you cannot visualize your experience of freedom within the framework of Being that is identified with the object? But does being able to imagine ourselves free mean only thinking concepts that describe freedom more adequately? As we can see, the question makes no sense, just as criticizing the idea of Being as object in the name of an idea that describes it more "adequately" or "reflects" it more "objectively" makes no sense.

At this point, those who see Heidegger's choice to embrace Nazism in 1933 as the "logical" outcome of his philosophy could be right. I say this paradoxically. Of course, it was logical and almost inevitable that the *Kehre* or turn toward the event should lead to a historical–political commitment as well as to the fact that this commitment was in part caused by a rejection of the dehumanizing industrial–capitalist society, which Heidegger (but let us not forget

Adorno and the Frankfurt School, at that time and later) identified with the society of the United States. Not without good reasons, he also looked favourably on the Soviet Union of his times.

Having followed him from *Being and Time* to the *Kehre*, we would not make the same decision today. I am not inclined to judge him, however, as though I were in Nuremberg – I am not inclined to condemn him in the name of humanity itself, laying down premises that would later justify NATO's "humanitarian" bombings of a number of countries in the world in the name of their right/duty to become "democratic." The question Heidegger, in 1933, believed he needed to answer, in the speech he gave on the occasion of his appointment as rector and the, albeit temporary, espousal of Nazism, remains open and with the same elements: how to remember Being, that is, get out of a metaphysics that had become total organization of the world, a world that is today much more unassailable than it was in his day, because it is much more nolitic, and, through the manipulation of public opinion (Doctor Goebbels was an amateur by comparison), transformed almost into a second nature of modernity. Are we dealing with an extraphilosophical problem that risks leaving the terra firma of our (up until now) respectable professions? But if not this, what could "do philosophy" mean?

5

The Future of Hermeneutics

As we can see from many of the essays in this volume, it is impossible to consider hermeneutics as if it were only one philosophical discipline among others (such as aesthetics or ethics), but at the same time it is impossible to consider it merely as if it were a philosophical school or movement (such as positivism, historicism, or any school of that sort). It seems quite plausible to think that the future of hermeneutics, whose traits we are seeking to define, will be constituted – even if not exclusively – by the dialectical relationship between these two meanings of "hermeneutics," in a sort of oscillation that will never be completely resolved one way or the other. Yet it is also possible to identify the future of hermeneutics as lying precisely in the progressive convergence of these two meanings: so the real future of hermeneutics as a philosophical discipline will depend on the recognition of hermeneutics as a general philosophical perspective or movement and not as a single "part" of philosophy. It is just such a view of hermeneutics (as specific discipline and general perspective taken together) that characterizes the modern history of hermeneutics from Schleiermacher onwards. Beginning with the modern origins of hermeneutics, the question concerning a rationally grounded understanding of texts has progressively tended towards the thinking of a general ontology. The traditional maxim that was already leading Schleiermacher's thought, according to which we must understand a text as well as and better than the author, cannot be considered a frivolity or joke.

Every text has its own life, rooted in the historical fabric in which the author as well as the reader (even if centuries after) are rooted. One cannot treat Gadamer's idea of "effective history"

(*Wirkungsgeschichte*) as just a matter of the historical "good fortune" of a text. In other words, the episodes in the history of a text's effects, the stories of its reception, and the interpretations it generates, cannot be reduced to the specificities of a single and determinate "history"; the historical effectiveness of the text consists in its being open to history in general – open to what Heidegger called the "history of Being" and nothing less. On this basis, the history of hermeneutics as a specific philosophical "discipline" does indeed appear as the progressive transformation of the philosophy of interpretation into a general ontology. Consequently, in asking after the future of hermeneutics what we must also ask is the following: what new paths await hermeneutics after it has assumed – with Heidegger, Pareyson, Ricoeur, Gadamer, and Rorty – the form of the only possible ontology? Following from this, we also need to consider another question contained under the general title "the future of hermeneutics": not just the question of what hermeneutics as theory will produce in its disciplinary future – different insights, ideas, and methods of interpretation – but what is the future that hermeneutics contemplates; what does the future look like from a hermeneutic perspective? As ontology, hermeneutics implies a certain philosophy of history – it projects such a philosophy, such a history and so provides its own interpretation of the history in which it is itself implicated. Yet renouncing, as any philosophy of interpretation must do, any metaphysics of eternal essences, hermeneutics is also brought to the point of announcing a sort of eschatology – the announcing of a certain ending of history understood metaphysically. The classical text of hermeneutics in the twentieth century, Gadamer's *Truth and Method*, prudently tries to avoid any commitment to a philosophy of history of the usual (metaphysical) sort. Similarly, with respect to his own central thesis – "Being that can be understood is language" (see my article "Gadamer and the Problem of Ontology") – Gadamer showed the same antimetaphysical prudence and always refused all extreme or metaphysical readings of the thesis.

Until the end of his life, Gadamer still complied – albeit with some concessions made in conversation with myself and Richard Rorty on the day of his one hundredth birthday (Heidelberg, February 2000) – with the classical distinction between the *Geisteswissenschaften* (the human or moral sciences) and the *Naturwissenschaften* (the natural sciences). The being that is language is what can be understood, and this "being" is not Being "in its entirety." Yet even given such a cautious qualification – in my view required by academic prudence – our "founding father" did not bring to an end the process of the "ontologization" of hermeneutics that, as I have noted already, characterizes the entire history of the idea of interpretation from Schleiermacher to Heidegger and Gadamer himself.[1] It may be that what will happen to hermeneutics in the future – to hermeneutics as an ensemble of texts, as a body of theoretical speculation, and also as a community of scholars – will be another step in this process of "ontologization." The battle of ideas concerning interpretation from its beginnings to the present – including debates such as that over Kuhn's idea of the "paradigm" or the more recent controversies concerning the question of "realism" (see my essay *Of Reality. The Purposes of Philosophy*) – can only move onwards inasmuch as the hermeneutic commitment takes the form of a political, or at least existential, commitment.[2] Such a development is unavoidable for those who take hermeneutics seriously and dedicate themselves to its practice. The history of modern hermeneutics, and, so far as we can imagine, also its future, is a history of "excess" – of the transgression of limits or, to use another expression, the history of a continuous "overflowing." From its origins as an inquiry into the understanding of the texts of the past, it developed into a general philosophy of existence and then into the only possible ontology: "*Sein, das verstanden warden kann, ist Sprache*" ("Being that can be understood *is* language"). Does this mean that hermeneutics must be understood more and more in idealist terms? Can we come to identify hermeneutics with an idealistic metaphysics? Does "Being" become "language"? If we are not to sever Gadamer from his Heideggerian roots, then we have to reaffirm that the *is* that is said of Being in this sentence of Gadamer's does not have a meaning that would allow that sentence to be construed metaphysically. The language in which Being consists (the language that Being is) is the language of *Gespräch* – of dialogue or conversation. This conversation is what we all are. It is the *Ereignis* – the event – that *happens* without being there. The future of hermeneutics must take the form of the transformation of hermeneutics into a practical philosophy or philosophy of praxis. This does not mean that hermeneutics, as philosophy of interpretation, somehow progresses in a positive sense through the increasing realization of its character as a philosophy of praxis. There is no object proper to hermeneutic thought that is better understood, described or represented through the progressive development of hermeneutics into an explicit philosophy of praxis.

At this point, we may have reached a moment like that of St Paul speaking at the Areopagus – the moment at which, incredulous and outraged by the absurdity of what is said, the audience gets up and leaves. The intolerance of any form of radical hermeneutics within academic philosophy is more or less a reaction in an "Areopagus" style. Hermeneutics is forbidden from transgressing the proper limits of academic "good manners," limits that are essentially those of "descriptive" metaphysics: there is a thing in front of me, *the world out there*, I describe it, I analyze it; I also judge it and condemn it (as absurd, false, morally unacceptable ...); limits that always depend on assuming the validity of the distinction between subject and object – the very distinction that does not hold within the *Geisteswissenschaften*, the human sciences, and whose rejection gives rise to the "excess" of hermeneutics – an excess that has an impact like that of a "terrorist" attack, even if it is an attack of ideas. Recognizing this, we can better understand how little an exaggeration it was when Nietzsche – a poor professor of ancient Greek at Basel and prematurely retired – described himself in *Ecce Homo* as a "mortal danger" for the world. If we dare, for a moment, to imitate Nietzsche, we can propose a "terrorist" vocation for hermeneutics. The adoption of such a vocation becomes more and more a demand, the more the metaphysical integration of the world increases ("Die Wüste wächst" ["The desert grows!"], Nietzsche, *Thus Spoke Zarathustra* IV: 76.1). In our late metaphysical world, determined by the triumph of technology and the technical, science and power reciprocally sustain themselves (see *Dialectic of Enlightenment*, in which scientists appear as respected officers perfectly integrated in a total *Verwaltung* or administrative/organizational system), and science, or what presents itself as science, itself becomes an instrument of oppression. Such a world can consider only as terrorists those who think, as Nietzsche did, that "there are no facts, only interpretations" (*Frammenti postumi* [*Posthumous Fragments*] *1885–1887*, 299) and who thereby threaten to unmask the complicity of metaphysical scientism and coercive power.

We are experiencing the transformation of the most "innocent" of crafts (see Heidegger's "Hölderlin and the Essence of Poetry") – so hermeneutics has often portrayed itself – into a sort of terrorist network constantly subjected to policing and attempts at control. Here "policing" takes many different forms: the "policing" of thought (notably the proponents of analytic epistemology), the "policing" of the leading classes (consider the "neorealism" of the international *mainstream* media), the "policing" of governments (in the form, for instance, of cultural policies "compliant with the current order," "neutral" audit and assurance exercises and processes, or "objective" evaluation of scientific productivity – the latter, starting with the privilege of English, represent a continuation of old imperialist and colonialist policies by other means). The transformation of hermeneutics into a dangerous praxis – and philosophy of praxis – goes hand in hand with what Heidegger taught us to recognize as the culmination of metaphysics in the form of what he called *Gestell* – "enframing" or "framework" – which is to say, the total reduction of Being (operating through different modes of "setting" or "positing" – *Stellen* to that which is calculable and manipulable – allowing its appearance only within that "frame." Through the progressive marginalization and obscuration – the forgetting – of what is not calculable or manipulable, *Gestell* reduces the world to itself – to *Gestell*. Maybe we can find here one meaning of Heidegger's ambiguous statement, to the effect that in the *Gestell* there is "a first flashing of *Ereignis*" (*Identity and Difference*) – a sort of *hapax legomenon* in his work (something spoken only once) that can be seen as an optimistic opening consistent with Hölderlin's motto: "But where danger is, grows / The saving power also" (quoted in Heidegger, *The Question Concerning Technology*). In the same pages of *Identity and Difference* where he alludes to this "first flashing," Heidegger also suggests an explanation of its occurrence: in *Gestell* man and world lose their metaphysical character; more specifically, they lose their character as subject and object. This explanation still leaves open, however, many different readings. On the one hand, one might suggest that Heidegger thinks of *Gestell* as the place of the overcoming of humanism – and so of the overcoming of the subject, of the oppositions of consciousness-thing, spirit vs. nature, and so on.[3] On the other hand, we can also interpret the matter as follows: *Dasein*, just as naked of its *humanitas* and reduced to a mere calculable entity, wakes up to the memory (of the oblivion) of Being. In either case, the progressive reduction to calculation and technical manipulation appears as preparatory to the overcoming of metaphysics. This is not to be understood merely as an objective "happening" in the world (how could such "happening" configure itself?) but is instead a change in the conditions of Being – it is something that happens to *Dasein* under pathos or suffering the reign of

Gestell. Can we suppose that *Gestell* simultaneously brings a suffering that wakes human beings to the memory of the oblivion into which *Gestell* throws it?[4] At the origins of Heidegger's *Being and Time*, as it stands in proximity to the spirit of the avant-garde of the beginning of the twentieth century, and already in the debate over the relation between the *Geistes-* and *Naturwissenschaften*, a revolt was underway against the dehumanization of existence, especially as that was evident in the "rationalization" of work (exemplified by the application of new modes of production and industrial organization in firms such as Fiat and Ford). Hermeneutics, so much taken up with a historical spirit (as *historisch*), so deeply linked to the memories of the past, has become more fully aware of its own "subversive" inspiration as the *Naturwissenschaften* have themselves been increasingly integrated into the global *Verwaltung*. Consider, for example, education policies as they are operative in schools and universities in most Western industrialized countries today – and especially the difficulty of defending the space of the humanities in teaching programs and in the distribution of research funds. It is no exaggeration to say that hermeneutics is now the expression of a mode of intellectual life and activity that has been progressively marginalized within contemporary academic hierarchies and in being so marginalized, politically as well as intellectually, is thereby pushed together with many other similarly marginalized groups (see my *Weak Thought, Thought of the Weak*). The latter remark would be quite inconceivable, however, within the frame of philosophy conceived merely as a "scientific discipline" – philosophy as the "science of Being" whether in the Aristotelian sense or in the sense of Kantian "critique" (and so as answer to critical questions about knowledge, action, and hope). If we compare hermeneutics with those two classical ways of doing philosophy, the distance (an abysmal one) is abundantly clear. It is true that the fundamental problems with which classical philosophy (descriptive metaphysics or critical metaphysics) began were often presented as pathos or modes of suffering or at least malaise, to which the philosopher responded by investigating. The liberation from the malaise, however, was always imagined in terms of the discovery of some incontrovertible given – some principle, authority, or evidence – even when presented in the form of an Other understood as a person (the God of Augustine). Yet the particular pathos that preoccupied Heidegger in *Being and Time* – that of anxiety or angst – cannot be overcome by a "given," since it is precisely the given-ness that is the source of anxiety (our anxiety arises out of our being). And such given-ness disturbs us even more unbearably as it objectivizes itself in a world progressively dominated by calculation and manipulation. To put the matter in slightly different terms: at the beginning of the twentieth century the revolt of the "humanistic spirit" against the self-imposition of social rationalization could still display the traits of an aesthetic revolution – the revolution of the artistic avant-garde and of a theological or philosophical existentialism, but during the past century such forms of "humanistic" resistance have appeared ever weaker and more partial. This is part of what is at issue in the *Kehre*, the "turn," associated with Heidegger's thought – one of the most damaging effects of which was that of bringing him (even if perhaps temporarily) to Nazism. The demand for authenticity that emanates from *Dasein*'s own Being cannot be restricted just to the existentialist perspective of *Being and Time*: the world as an ordinary talk was the primary sign of inauthenticity in that work, but the same inauthenticity is even more clearly evident in the world of the great capitalistic organization of industrial work that belongs to *Gestell*. Similarly, Gadamer's critique – albeit respectful and polite – of the hegemonic scientism of the philosophy of his time (including that of neo-Kantianism) could not be contained within the limits of that academic debate alone but extends to all domains, as does hermeneutics itself. At the same time, it has to be acknowledged that Heidegger's Nazi "misadventure" can also be seen as the effect of the transformation of hermeneutics into praxis and its philosophy. Yet whatever the dangers, it is impossible to practise an antimetaphysical thinking by purporting to maintain the position of a neutral observer – of holding to "a view from nowhere." The hermeneuticists, if they are to become serious, must also become, fatally, militants.

The question is, for which "cause"? Now we can consider the question concerning the future of hermeneutics in the second sense identified earlier. Not only because hermeneutics stands opposed to metaphysics but also, and above all, because hermeneutics must measure itself against the future; hermeneutics has no world "outside" to take as its own "given," not even as a norm written into Being (which is nothing but event). Of course, talk of *Gestell* may seem to imply something, some "phenomenon," that is indeed "outside" and autonomous. But were we led, for a very good reason, to speak earlier of the possibility that *Gestell* may itself be accompanied by a certain pathos or suffering. What helps us here is Foucault's notion of *ontologie de l'actualité* – "ontology of actuality" – which I have tried elsewhere to reinterpret from Heidegger's point of view: remembering Being can refer only to the attempt to understand how Being gives itself to us in this moment, in the event that properly concerns us and in which we are caught up – it can refer only to the attempt to understand what it means "to be" today. The terms in which Foucault introduces this notion of an "ontology of actuality," which he contrasts with an "analytics of truth," originally seemed to me to be overly psychologizing – as if such an "ontology" concerned nothing more than a certain mode of biographical–historical consciousness. I recognize now that such a reservation can lead to an overlooking of that crucial element of pathos or suffering: it is this element, and only this, that allows hermeneutics to be a philosophy of history without being at the same time an objectivist metaphysics. *Gestell* is thus "described" only from the perspective of its effect on us, and thus in terms of the pathos that it brings, and not from the perspective of some panoramic view – giving a particular significance, in this context, to the Greek phrase *pathei mathos* (suffer and learn).

But someone might ask: will the militant hermeneuticists undertake some sort of historic action – look to some sort of transformation of the world – on the basis only of their personal suffering and what happens to them alone? The frequently repeated demand for an ethics based on universal principles appears here in all its (metaphysical) force. How can the principle of one's own action – as Kant asks – be legislated as universally valid if the starting point is one's own individual situation and individual pathos? Here it should be remarked – although it may seem outrageous – that Heidegger refused to formulate an ethics since doing so would have forced him to develop a metaphysical discourse. Moreover, the Kantian imperative, which is absolutely uncontaminated by any purpose external to itself (it is categorical not hypothetical), is a fact of reason – we may also say it is a "given" – and as such it is something that is indeed metaphysical from Heidegger's point of view. Consequently, if hermeneutics "has" a future (or an "image" of it), this can only ever appear as a project and never as something "given" (as a categorical imperative, for instance, or a natural essence from which norms of actions are derived). What Benjamin says of the revolutionary in his "Theses on the Philosophy of History" seems here to be especially apt: the revolutionary who fights for change in the world is not inspired by the image of a future new order but by the memory of past horror. Here we can add a thesis advanced by Emmanuel Lévinas: ethics arises only by listening and responding to the request for help that the other addresses to me and not from any rational awareness of what "is" good or bad. "Until we are a dialogue …" ("Conciliator, you that no longer believed in me"), Hölderlin would say: truth happens only when we are and remain in a dialogue. The foundation of a hermeneutic ethics constitutes itself when we are doing something with others – reacting to a pathos or suffering that we discover is common and that gives "content" to the dialogue itself. Such suffering is not only the suffering that is experienced in the moment but also the memory of the suffering of those who have gone before – the memory of a history as it constitutes itself and as we are constituted by it.

Can such a project be a "project" for a world? Reduced to their essential terms, the considerations at issue here recall not only Benjamin and his philosophy of history but, more radically, the passages in the Gospels in which Jesus refuses to answer the questions of his disciples regarding the means by which the Messiah may be identified on the day of *parousia* (see Matthew 24:3). There Jesus warns not to believe those who say to them that he is the Messiah, at the same time as he refuses to provide any positive descriptions – refuses to provide objective "signs" of the sort that may be demanded by the metaphysician. In these Gospel passages are the roots of ontological difference. The undoubtedly "apophatic" tone (the tone of denial or negation – from the Greek *apophe-mi*, meaning "to deny") that is present throughout Heidegger's thought is at the same time a characteristic tone within hermeneutics. That is something that can be found in some of the most important pages of *Being and Time*, in the passage from the existential analytics to the ontology. In §44, at the end of a long excursus on truth, Heidegger writes, "Being (not entities) is something which 'there is' only insofar as truth is. And truth is only insofar and as long as *Dasein* is" (*Being and Time*, 230). Such a statement cannot be taken merely as the concluding synthesis of previous analyses. Instead it must be interpreted as intending a program – a project. The endeavour to remember Being against the oblivion of metaphysics – not to forget ontological difference – aims at letting Being be through attending to singular beings. Yet the happening of truth, as this occurs in the conversation or dialogue that we are, is not a matter of bringing those beings to appearance merely as "true," as "given," or as fully "present." The occurrence of truth places the individual being in the light of the true precisely because it staves it off – it places it, also and especially, in the background. We could say, at this point, that the future of hermeneutics does not appear only in terms of some prediction as to what we think will happen to the theory of interpretation in the years to come. What is said here assumes the meaning of a radical subjective genitive: the future will belong to hermeneutics – or it will not be at all. The world of the future – as seen by hermeneutics, as searched for by hermeneutics – is a world where the "objective" constraints, the "principle of reality" (which is increasingly indistinguishable from the laws of corporate capitalism) must increasingly be challenged by the world of dialogue and conversation, by the world of the truth event, by the world of a progressive symbolization in which objects move into the background as that which supports the engagement between subjects and in which the violence of immediacy is also there but reduced. What is at issue is nothing less than a reformation of the world. A reformation that must be undertaken by a militant hermeneutics with all the tools of the humanities at its disposal – philosophy, theology, fine arts, law, politics – and that will draw the world ever closer to being what for Hegel (and later for Marx) is the place of the spirit, where the spirit feels itself finally (but never thoroughly) at home.

6

The Consequences of Hermeneutics

One could argue that fifty years after the publication of *Truth and Method* hermeneutics has rediscovered some of its roots – which were already present and brought forth in the history reconstructed by Gadamer – and has placed others in parentheses. Gadamer always insisted on the importance of biblical hermeneutics and juridical hermeneutics in the development of the reflection on interpretation, but in reality – according to a line that can be similarly recognized in the development of Heideggerian philosophy – he had above all emphasized aesthetic experience in his theory. Contrary to the "neutralization" which took place in the developments of Kantianism, it was in fact the experience of truth encountered in art that was the essential keystone to Gadamer's work. Or at least it appeared so to the first readers during those years. Today, without trying to reconstruct all of the decades of Gadamer reception, what one sees more often is the emphasis that hermeneutics takes on either through the reflection on religion or through the consideration of politics. For some reason the reflection on aesthetic experience as the authentic experience of truth no longer seems to allow for significant developments, even though during the years of the publication of *Truth and Method* it corresponded to the actuality of the practice of the arts and to the apparent conflict between a philosophy of "aesthetic disinterest" and the rightful claims of artists of the time, especially in the avant-garde, whether they were presented in the classical theories of engagement or in the pointed critiques of the existing society (up to the silence of Beckett as theorized by Adorno). Art's claim to truth seems by now firmly established and has found in Gadamer himself (see *The Relevance of the Beautiful*) a formulation that appears definitive: art is the happening of truth as it grounds community, shared styles of life, usually through the happening of choral experiences (Gadamer has reached the point of citing big musical events). More or less paradoxically, it is no longer a matter of vindicating the truth of the avant-garde but rather of opening up to the consideration of the truth of the arts of the masses, which in the meantime have assumed a rather broad horizon of meaning, so as to justify the idea of a sort of generalized aestheticization of existence. It is worth noting that the first author who had the courage to bring into question the "auratical" values of art in the name of a more open acceptance of the arts of reproducibility, Walter Benjamin, put forward his theses in an essay that concluded with an appeal to the politicization of art in a perspective of communist revolution, one that evades the fascist "aestheticization of politics" which he had rightly seen as a reactionary and totalitarian outcome. It would be difficult to prove the hypothesis that Gadamer had knowingly pursued this conclusive position of Benjamin. But certainly one could at least take as emblematic of the development of hermeneutics this evocation of the arts of the masses by a teacher as prudent and often conservative as the author of *Truth and Method*.

Whatever the value of the hypothesis put forward here – to assume also the final positions of Gadamer on the actuality of the beautiful as a sign of the "political" vocation of hermeneutics – one cannot deny that the directions in which hermeneutics shows it possesses a searing actuality today are the two that I have pointed out and that after all carry hermeneutics back to its historical "origins." As we know, even in the past hermeneutics had a weight and a timeliness primarily as the theory and practice of the interpretation of laws and of sacred scriptures, often with a very explicit link to the problems of social hierarchy and power. Now this connection is presented in forms and with an urgency only slightly different. It is clearly visible in the importance that it assumes in the preaching of the various faiths, which have been restored by the general renewal of religiosity in recent years – the consequence of the unrealized and yet worrying character of the problems arising from new technologies (bioethics, environment). And as for the political implications, the question of the multicultural society in which we live is by now in play on a "hermeneutic" level. For many reasons tied to this new condition of today's social panorama, hermeneutics can no longer be presented, if it was ever able to be, as an innocent theory of the interpretative character of every experience of truth. For example, while for Gadamer the relation between "hermeneutic" forms of knowledge and the positive sciences seemed relatively peaceful, almost a tacit renewal of the Diltheyan distinction between the human sciences and the natural sciences, in the current situation this sort of pact between good neighbours no longer has any possibility of functioning. Multiculturalism is born when European political and cultural colonialism are brought into question, and the awareness of this fact has not left the world of the experimental sciences, and above all of the technologies that depend on them, intact. The question is not to establish whether science thinks or "does not think" (according to Heidegger's thesis) but to establish the extent to which the experimental and technical sciences are aspects of the Western culture that postcolonial countries are no longer disposed to identify with the one, true human culture. Moreover, beyond the relations between diverse worlds and cultures, what does it mean to recognize the interpretative character of truth within individual national situations where they find themselves confronted with an unrealized presence of multiple worldviews, with which they are often unprepared to coexist (and which also and above all present them with problems of power, of rights, of distribution of wealth, and of work)? In this intercultural opposition that is for the most part the conflict of power and therefore political, the churches – in Europe above all the Catholic Church – have their exclusive truth claims, which they believe to read authoritatively in the texts of their tradition, brought into question. Is a conception of the sacred text, seen as an undeniable given, compatible with the Gadamerian thesis of *Truth and Method*? And if, as certainly the Catholic Church has taught us to do, it is read solely within the living context of the tradition (according to the Catholic catechism the sources of the divine revelation are two: Scripture and tradition, that is, the living teachings of the Church itself), one cannot ignore that the very text of Scripture is already the work of the Church: it is not written directly by God and not even, in the case of the Gospels, by Jesus. When, as always happens and recently more often (not surprisingly, the infallibility of the pope was defined as dogma little more than one hundred years ago), conflicts of interpretation over the sacred text arise between the ecclesiastical hierarchy and worshippers, the appeal to the authority of the tradition becomes a weapon that cuts both ways hermeneutically: the tradition is precisely the common opinion of the faithful brought together in the ecclesia. Many of these questions are anything but new, given that they were also the basis for the Protestant Reformation. But today they gain a new weight and a new visibility, due to the media-driven revolution in which we live, one that also cuts into faith much more than the Gutenberg revolution did.

It is not necessary to spell out the reasons for the actuality of hermeneutics. One must, however, demonstrate to what extent hermeneutics can provide answers to all of these questions – no matter how difficult they are to formulate in rigorous terms nor how sensible they seem to common consciousness. If one tries to unite the "questions," implicit or explicit, that confront hermeneutics today, one immediately encounters the problem of the truth claims of the Church and of the dominant political authorities. It does not matter whether these claims, especially in the case of political power, are ideological masks however knowing or unknowing – of other more concretely material interests (the example of Bush's war in Iraq, Afghanistan, and so on, is typical: that he presents them as ways of asserting universal human rights against the barbarism of Islamic extremists). While in the 1960s the task of philosophical hermeneutics was to affirm the value of the truth of art against the exclusive claims of the experimental sciences, today it seems to be that of defending the concrete historical experience of various cultures against the claims of an absolute truth that is presented as the only one able to guarantee peaceful coexistence. The polemic of the Roman pope against "nihilism" and "relativism," as with the recurrent preoccupation of governments to keep us safe from the dangers of "terrorism" – namely, of every cultural, religious, and ethical dissent on the part of groups or communities (were the events at Waco really so far in the past?) – are all part of a general movement, so to say, against the establishment of that which many have called *pensée unique* (single thought). Many signs seem to point toward a society that, so intensely globalized and saturated with information, cannot escape the destiny of a growing totalitarian order. Faced with this risk, which it perhaps first taught us to recognize as such, hermeneutics today has a twofold task: that of refining its own critical capacities by demonstrating, beyond every dogmatism similar to Marxist historical materialism, that the claims of truth are always, also, and above all claims to power; and that of demonstrating, first of all theoretically, but also with an active presence in public opinion, that rational human coexistence is possible without "the truth," namely with regard to the plurality of values and worldviews that constitute the richness, rather than the danger, of humanity. As for the first task, hermeneutics moves in the same direction as the ecological movements that are committed to defend the survival of the human species on earth. The continuation of life requires that the event of Being is held open, and this can happen only if, as Rorty writes, "the conversation continues" (*Philosophy and the Mirror of Nature*, 304). The history of Being and the history of interpretations, of worldviews, of "openings" or of "paradigms," are the same thing. If one were to impose – as every type of "authority" does – the one Truth, with a capital "T," human life itself on earth would be threatened, in the same way that the loss of breathable air and drinkable water threaten it.

Is it possible that hermeneutics also attends to its second task: to claim a rationality that does not have as its ideal directive the achievement of the one truth such that it would feel committed, as in Plato's *Republic*, to "tear out by the hair" those in the cave of opinions who resist the duty of seeing the one authentic truth? Here, we are faced with one of the most radical consequences of Heidegger's critique of truth as reflection, namely, of the Platonism that dominates the history of metaphysics. It is the idea of truth as the reflection of a given, and by definition good, objective order that has always inspired (at least from the beginning of the history of European thought) our ideals of life as directed toward the unity of opinions in the true, of suffering in the peace of the one who, as St Augustine says, finally "rests in You" (*Confessions* 1, 1.1) and the end of the anxiety of becoming in unchanging Eternity. Now – and this is an aspect of the completion of metaphysics that, according to Heidegger, discloses it as unachievable and unacceptable – the unity of the human species has become in reality possible, indeed in large part real, due to the establishment of a universal discipline, of the absolute control of *power* over our lives. The conflicts that still flare up around the world are connected only, from this point of view, with problems "of public order," and the dominant power cannot see them except in this way. Every conflict is but a residual phenomenon without legitimacy. And thus the label "terrorism" is given to every instance of dissent, even the most peaceful: even these acts of dissent, in fact, being without legitimacy in respect to the ideal of unity, are only considered as knowing or unknowing forms of support for terroristic activities.

To ask hermeneutics what the ideal life would be, as an alternative to that "lethal" one of metaphysics, is usually a weapon in the hands of authorities of every type in order to consolidate their own power. Does hermeneutics perhaps want to reestablish (!) the war mentality of all against all, which supposedly preceded the social contract and the birth of civilization? The answer can only be the vindication of the unity of theory and practice championed by Marx, even if in a context too "scientistic" for the palate of hermeneutics. A philosophy capable of defining in purely theoretical terms a nonmetaphysical ideal of humanity would be precisely the umpteenth form of Platonism and thus of the metaphysics of Being thought as stable structure and the source of an authoritarian rationality.

Everything said thus far certainly could use a more systematic development, but at least it shows how hermeneutics is wrapped up, well beyond purely theoretical disputes, with that which Hegel in the *Aesthetics* called "the general condition of the world." The critique of the metaphysical notion of truth leads hermeneutics to collide with the political and religious authoritarianism that, at least as it seems to me, tends to impose itself with great force in the world of economic globalization. Such a world is driven by the ideal of the market, which, by producing crises like those currently under way, call for – everyone says so, and even this is an aspect of *pensée unique* – an ever more vigilant political order on the world stage.

Shifting the "focus" of hermeneutics, from the claim of the extramethodical experiences of truth, first of all that of art, to political–religious critique, has its own logic that does not depend on the preferences, prejudices, or arbitrary orientations of individuals. Today those who, even in the pure realm of theory and of philosophical debate, propose radical hermeneutic positions ("There are no facts, only interpretations, and even this is an interpretation," Nietzsche, *Frammenti postumi* [*Posthumous Fragments*] *1885–1887*, 299) find themselves confronted with objections that claim to reduce their theses to "historical–political" absurdity. In the end, hermeneutic thinkers are more or less explicitly accused of being cryptoterrorists and fomenters of social disorder. Confronted by the tightening of the social order that accompanies globalization, hermeneutics becomes aware of its own nihilistic vocation, and it takes note of the menace that every pretence of absolute truth represents for freedom *and thus* for the history of Being. This nihilistic variant of hermeneutics is not a pure theoretical turn or the contrivance of some eccentric disciple of Heidegger and Gadamer. What is happening here is analogous to what occurred to Heidegger in the 1930s, at the time of the *Kehre*: philosophy can no longer remain detached from reality, debating the validity of this or that theoretical argument. It finds itself – as it certainly has always but never in such explicit and cogent terms – within the historical process where the Being it cannot speak of from the outside, or *from nowhere*, "happens." Today, to affirm that (the experience of) truth is interpretation means to find oneself immediately in conflict with the absolutist claims of the apparatus of power, both civil and religious, which is always more committed to the preservation of its own authority and the privileges of the classes that sustain it and feel they are represented by it. I am aware that a philosophical assertion has always claimed to have an application to concrete historical reality, but without ever abandoning (save perhaps in Marx) the metaphysical persuasion of being theory that speaks from a place not immediately and completely historical – undoubtedly, the Platonic ideas and fundamental truths have always been conceived of as outside of time. The connection between hermeneutics and nihilism does not mean solely that, if one theorizes the interpretative character of the true, one can no longer allow any ultimate foundation for knowledge or for morals. Hermeneutics and nihilism, instead, have in common first of all the characteristic of being not "theory" but event: when Nietzsche spoke of nihilism as a historical destiny, he was certainly not only thinking of the "logical" consequences of the contradictions in which the metaphysics of the past were caught up. Rather, he described, or in fact noted in himself and in his contemporaries, the "death of God" as the determining event of the entire historical condition of his time and certainly not only the affirmation of atheistic ideas in the minds of the majority. Hermeneutics has become a philosophy of history in the double sense of the genitive: it proposes a reading of history, but this reading is itself history; in order to claim its own "truth," namely, its own preferability in respect of other theories, it can appeal only to the experience of what happens, to that general condition of the world that includes it and in many senses determines it. For hermeneutics, to assume its own historicity means first and foremost to feel engaged in the contributing that determines the history into which it finds itself thrown. If one reads contemporary history as a threatening of the event of Being in the name of affirming *pensée unique* and the globalized order, one cannot but feel engaged in the concrete struggle to keep open the conversation on which Being itself depends. Perhaps the idea that hermeneutic philosophers are dangerous for those who want to preserve the existing "order" at any cost is not, after all, just an illusion of power.

7

Hermeneutics of Outrage

The term hermeneutics of outrage has two meanings: on the one hand, it refers to the sense that it assumes as its proper object that which we have learned to call outrage or indignation according to Stéphane Hessel's booklet *Indignez-vous!* (*Time for Outrage!*), the actions of the Spanish "indignados" movement, the Greek expressions of outrage, and the Occupy Wall Street movement in America; on the other hand, it refers to the indignation in a subjective sense of the genitive – the interpretation motivated and inspired by the indignation of the "indignant." Nonetheless, who best to interpret this outrage but the outraged themselves? Not at all, one may object; indignation is an emotion that risks obscuring intelligence and that does not allow us to have an adequate understanding of what indignation means as an "object." As always, when one introduces a term – even the term hermeneutics creates a sort of short-circuit – the *intentio recta* (cognition of the true object) immediately becomes oblique; everything becomes complicated. This is probably due to the fact that the term interpretation itself has a double meaning: it is suggested that it generally stands for the method of grasping the "real" meaning of a statement or of a "fact," bracketing the appearances tied to the contingency of situations, including the subjectivity of the interpreter; on the other hand, the subjectivity of the interpreter – in the pure etymological sense of the term – cannot be excluded, inasmuch as he or she is an interpreter and has an interest, which is an insurmountable condition of interpretation. As for the "indignant" and indignation, it is clear that the fact itself of posing the question of a hermeneutics of indignation opens up a horizon of political and philosophical discourse that does not permit itself to be reduced to strictly theoretical limits.

What do the outraged ask for (want)? To answer this question is to "interpret" the meaning of their indignation. We note that the "inter" prefix of interpret also conveys the sense of "translation." Do the outraged, then, need to be translated? We know that this implies the problem of the "representation" (political, parliamentary, etc. as well) of indignation, and in more specifically philosophical terms, we cannot overlook the importance of the issue (impossibility) of a "radical" translation. I have in mind Quine and Davidson and the fact that they introduce a "principle of charity" precisely into the issue of translation. In other words, (I translate) we cannot guarantee that a sentence in one language can be translated perfectly into a sentence in another language given that we do not have a universal or absolute metalanguage (do you recall the problem of translating the famous term *gavagai*: the rabbit that runs, the run itself, the rabbit ...)?

In the specific case of *gavagai*, we usually accept Wittgenstein's solution: in order to learn a language, we need to share its form of life, to the establishment of which it contributes; we need to love the life of those who speak that language, play their games, etc. We do not need a manual, which merely provides imperfect "translations" – although obviously useful – that ultimately require that we apply the principle of charity. It seems, therefore, that in order to understand fully what the "indignant" want, we need to share their indignation. There is, however, a subtle difference between understanding what the outraged *want* (for example, the abolition of war, etc.) and what they *want to say*. This subtle distinction conceals a very important issue, which relates to that of political representation: the outraged tell us something they want us to understand; this presupposes that they speak in an understandable language, either ours or another. It is clear that, without exaggerating the importance of this observation on the theoretical level, the wanting to say something, on the political level, always implies a kind of compromise. In the poem "To Those Born Later" (1939), Bertolt Brecht writes, "We / who wished to lay the foundation for gentleness, / Could not ourselves be gentle." And the lines prior read, "Even anger [indignation] against injustice / Makes the voice grow hoarse." The objection that is always raised to protesters, not only the most recent ones, is that they do not have a positive program that can be discussed and that they limit themselves to criticizing, at times resorting to violence, the status quo without knowing well what they want to replace it. Fear of sheer chaos results.

Furthermore, without a true crisis that touches people deeply, there will not be any political change, such as a new electoral majority, etc. Naturally, we cannot wish for, or indeed foment, a disastrous crisis in the hope of provoking change. At any rate today, at least in Europe, the crisis is real and does not need to be provoked. This is not a sufficient reason, it would seem, to touch off a revolution, although social demonstrations are becoming increasingly intense. The very idea of a revolution in a "Western" state, which is to say in one of our industrialized countries – the very ones that are enduring the current economic crisis – is unthinkable: imagine the French of the eighteenth century who killed their king! Today, NATO and the European Union, the United Nations, or the International Monetary Fund would intervene to restore order (or, in the case of Libya, drop bombs in order to protect the citizens against violence). This means that today, more than in the past, the notion of indignation is thought of in terms of pure negation without a foundation of truth. Here we have one of the meanings of the idea of Walter Benjamin, described in his "Theses on the Philosophy of History," that what sets revolutionaries in motion is not so much the vision of a happy world that they will build for their descendants as the memory – the indignation, we might say – of the oppressed (enslaved) ancestors. Power, in its turn, always consists in the inertia of the existing situation. Who knows what can happen if we were to change this or that thing.

A hermeneutics of indignation raises all these questions, especially the one that emerges from the fact that in our increasingly integrated (totalitarian) world changes in habit become impossible or at least unthinkable. This can cause us to doubt once more the validity (goodness) of the project of unification – of states, continents, or the world. Poor Kant, with his ideal of a cosmopolitan republic governed by a single law, could not foresee the degree of control that has been made possible for the powerful of today. In our times, in the age of a totally administered society, we have the overturning of Hegel's principle that "the truth is the whole," which, according to Adorno, should be read as "the whole is the false." Adorno very probably thought that even revolution, if ever it was possible, would spill into "the whole is false," which is what happened (according to his viewpoint and that of conventional history) in the case of the October Revolution and Stalinism.

The demonstrators in Madrid and New York cannot possibly believe that they are carrying out a revolution; at least, they are no longer inspired by the ideal of a new society that is to be constructed. They are called "indignant" and not socialists or communists. Their misfortune, and ours, is having been robbed (deprived) of the very possibility of a positive dream; rather, they resemble a sort of Marxist proletariat, and, in psychological terms, they no longer have anything to imagine, having been reduced to the level of refusal, resentment, and vengeance. I am not constructing a "rhetoric of indignation." It is not even an overly pessimistic or overly literary image of the "rebellious" youth of our cities – Rome (15 October 2011), Madrid (15 May 2011), London (15 October 2011) – as well as the so-called Arab Spring. The young people who occupy the city squares and threaten to remain there for long periods of time are generally people who are involuntarily unemployed and can be compared to inhabitants of the poor quarters of third- or fourth-world countries. A recent study has shown that in Italy there is a worrisome percentage of young people (ages eighteen to twenty-five) who do not have a job even though they are not students. Social anger, more than indignation, can only grow. If they were to take drugs or embark on a life of more or less violent crime, it would not be surprising in the least. They are in every way similar to the young people of the western Sahara that I met during a trip I took as a member of parliament: no job or school during the entire day, no experience of "city" life because they are prisoners in a refugee camp. No city, no political life, only a mindset and a culture of pure material survival, and their only hope is that of escaping to Europe one day. There are, obviously, differences between our youths from the poorer quarters and this even more wretched generation. The indignation of the rebellious youths also expresses all this, although our angry young men and women are generally more educated and less poor. I have been told that the riot in London broke out because the protesters wanted brand-name sneakers, the latest cell phones, and such. Even if these were the reasons, then what? Let us, instead, ask ourselves, who and what brought them up in the cult of brand names and superficial things, if not the very banks and governments that now try to impose austerity on them? These young men and women are the real proletariat of today, and their imagination has been taken from them. In this regard, we should not forget that former Italian prime minister Silvio Berlusconi, the richest man in Italy, used to spend his evenings away from institutional duties in the company of third-class comedians, prostitutes, and pimps, in short a rather mediocre bunch, and never extended an invitation to artists, Nobel Prize winners, or scientists. Too boring?

What is one to read, therefore, in the indignation that we wish to interpret? We are faced with a symbolic case for hermeneutics: there is no acceptable interpretation without participation, as in the case of the ethnologist who attempts to understand the word *gavagai*; he or she does not understand anything without some kind of participation in, or sharing of, culture. If the indignation did not concern us or if we simply wanted to carry out a journalistic inquiry or a sociological *wertfrei* (free of ideological, moral, or cultural biases), as Max Weber would say, we would be merely functionaries of the system ready to exorcize it. To what extent does the proletarian status of the young protestors concern us? The question is not, once again, of the "epistemological" kind, as it would be if we were trying to put ourselves in the position of understanding better, describing objectively, *sine ira et studio* (without anger and passion, Tacitus, *Annals*), a phenomenon that eludes us. The question concerns us to the extent that we are part of society taken – embarked on, Blaise Pascal would say – into the conflict, but bankers and proprietors of large data groups or shareholders of multinational corporations are entangled (incorporated) in the play, each according to its status as interlocutor in a dialogue or a conflict. In philosophy, at least starting from the nineteenth century (I recall the discussion on Dilthey's spiritual sciences, etc.), this problem has already been studied in the form of the possibility of knowing history "objectively," given the fact that, to an extent, all the history we study touches us and conditions us in that it is our history. It was thought that the problem could be solved by means of such concepts as *Erlebnis*, or empathy, i.e. a form of imagined identification with the objects of historiography, an identification that remained more or less aesthetic in nature. This can be seen primarily in Dilthey, for whom aesthetic pleasure is almost entirely reduced (ascribable) to the "estrangement" effect, the capacity of a literary, musical, or theatrical work to enable us to experience, via our imagination, other forms of life (here once more a term analogous to Wittgenstein's), which brings us pleasure because in our quotidian lives we find ourselves always tied to a limiting condition, a job (never forget this), a social context. This reference to aesthetics is not so extravagant (or unfounded), after all. In my effort to interpret the indignation of the outraged, there is always the risk of looking for an imaginary (ultimately aesthetic) identification with the "movement." Some of us may remember leaving for Paris in 1968 in order to take part in the student protests at the Sorbonne, which also had a strong component of passion, sexual freedom, etc. Should we be embarrassed today by such an aesthetic element in our (my) effort to share the indignation? It is true that protesters are, generally speaking, young, often attractive, and endowed with an energy that many of us lost a long time ago. Once again: why not? Because the protest should not be a party, an emancipation in the fullest sense of the word? The desires to change society are desires too and not, properly speaking, exigencies of "rationality" based on utilitarian concerns or the claims of "human rights" as articulated in a philosophy. The mistrust of revolutionary parties in the face of desire, when it is not a means for defending the privileges of bureaucrats, is a form of Stalinism. Precisely as did Stalin, who had to become a bloodthirsty dictator because he wanted to achieve a kind of capitalist-American form of industrialization, revolutionaries often adopt the repressive ethics of their enemies.

As you can see, this discussion on the hermeneutics of indignation takes us far and perhaps straight into a *Holzweg*, quoting Heidegger, that is, a narrow path that disappears into the woods. Indignation is not a work of art or a text from the distant past that we can revisit for the purpose of deriving from it "aesthetic" pleasure or a sort of break in our daily lives (for Hegel, art is "the Sunday of life, which evens everything out and discards all that is bad," in *Estetica* [*Aesthetics*] III, 129–30). Escaping the everyday condition, which we do not like or which bores us, can be something more concrete and "real" than a simple play of the imagination. Today art itself often refuses to subscribe to this pleasure that forgets. Bertolt Brecht had an epic, not an Aristotelian, theatre in mind, that is to say, not a cathartic but, rather, revolutionary one. Hermeneutics itself does not merely interpret indignation; it is called into question by the fact that it is faced with phenomena of this kind. We should not forget, however, that Heidegger started his philosophical journey, at the time of *Being and Time*, by reflecting precisely on Dilthey's work and the question of our relationship with the historical past. He felt like a student of Dilthey, whose legacy he wanted to continue and make the importance of his thinking known. So, having started with the simple reflection on the title of this paper and with the idea that we should confine ourselves to applying the hermeneutic "method" to the phenomenon of indignation, I find myself urged (pushed), like Heidegger himself, toward a practical-revolutionary conclusion. Obviously, no one is, for the moment, ready to set out to conquer the Winter Palace of the International Monetary Fund. But, if we want to take into serious consideration what the movement of the outraged has taught us, we could at least begin to think about it.

8

Hermeneutics of European Nihilism

To begin with, the term hermeneutics of European nihilism does not mean only what I propose, in the following pages, to clarify in respect of such a complex phenomenon. I underscore the fact that here the genitive is considered in both the subjective and the objective sense. Hermeneutics itself, which is not solely a method for deciphering a text, is part of the very process of attempting to understand. It is precisely in the process we call European nihilism that hermeneutics is defined as both a method and a general philosophical theory. In one of his notes from the later period, Nietzsche writes that, in the age of accomplished nihilism – which was his own and is especially ours – if one does not become an *Übermensch* or overman, he is lost; the individual no longer exists; he is no longer recognizable as such; it is as though he were eliminated. So, the *Übermensch* that Nietzsche has in mind in these notes is neither the superman we find in comic books nor the "blond beast" of Nazi ideology. Rather, he is someone who interprets, someone who does not passively receive the real data of the world that, due to nihilism, no longer has an objective character but someone who assumes the responsibility of interpreting (here we could cite once more Marx's eleventh thesis on Feuerbach, but with an opposite reading: what is to be done, in the end, is interpret the world; this is because the activity of one who expects to change it is thoroughly conditioned by the nihilism of technology, the economy, development, etc.). In fact, this is the very concept of nihilism that we inherit from Nietzsche: the dissolution of all values (the polytheism that Max Weber talks about). But the many gods are not the realities "out there"; rather, they are interpretations, cultures, religions that appear on the stage of a globalized world. In this first meaning, accomplished nihilism evokes and makes hermeneutics possible, necessary as a matter of fact.

With this first historicodestinal meaning of hermeneutics, we find ourselves engaged in the enterprise of interpreting nihilism. According to the classical definition of the term "interpretation," this means that we cannot ascertain or even describe a phenomenon, but it is perceived as a problem, a point of departure, or a situation that involves us and asks us to take a position. The interpreter is never a disinterested eye; this is confirmed even in our everyday speech. What does nihilism look like to an interested eye that always finds itself (*immerschon*) involved in interpretation? It looks like a situation of universal equivalence, a multiplicity that does not allow itself to be described "aesthetically" but that engages us immediately. In fact, if we expect to remain a disinterested eye, we "vanish" in the Nietzschean sense – assuming that it is always possible to disappear in such a complete way; even the choice not to engage is a choice, although it is a self-destructive one. Let me state this more clearly: the need to become an interpreter reveals the nihilism of which hermeneutics is both the consequence and the effect. Consider the most banal of examples: in the world of widespread information, we are obliged to choose a point of view, a newspaper, a television channel, a news agency; otherwise, we can no longer speak or think about anything.

The disgust felt in the face of the politics we see in our society today is surely informed by the corruption we notice everywhere in our representative democracies, but it is also very likely an effect of the babel of information that, precisely because it is continuous and widespread, produces a neutralizing confusion. Proof of this is the fact that, in the field of politics, the only categories that still seem to still hold true are indeed the elementary ethical categories: ideologies are no longer relevant, much less programs (which are discredited as a result of nihilism) but only the immediate trust of people. But personal honesty has a degree of neutrality as well: one can be an honest condominium manager and an honest administrator of a gulag; value is measured in relation to the assigned function. It is precisely the political news – not only the Italian political scene, which I consider to be emblematic of a more general process – that suggests the simple conclusion: European nihilism is simply the triumph of technology. As everyone knows, for at least a year now,[1] Italy has been governed by a "technical" executive, which is to say, one composed of economists who are well known in academic circles but who have never engaged in political militancy. They were never elected by the people, although, after they were appointed by the president of the republic, their appointment was confirmed by the parliament, specifically by all the parties established by Italy's constitution: the left, the right, and the centre. This vote of confidence was requested and presented as the only way of getting Italy out of the financial crisis and of making the Berlusconi government fall, though it had not formally lost its parliamentary majority. This is a well-known story that I do not need to expand upon here. The "philosophical" interest – I insist on using this term – lies in the fact that the entire process was justified (subsumed) by the notion of "technical" government. The professors who comprise the cabinet of Mario Monti are technicians; their "scientific" neutrality guarantees the fact that they will do only what is required to solve the economic problems. All this was presented to the public as a temporary measure needed to restore the machinery of democracy itself; the temporary measure, however, is now becoming permanent, since Monti is running in the next election as leader of a group of "centrist" parties, soliciting the vote of the citizens, backed by the large corporations, "independent" newspapers, the so-called pro-European Union, and basically nihilist, forces – there is nothing more clearly European and nihilist. This, in the most elementary sense of the term, inasmuch as the "good" European reasons are the reasons of the functioning of the financial machinery, which is, however, in the hands of people who are not at all pure academics but who have a long history of collaboration with the large international banks (Goldman Sachs, most prominently). The technical element that replaces politics is nihilistic because it does not have to deal with the "highest" values, and this constitutes its certificate of merit; technical expertise does nothing other than ensure the functioning of the financial machinery, if you will, and therefore of the system, without asking the "ultimate" questions. Here, the Nietzschean notion of nihilism encounters the Heideggerian notion of the end of metaphysics: the total reduction of Being to the thing, the forgetting of Being itself, which also means the forgetting of all the problematic aspects of experience. It is a fact that metaphysics had always tried to master the "ultimate" principles, first causes, etc. But this very obsession was also its critical force, as in the case of Leibnitz's famous question: why is there something instead of nothing? Some looked for an answer and others did not, but in either case the question only suspended the peremptory authority of present entities. Technical skill knows only intermediate values, instrumental reasons. The power of the Kantian distinction, which Heidegger takes up and exaggerates scandalously, between knowledge and thinking, can be seen here: the object of rational knowledge (*ratio* = calculation) is the totality of phenomena, cause and effect connections, which is to say, measurable (computable) predictability, etc. The totality of the world is nothing more than the contents of an idea, a regulatory one, but never applicable to a given phenomenon. Knowledge apprehends only objects; Being can only be accessed via thought (in Kant, beyond the phenomena there are the *noumena* or "what is thought"). Here we see how pure phenomenal, scientific–rational knowledge is always confined to the world of cause and effect (causality was one of the a priori constitutive of knowledge of the world of phenomena). The metaphysical forgetting of Being, which Heidegger wants to "overcome," is purely the reduction of the world to instrumental rationality: which is nothing demonic except that, in principle, it excludes freedom. For it to be what we intend by this name, metaphysics demands the capacity to ask the "big" questions. We may ask ourselves here if the emptying of the highest values about which Nietzsche talks is the elimination of freedom. At any rate, whatever Nietzsche's own intentions may have been, Heidegger's taking up the idea of nihilism is oriented toward the other term used by Nietzsche when, after the death of God (*Umwertung der obersten Werte*), he hopes that many gods will be born. The multiple highest values, which I interpret (read) in terms of the plurality of cultures and ethics that characterize late modernity, are like metaphysical systems *verwunden* (employed) ironically, secularized religions that are capable of giving unity to our lives and of producing the continuity of individual or communal subjectivity, without any pretence to being definitive. Another aspect of this is what Heidegger calls *Verwindung* (resignation–distortion) of metaphysics, which can never be *Überwindung* (going beyond): it cannot be overcome and discarded like an old suit, but it can and must be "distorted," an allusion to twisting and torsion, but also to irony in order to keep existence from falling prey to the absoluteness of technological necessity.

We have here a picture of the link between hermeneutics and European nihilism and the task of thought in the world of technological neutralization: to not forget Being, as horizon of utopian – I might say – totality, which suspends the definitive claim of the thing, at the cost of always falling back into a state of conflict. It is not difficult to follow Heidegger's ontological meditation: if Being is not what is there – since always and for all time – it "is," instead, the event. The latter occurs when we change the order of the entities, of the "world," if you will, or what Thomas Kuhn calls paradigms, while technology and the rational science that directs (guides) it are only solving "puzzles" in a given paradigm. New paradigms are not something that fall from the sky or that depend on a transcendental necessity; Heidegger compares them (in *The Origin of the Work of Art*, 1936) to poetic creation, but, in the same book, he also has the establishment of a political order in mind. We can certainly talk about revolution. Even in the case of the work of art (the most innocent of activities for Hölderlin), we need to talk about a struggle – between earth and world, says Heidegger. Neither event, i.e. the work of art or revolution, comes about without the destruction of the established order, that is to say, without conflict.

Now the growing predominance of technology in our world – consider the successes of governments, called, precisely, "technical," which today prevail in Europe, not only in Italy – aims to silence all conflicts in the name of a scientific, "objective," seemingly "neutral" rationality, wherein ultimately even the distinction between good and evil disappears: "evil" are simply those who do not fit into the order envisioned by the United Nations, the international communities, the International Monetary Fund. In this system (regime) of neutralization, the task of thought is evidently to "describe" and to know, as opposed to interpret actively the call (appeal) of Being and not the reality of the thing. This, at the cost of combatting all forms of scientific, and ultimately "aesthetic," neutrality in the face of the imposed order. What is at stake is not only our freedom but the question of Being (event) itself, as well.

9

Hermeneutics: Crossroads of the Critique of Globalization

The recent wave of philosophical "new realism," which to me continues to appear theoretically empty and essentially inspired purely by media marketing reasoning, at least has had one merit: that of delineating the difference between the explicit argument in favour of a philosophical "return to order" on the part of the "new" (?) realists, on the one hand, and the commitment of hermeneutics to reading the signs of the times in progressive, emancipatory terms, on the other hand. Not too paradoxically, with their cult of what there is (see Quine, *On What There Is*), the new realists are adversaries who push hermeneutics to see itself more clearly as a philosophy of praxis, which it was and must be from its Heideggerian origins. Finally, even the debate instigated by the publication of the *Black Notebooks* has the same meaning or at least points in the same direction. I would summarize this meaning by saying that the same reasons for which Heidegger supported the Nazis could have (should have) pushed him to choose communism. It was due only to the historical contingencies in which the choice was made – among other things, the antisemitism that characterized the cultural and philosophical German tradition (on which extensive documentation can be found in Di Cesare's *Heidegger and the Jews*) and the threatening aberrations of Soviet Stalinism – that Heidegger chose to side with Hitler. But, this same decision – in particular the decision to commit himself politically and to support the Nazis – today is justification for speaking about a leftist Heideggerianism and a "communist hermeneutics."

First of all, we need to keep in mind the reasons for which today I am speaking of hermeneutics as a criticism of globalization. At first glance, it appears that the discussion can be limited to asserting the essential plurality of cultures, which works against the "neutralizing" effects of unitary thought, the homologization of everything in the great dream world of merchandise. Why can this theatre not be hailed as the realization of a "humanity" that is at long last united by the infinite availability of material goods, the profession of a single faith, and the use of one language as in pre-Babel times (Anglo-American English, whose primacy is challenged, interestingly, only by the spread of Spanish of migrants of all races?)? *Materia signata quantitate* (determinate quantity) comes to mind as an initial response. *Principium individuationis* (the principle of individuation) of medieval scholasticism appears to me here without any urgency or theoretical rigour: it simply indicates that materiality is what makes the dream of globalization fail; this is because there are not enough goods for everyone and not every type of good can satisfy the hunger of the world. Materiality individuates as well because it immediately reveals scarcity and because it makes us aware of the differences between individuals and groups, including cultural ones: if your child asks for bread, you cannot give him or her a stone – consult the Gospels. Are we uncovering the rationale of the "new" realism, which, as we know, chastises the excessive postmodern optimism of hermeneutics? It does so, however, from the standpoint of a principle of reality presumed to be "neutral" like the natural sciences, as claimed by realists. No proponent of hermeneutics forgets that, when we say "it is raining" – and therefore we place ourselves in the hands of Alfred Tarski and his definition of true sentences – ordinary speech generally adds "blame the thieving government" (a common expression in Italy whereby anything that happens is blamed on the government). Philosophy does not deal with facts but with interpretations: the reality it speaks of is the *Wirklichkeit* (reality) that produces *Wirkungen*, that is to say, the effects on subjects and never on abstract events measured geometrically. The countereffects of globalization, what is happening *to us* precisely because of it, give rise to the criticism of hermeneutics, which does not suddenly come to realize that there is something theoretically unsustainable in the idea of globalization, some internal contradiction. What is happening here is what happened in Heidegger's decision to reformulate the question of Being in *Being and Time*: the reduction of Being to the object, its identification with the thing, did not lend itself to a critical theory, as though it were an error that had to be corrected. It required the rethinking of the question because it produced unacceptable consequences for the existence of Being itself. This connection between *Being and Time* and the intellectual avant-gardes of the early twentieth century, as well as the awareness that it inspired in them, i.e. the repudiation of the society of total organization that emerged powerfully at the time. Although it is very different from that one, the age in which we live suggests much more than simple analogies. What Adorno and Horkheimer called, a few decades after the publication of *Being and Time*, a "dialectic of enlightenment," in other words the turning of social rationalization into generalized repression, has become infinitely clearer. The globalization of which we are both the victims and the protagonists today represents only a more advanced phase, and perhaps for this reason less recognizable since it is more consolidated and "obvious," of that process. Even in that part of the world where globalization does not yet appear to have produced disastrous effects like those that are visible on the periphery – which we have learned from Zabala to call "human waste sites" on the outskirts of our societies – the existential, and thus material, intolerable aspects of globalization are noticeable. Those who still have a job in the West are witness to the continual reduction of their rights, as well as an unprecedented intensification of discipline and social control. The destruction of the *Lebenswelten* (life world) of nations and communities, and therefore of their cultures, in favour of the homologization imposed by centralized production and markets is what is most striking from the hermeneutic perspective, as is the progressive (and statistically worrying) disappearance of languages and dialects, a disappearance that likewise damages "cultures," which are reasonable modes of human survival in the world. Here I am thinking of the unmitigated plundering of still "primitive" worlds carried out by large pharmaceutical companies that appropriate plants and other natural resources in order to patent and "valorize" them in the capitalist market. As regards such phenomena, it is difficult not to succumb to the temptation to stop resisting and surrender to some form of naturalistic, antiscientific, anti-industrial obscurantism. The image of a Heidegger attached to the traditions of the Black Forest and fatally a victim of the Nazi myth of *Blut und Buten* (Blood and Soil) looms before me in all its dissuasive power. And yet, the problem that he saw clearly and that he was able to resolve by joining the Nazi Party today resurfaces in more or less the same terms. It is what he called the question of the overcoming of metaphysics, i.e. the construction of a society in which material progress does not mean the destruction of life and human freedom. Those (like me) who talk of hermeneutic communism are well aware of Lenin's remark that defined communism as the Soviet government plus electrification, and they recognize its programmatic value, even though it was little more than a slogan.

Almost as vague as Lenin's definition appears to be, obviously, is the expression hermeneutic communism, which, if we want to be even a little bit precise, indicates a theoretical position that aims to overturn the pretence of science on the part of Soviet communism and, in general, of the Marxism that believed it was criticizing ideologies from the standpoint of metaphysical realism, which is for me untenable and which I am tempted to see as the source, if a remote one, of the totalitarian aspects of present communism. Metaphysics, i.e. essentially authoritarianism, is everything that claims to legitimate itself with a description of how "things really are." Hermeneutics always responds to these claims, which are the domain of the experimental sciences, with the question: who says so? Thus, it brings into play the responsibility of the interpreter.

But to speak of hermeneutic communism does not mean only to state a theoretical position against other ways of understanding communism. Precisely because it is hermeneutics, this communism requires theoretical–practical reference to the subject who talks about it and who intends to practise it (another analogy with Heidegger's situation in the Germany of his day).

While it seems understandable that associating communism – whatever it may mean, starting with Lenin's definition – with hermeneutics might give it a more positive quality, we have to ask ourselves what hermeneutics has to share with communism and if and why this connection is justified. Does hermeneutics have a vocation for communism? Or, in more general terms, does the choice of philosophizing within the hermeneutic horizon, the choice to be hermeneuticists and not, say, positivists or (neo?)realists, imply a particular political leaning toward communism? Furthermore, is it correct to think that a philosophical position has an "application" and a grounding in a political option? One might respond that this very illusion was the cause of Heidegger's fatal Nazi mistake: supposedly, he not only made a bad choice by joining the Nazi Party but, more importantly, he supposedly sullied his own theory by taking a "political party" position, a biased choice in contradiction of the "neutrality" of a universal truth, which should be a philosophical doctrine. As you can see, we are on "slippery" terrain, as is always the case when we abandon the comfortable position of theory (you may recall Gadamer's account of the *theoros* [representative] sent to the city to take part in the festivities: he was, nonetheless, a "political" envoy) and mix it with praxis. But as "hermeneuticists" we cannot choose the "comfortable" position of the neutral spectator. Nietzsche's very controversial statement, "There are no facts, only interpretations," is followed by an often-forgotten addition: "And this too is an interpretation" (*Posthumous Fragments 1885–1887*). The truth of hermeneutics is not the value of one theory that is arguably preferable to others; above all, it is a way of practising philosophy in a non "objective" way, precisely because the interpreter is himself involved in the process about which, and within which, he speaks. One cannot do hermeneutics without taking sides. What distinguishes hermeneutics from the "descriptivism" of positivist metaphysics if not the fact that it implicates the philosopher in making the position of a neutral observer impossible for him or her? It is obvious that, here, we are not dealing only with the position of the philosopher, a specialist who, according to a certain tradition, is supposed to see that his profession has changed. We might say that we are facing an ontological turning point. The truth is not a mirror reflection; the position of the subject is not that of the image on the screen on which realities are created, and Being is not the "given" but the event (which, as appropriating and expropriating *Ereignis*, is much more than the dynamic nature of what occurs; it is the occurrence of Being).

Is this, then, why I bring communism into the discussion? The media controversy of the neorealists has, in fact, shown hermeneutics to have a political position as well. Hermeneuticists are their "adversaries," not simply scholars of another school within the ideal, imaginary museum of philosophical doctrines. What is more, realistically, neorealists do not "describe" us; they attack us. And we, for our part, given their insubstantial arguments, can only ask ourselves what or whom they serve. The hypothesis that seems most probable to me is that their work, which is not justified by any imminent danger to thought and not imposed by the possibility that Nietzsche's statement might produce confusion in the minds of ordinary people, chaos in air travel and in weather predictions (this was raised as an objection!), is only a way of making philosophy participate in the general "return to order" called for precisely by globalization. Convincing signs of all this can be seen in the reports, essentially by the media, of the birth and spread of neorealism.

To claim that hermeneutics has a "communist" vocation merely means taking note of this state of affairs. In some sense, it is still the "enemy" that defines us. This is similar to the point in time when we became aware that the realists were attacking us because hermeneutics was "bothersome." Not that any opposition to the domination of metaphysics, i.e. the technological–scientific globalization of the world, is per se communist. But to call it this means to reduce to a single term all the reasons for that opposition: globalization is purely electrification, to use Lenin's term, without the Soviet, without the involvement of the people affected, and without the participation of the citizens in the decision-making process; in other words, without the responsibility of interpreters. We should, therefore, design a society similar to the Soviet or the Chinese society, with five-year plans, the KGB, etc. Hermeneutics obviously has nothing to do with all this. If it evokes the term or the notion of communism, it is because this term and this notion were critical of the dream of transformation of the exploited classes in most of the world. The "scandal" of taking up these terms now arises from the fact that, because of the pressure exerted by the capitalist world among other things, the communist ideal allowed itself to be contaminated by the scientistic mentality that dominates metaphysics. Metaphysics – as scientistic objectivism that reduces the object and the being-there to a measurable object, a *Bestand*, or an exploitable resource – is essentially capitalism, at least in our historical period. Purified of the prejudices and mental habits that he too was guilty of by engaging in that situation, the reasons that prompted Heidegger to side with the Nazis are still with us today: there were not then and there are not now any "metaphysical people" allegedly responsible for the betrayal. At the time, Heidegger already thought he was fighting the globalizing logic of capitalism, which had imposed itself not only on Hitler but on Soviet communism, suffocating the *originary* revolutionary impulses under the historical necessity of "copying," in obligatory stages, the structure and means of production of American Taylorism. In short, Stalin was corrupted by the example of Western capitalism, and it is for this reason that today it is scandalous to talk about communism.

But what about praxis? Those of us who do things? The question of intellectuals in Gramscian terms? I think that we do not need to be ashamed of practising a militant philosophy and accept responsibility for our past as *Gewesen* (what has been) and not solely as an archeological datum.

10

Democracy and Hermeneutics

Richard Rorty writes that "the hermeneutic attitude [is] in the intellectual world what democracy is in the political world" (Rorty, Vattimo *Il futuro della religione. Solidarietà, carità, ironia* [*The Future of Religion. Solidarity, Charity, Irony*, 2005], 73). The validity of this claim is becoming increasingly evident, even if not in its apparent meaning, which instead runs the risk of becoming banal. I would like to propose that we think of the parallel between hermeneutics and democracy as the sign of a shared crisis. Putting it bluntly, both hermeneutics and democracy today seem so obvious and innocuous as to have no concrete impact on the intellectual and the political level.

The source of this growing loss of credibility can be identified by means of a term used by Carl Schmitt: neutralization. We have recently become accustomed to speaking of "single thought" or, more specifically, "Washington consensus." Washington and its orthodoxy only appear to have nothing to do with philosophy and hermeneutics: the "new" realism of philosophers like John Searle (celebrated by George W. Bush a few years ago)[1] and a monstrous alliance of remnants of phenomenology and postanalytic philosophy – which is replacing the metaphysical epistemology of the previous decades – are really the "intellectual" support of the neoliberal world, which is increasingly built on the imperialist power of the United States and multinational capitalist organizations headquartered in Washington, DC. The Searle–Bush new realism has tried to erase hermeneutic "relativism," which is actually the primary and most important aspect of hermeneutics, as well as the element that supports political critique and democratic practice. In the eyes of the new realists, what should counter the dangers of hermeneutics is obviously "science," whose connections with the dominant powers are almost too obvious, given the enormous amount of financial aid that is requested for research, especially in military programs. Hermeneutic distrust of the role of the experimental sciences is largely due to the thesis encapsulated by Heidegger's statement that "science does not think." This claim is much less scandalous than one might generally suspect. In fact, this is a rigorously Kantian assertion. Science does not think, but it knows: it does not access the *noumenon* but only the phenomenon. The *noumenon* – what can only be "thought" – is the domain of freedom, values, morality, etc. And, it is the domain of politics.

As I was saying, democracy and hermeneutics are experiencing a crisis that, to use a Heideggerian expression whose meaning is similar to Schmitt's "neutralization," we can define as "absence of emergency." In many senses, we must recognize, along with Heidegger, that Being is event, *Ereignis* and that, paradoxically, in a world dominated by the "Washington consensus," nothing happens. Hence, I continue to consider the wave of democratic (I would say socialist) transformations in Latin America as the only "novelty" in recent decades. Are these transformations based on, or accompanied by, the growing popularity of hermeneutic philosophy? I would not go that far. But, it is true that, if we could imagine a philosophical foundation for politics as practised by such figures as Lula, Morales, Chávez, Correa, etc., it could not be the orthodox Marxist tradition (allowing, but not conceding, that such a thing exists) or the rhetoric of democracy that dominates the cultural climate and *mainstream* European and North American media. Here I have in mind a philosopher like Habermas, whom I admire and respect but who gradually became indistinguishable from "moderate dissidents" (I would say, "integrated") like Michael Walzer, Amartya Sen, etc. (on whom we have insightful reflections in Danilo Zolo's *Il nuovo ordine mondiale* [*The New World Order*]), who believe (that they believe) in a possible international order guaranteed by the United Nations and other pseudodemocratic institutions. In its most radical and anarchic version, hermeneutics is the only possible candidate to propose a philosophical foundation for the "emergency" of democracy, in two senses: hermeneutics interprets the absence of emergency, which is also the state of the crisis in democracy, the loss of vigour and credibility of representative institutions throughout the world, and, at the same time, it asserts the possibility of understanding and advocating the emergence of new forms of popular participation in power. The fact is that hermeneutics itself is in the process of radicalizing its own theories under the impetus of what is happening to democracy. Can we still quietly idealize "dialogue" in a world where all forms of dissent are either "integrated" or criminalized by the overwhelming power of the military–industrial–media complex from which we cannot escape? The assertion of identity formation like that occurring in Latin America and its capacity for combatting oppression under the power of the economic "laws" of capital are an extraordinary call to construct a true hermeneutics of otherness, based on what seems today the only possible form of "emergency."

Can hermeneutics truly support people's struggle against international capitalism? As a philosophy, should hermeneutics not be a "neutral" doctrine that seeks "objective" truth? This idea of truth as something that goes beyond all biased, interested points of view has always been the basis for justifying the supposed "neutrality" of culture; a supposition that, in reality, was a way of submitting to power because in a situation of desperate inequality – wealth, military power, intellectual apparatuses, expressions of self-consciousness – neutrality simply means acceptance of the status quo. The daily repetition of the accusation of "relativism," considered – quite reasonably from this point of view – to be a dangerous doctrine for the social order, has a very clear meaning: we (the social order, i.e. the victors) need truth, meaning the ideological legitimization of our domination. It is not so paradoxical to think that "objective truth" serves to underpin power; for example, we could claim that, essentially, God must exist, as an entity that exists somewhere and somehow, in order to legitimize the power of the Church. Who are the people that are afraid of relativism? Surely, not the vanquished in the social and economic game, those who are usually not concerned about determining what is absolute and what, in theory, is "relative." When they speak of truth, they do so, generally, in order to challenge or deny the truth claim of those who support a given power. The emblematic case is the appeal to human rights that we see in many revolutions. To the extent that this recourse to natural, essential, metaphysical rights is used as a weapon against the (co-called divine) rights of the dominant class (I have in mind the divine right of the royal families), it is perfectly legitimate, but in the case where the revolution succeeds, the claim to "natural rights" becomes the basis for all types of Stalinism.

In its anarchic and radical version, hermeneutics can be a philosophy of revolution, starting with the (negative) experiences of the greatest revolution of the twentieth century, that of communist Russia. Am I saying that if he had read *Pensiero debole* (*Weak Thought*) Stalin probably would not have been a bloody dictator? No, this would obviously be absurd. I mean to say, instead, that Stalinism was, in general, an effect of metaphysics, in the sense that Heidegger attributes to the term: Stalinism was inspired by the belief that some possessed the definitive truth of history (the proletariat was qualified to know it because, not having any interest to defend, it was considered to be free of all ideological veils and, therefore, capable of seeing "objective" truth) and by the belief that an economic, scientific doctrine was being applied. The "scientificity" of the economy and of social organizations is, at once, the adoption of triumphant capitalism, for which the free market remains the only means for creating wealth, irrespective of the number of victims it created through necessary (humanitarian, obviously) wars and the intense exploitation of resources.

Summarizing what I have proposed to this point: there is a clear parallel between hermeneutics and democracy not only, and not primarily, because hermeneutics, being a philosophy that calls for dialogue, evidently proposes a democratic order rather than violence or authoritarianism but also, and more importantly, because democracy and hermeneutics are experiencing a crisis of credibility in a world dominated by neutralization and the absence of emergency. Hermeneutics aspires to be a philosophy of social transformation based – as occurs today in many Latin American countries – on the affirmation of cultural identity as a weapon to use in the struggle against the capitalist and imperialist order. The parallel between democracy and hermeneutics does not consist solely in their shared destiny of crisis but also in the support they offer each other as they revise and restructure their specific meaning. In this sense, the truly important dialogue is not what hermeneutics seems to "preach" for the attainment of a serene collective life but the exchange that hermeneutics and democracy can put into practice in order to understand the meaning of their crisis. For both, the critical factor is the appeal to a universal objective truth. On both the theoretical level, that of worldviews, and the practical level, that of political praxis, presupposed neutrality and universality do not have the slightest meaning. These are simply the ideological masks of the dominant interests. This conclusion, however, is not, in its turn, a discovery or an "eternal" metaphysical truth; it is merely the result of the experiences that modern philosophy has produced having followed, across the centuries, the fortunes of Western imperialism, an experience that, indeed, becomes evident today when the "civilizing" West is starting to see its own vision challenged by another pseudo-universal (Islamic extremism, which has the same monotheist roots that we do) worldview, forcing all of us to acknowledge that objective truth is nothing more than the ideology of the victors.

The critique of the notion of an objective and universal truth seems to bring with it praise of the *bellum omnium contra omnes* (war of all against all) – the *originary* war of survival prior to any social contract. In reality, we should not forget that, at least in the crudest and most realistic of contracts, that of Hobbes, the line *bellum omnium contra omnes* required the acceptance (obviously not through democratic elections) of a tyrant, ruler, etc. on the part of the people. Having seen what democratic elections have become in the late-modern world of domination, radical hermeneutics proposes the recovery of the *originary* freedom *pro omnes* (for all). Naturally, this is only a paradox, but it is a paradox with which we must come to terms, precisely because of the extreme gravity of the crisis in which democracy and philosophy find themselves today,

No ideological and hypocritical "universal truth," but what then? What does hermeneutics offer, not in purely negative terms, in order to escape the enslavement of *omnium sub paucis*, that is to say of everyone (or of the masses) by the few? The idea of revising the social contract at its roots, starting over again but eliminating the "sacred" respect for what has been "established" for centuries and which some want to impose as "natural" (consider, for example the sermons on "biblical anthropology" of the Catholic Church: monogamous marriage, etc.) is already an obvious effort to "legitimize" (or champion) the cause of revolution. Clearly without relying on metaphysics, such as would be an appeal to natural laws, hermeneutics does not believe that human beings are naturally free; freedom can be affirmed only through the act with which it is conquered.

But why should hermeneutics promote revolution? Since it is not a metaphysical philosophy, hermeneutics has no "reasons," in the strong sense of the term, for preferring one social order or another. And it is not a metaphysical philosophy because – even in the absence of objective evidence – it believes (that it has understood) that metaphysics, in any form, is merely the ideological legitimization of the existing forms of power. Therefore, neither the choice of preferring hermeneutics as a philosophy nor the choice of promoting revolution is metaphysically grounded; as was the case for Heidegger, who in *Being and Time* rejected the notion of truth as *adaequatio* (correspondence) without offering another "description" of truth (that might be more adequate!) but only the existential need to oppose the beginnings of total *Verwaltung*, the organization of social life as a production machine based on the scientific division of labour,[2] in the same way that hermeneutics claims its own validity by simply appealing to a (possible) conviction based on a shared experience. If the experience of freedom and the need for the increasing amounts of freedom that we see in our life have a meaning, this cannot be "explained" by returning to a world of objective (essential, metaphysical) truths. In many ways hermeneutics cannot be a "theory" without contradicting itself, that is to say, assuming that "there is" an objective reality in Nietzsche's claim that "there are no facts, only interpretations. And this too is an interpretation" (*Frammenti postumi* [*Posthumous Fragments*] *1885–1887*, 299). More or less paradoxically, the famous eleventh thesis on Feuerbach, with which Marx appears to condemn interpretation, is perfectly "satisfied" by the radical philosophy of interpretation, which cannot be a theory but only a practical act, a choice, a revolutionary decision.

Should we not read the Heideggerian expression "lack of emergency" as another version of what we could call "lack of revolution" – an absence that Heidegger himself could have explained through the notion of Being as event? Running the risk of sharing the biologistic preoccupation with survival, we could say that, from a Heideggerian and hermeneutic point of view, the only way to respond to the call of Being is to facilitate the occurrence of the event. Who promotes and who obstructs the event, i.e. radical change? Obviously, the enemies are the victors in history, who (Walter Benjamin would say) are convinced that the world is absolutely as it should be. Although a philosopher has no "reason" to prefer the weak and the vanquished, except the fact that he probably is weak himself (not being a physical or natural scientist!), he should, nonetheless, heed the call of Being, which is to say, tend to the occurrence of the event. From this perspective, hermeneutics is an ontology of revolution.

11

Emergency and Event: Technique, Politics, and the Work of Art

There is a sentence by Heidegger that I find absolutely pertinent to the current European political and economic situation. According to Heidegger, the only "emergency is the lack of emergency." I interpret emergency as "opposition," and this brings me to the core of the argument I wish to make. In the last few years, in Europe as a whole and in the individual countries of the European Union, we have witnessed the progressive dissolution of every form of opposition. This is especially the case with the financial crisis of the past two years,[1] during which we have witnessed the shocking disappearance of every political alternative. In various forms and to different degrees, each country must follow a series of regulations established by economists who present themselves as mere "technical experts"; there is a fiscal system that must "function" and consequently it must respect specific economic parameters, first and foremost the balance between revenue and expenditure. Italy is a perfect example, as it became the site of Europe's first *technocracy* (government by technical experts) that emerged through the autocratic decision of President Giorgio Napolitano. Originally a communist who has since moved to the centre and converted to the ideals of Atlanticism, Napolitano convinced Prime Minister Silvio Berlusconi to resign despite his parliamentary majority. (The content of the negotiation is unknown, but one suspects that the president promised to gradually relieve Berlusconi's various legal problems, problems that in fact have been recently disappearing.) The president then entrusted leadership to Mario Monti, an economics professor who is morally irreproachable (and therefore immediately welcome in the wake of Berlusconi's improprieties), but who is ultimately tied to the largest international banks. The president charged Monti with the task of saving the Italian economy (ultimately its finance industry) with Greek-style austerity measures. The technocracy does not conform to the agenda of parties that support it from both the Right and the Left. It is, instead, politically neutral and therefore politically unaccountable. I do not have space here to recount this story in more detail, but most readers should already know that this is taking place elsewhere in Europe. European politics is also dominated by problems with its finance industry, banks, and the threat of government insolvency. We are all well aware that economics is neither an exact nor a neutral science. Parties of every political orientation, as well as the big media ("independent," "nonpartisan," and obviously "technical"), relentlessly impose the idea that these special circumstances require a sort of *union sacrée* (sacred union): the suspension of political confrontation in order to fix the economy (ultimately to shore up international financial power).

I do not think it is unreasonable to see this situation from the point of view of a philosopher, namely Heidegger. Perhaps only he can provide the foundation from which to refute the presumed neutrality of "technical experts" and the presumed objectivity of "science" that claims to produce consensus in the name of universal needs, etc. It is precisely this philosopher who is more and more frequently attacked by today's mainstream thinkers for joining the Nazi Party in 1933, who would most radically oppose the levelling of every political discourse to make the system "work well." Let us connect this current triumph of pure technique (in all areas formerly the terrain of politics) to the intensified bureaucratic controls (again by technical experts and in the name of "security") and police controls on the lives of citizens (from electronic surveillance on private communications, to the fact that all Internet communications travel through American servers ...). We will then realize that the loss of political opposition is an unprecedented historic event, a sort of anthropologic mutation that is not merely the great ideological deception that the rich ("the victors" as Benjamin called them) employ in an attempt to preserve and expand their privileges. Instead, we must consider this in the light of Heidegger's "history of Being."

By now the interests of wealth and power have themselves become a pure function of the system; it is in fact impossible to understand what personal motivation may lie behind the constant increase, in the face of economic crisis, of the bonuses and privileges enjoyed by those at the highest levels of the capitalist system. Greed and avarice are by now "original" sins, somewhat similar to lust at a time when bodies are being substituted by their electronic prostheses. If we see the situation in these terms, it becomes more evident that the working classes – whose wealth amounts to the capacity to reproduce – is the last refuge of authentic passions, including sexual desire and fundamental economic needs. The *Guttungswesen*, the generic essence of human beings, still exists only where it is threatened by exploitation and by a generalized tendency to consider humanity in terms of efficiency and functionality.

What is becoming increasingly evident in the wake of every new tsunami, earthquake, and meeting of experts who remind us of the climatic catastrophes produced by CO_2 is the possibility that a sudden and decisive manifestation of the force of "nature" will make up for our lack of emergency and the unlikeliness of an "event." This will not only take the form of human bodies that sooner or later will claim the right to survival but also of climate change that will force populations to make radical changes in their lifestyles and institutions. As in the case of the Apocalypse – "Pray that your flight may not be in winter or on the Sabbath" (Matthew 24:20) – perhaps we should pray that this awakening of nature does not occur all at once, like a catastrophic emergency, but rather through gradual adjustments and a rhythm that is conducive to human adaptation. But, again, taking into account our historical inability to transform, it is difficult to imagine that our prayer will be answered. As Heidegger's history of Being moves (only?) with the *diken didonai* (giving of justice) of the generations that, in turn, make way for one another (and maybe here we have another meaning of Being-towards-death in *Being and Time*), the event of Being happens only in the dialogue with the other that is not world but earth. Ultimately, even the Marxian dialectic between the forces of production and the relations of production is something of this sort. History does not move on its own; on the contrary, when it presumes to exclude every foreign element through an all-encompassing plan (i.e. levelling), it produces the depleted state in which we presently find ourselves. It is the "end of history" that Nietzsche already discussed in the second of his *Untimely Meditations* and that is addressed by some contemporary theories that function as exorcisms rather than prophecies. We might instead stand on the side of those who, almost from the beginning of human history, idealize "barbarians" as saviours because they come wholly from the "outside" (Kavafis wrote a fine poem about the anticipation of these saviours). The truth of Marx's thesis that capitalism harbours within itself the forces of its own destruction is the same truth we find in the passage of the Gospels, "You will always have the poor [or the barbarian] among you" (John 12:8). To put it in Heidegger's terms, only the work of art "produces" the earth, by putting forward the other who suspends the ordinary plausibility of the world, institutions, and routine. The absence of emergency can be felt only within the world of domination, as dysfunction, disturbance, and interruption, a *parole* that acquires meaning in its ability to disturb the quiet of the *langue*. The lack of emergency is also the lack of a concept of the history of Being that accounts for this unresolved dialectic between the world and the earth in every event worthy of its name, not only in the work of art, to which Heidegger restricted himself in his 1936 essay, after his unfortunate Nazi experience. But even this political misadventure of Heidegger's testifies to the fact that one can never simply theorize the lack of emergency without considering a shift to praxis. In this situation, multiplying the conflicts at every level (union, neighbourhood, political, economic) is more important than theorizing. To cite again the Gospel, "For whoever wants to save (perhaps) his soul will lose it [i.e. risk it in conflict]" (Matthew 16:25).

12

Democratic Fundamentalism and Dialect of Thought

I think that it is politically important to reconsider the meaning of such terms as "deep democracy" and "emerging subjectivities" in order to grasp fully the current state of affairs. I interpret "deep democracy" as an allusion to the crisis that representative democracy of the "Western" type is currently experiencing. Not only after Bush adopted the word "democracy" to justify his politics of war but also for more physiological reasons, since the "formal" democracy enjoyed, so to speak, by the industrialized nations of the West increasingly finds less merit in the minds of those disposed to moderation. The media advertising system has placed the election fortunes of the political parties increasingly in the hands of big capital, which controls the economic resources, and which is increasingly less private capital since, in order to grow and prosper, it needs the complicity of the politicians, which is secured through the massive financing of election campaigns. Pure private capital, instead of improving the situation from the democratic point of view, merely represents yet another aspect of the deterioration. In the West a type of new class has more and more affirmed itself, a class composed of the heirs of the industrial wealth and managers (for the most part publicly appointed) of the capital administered by banks and industries that are now semiprivate; this is a new class that deprives the government of the capacity to reform its policies for intervening in the economy. This marriage of powers appears at times to spark conflicts, which, however, lack real political and social weight, being limited as they are to power games played out completely inside the "caste." Thus, who would ever take an interest in big bank mergers that, occasionally, fill the front pages of newspapers? Or the privatization of this or that economic enterprise, for the most part carried out at the expense of the state and to the benefit of private groups with ties to political parties? The case of the post-Soviet Russian economy, with its increasingly wealthy and arrogant oligarchs, is symbolic of what is happening throughout the West, which was once social-democratic and today is totally a slave to market ideology.

In the face of all these changes and the real deterioration of hope for history that they generate, the distrust that for some time filled us, when Marxists talked to us about the difference between formal democracy and "substantive" democracy, loses all trace of a *raison d'être*. It is more and more obvious – and the so-called "stability" of Western regimes confirms this – that representative democracy in which we live (the best possible system, Winston Churchill would say, but only under certain conditions – for example, the condition of being Churchill or, at any rate, another member of the dominant class) is nothing but a means of ensuring that nothing changes from one election cycle to the next. The apparently random fact that even the presidency of the United States has now become a hereditary power (from Bush senior to Bush junior, and probably from Clinton the husband to Clinton the wife) can safely be cited as confirmation of these observations. What is happening to us is analogous to what Europe experienced at the time of the *Blaue Reiter* (Blue Rider), when the avant-garde, from Kandinsky to Picasso, saw African art as a new formal world capable of replacing the, by now, worn out figurative forms of our tradition. It was the eve of the First World War, and, in this regard as well, which brings shivers to my spine, we cannot be very optimistic: the plans to wage war against Iran are much more than an abstract scenario within American military circles. But, apart from these catastrophic hypotheses, albeit tragically real, what we, Westerners disappointed by our formal democracies, suffocated by North American imperialism that is solidly allied with multinational capital, are looking for increasingly are potential democratic regimes that are no longer based simply on the pure and simple equation "one person, one vote" without being concerned about the problem of who the persons that, in principle, we consider to be equal are, or were, inclined to be. The equality of the rights of every individual – certainly for a long time a progressive principle in European modernity – has increasingly become a sort of dogma that precludes all less atrophied forms of democracy. Yes, I must confess that I have in mind (notwithstanding the perversions that it has undergone not for "logical" reasons alone) the Soviet model and the effort that certain revolutions – at the time that of Russia and more recently those that Chávez and Castro – made and are making to ensure that the consensus of the citizens and their choices are formed on the basis of a political life that is less suffocated and less enslaved by television and media propaganda. When, in *Democrazia ad alta energia* (*Empowered Democracy*), he talks of high-energy democracy, Roberto Mangabeira Unger is essentially thinking of a democratic public opinion that thrives on a more constant presence of local institutions, from neighbourhood committees to the public drafting of municipal budgets, which are being tried in some regions of Latin America. With all the reservations I must impose on myself, owing to a partial knowledge of the models of the new Latin American socialism, among other reasons, it is not unreasonable to ask if it is possible that from local traditions, different from the Western European tradition, which have preserved a community practice different from the one that has disappeared in the West due to capitalist rationalization, we can find important and useful examples of a better practice, a way of conceiving and practising a democracy capable of averting the crisis we see today. It goes without saying that it is not a question of applying the structures of Castroism and Chavism to European democracies. As for the more "repugnant" traits of these regimes, i.e. their populism or "Caudillismo," we can at least learn from these examples that the growth of the power of charismatic leaders, whom we find more and more in our formal democracies (Berlusconi, for example), may not become totalitarian or fascist if there is an active presence of local institutions, which is precisely what the atomization of our society by television tends to make impossible. What remains of Western constituent parties? This is a question that brings a shiver: everything now comes from the top, i.e. central secretariats, which are allies of the dominant economic powers whose people are an integral part they control down to the last detail of the majorities and minorities in the "elected" institutions (the recent consultations with the base in Italy, from the union-sponsored referendum on changes to the welfare system, to the so-called primaries for the selection of the leader of the new Democratic Party attest to this very fact).

We can, therefore, try to respond to the undeniable need for a "deep democracy" by paying more attention to the other social and cultural worlds on which until now our Western world has tried to impose its lifestyle of consumerism and its own protocols, above all economic ones, by waging bloody "humanitarian" wars led by the United States. Is such attention only the expression of the need, largely "on the part of intellectuals," for renewal, a demonstration of the unease of the socially maladapted who are always dissatisfied with what they have and who, for example, do not have the required gratitude toward the United States, the saviours of the "free world," first from Nazi brutality and then from the Soviet bear and its gulags? Here too a similar thought, such as suspicion as regards the concept of substantive democracy, has become impracticable by now in the face of the massacre of democracy and humanity that goes hand in hand with "humanitarian" wars waged by the United Nations and Bush, on the one hand and, in consideration of the growing importance of the experiments in socialist democracy that we find in Latin America, on the other hand.

In short, if there is a path to the salvation of the democratic tradition and the solidarity of "old Europe" (you may recall Rumsfeld's disparaging expression) it runs through a new alliance of all those countries that want renewal – a high-energy one but I would say an imprudent "Soviet" one – of the moribund Western democracy. Also, and above all, as a European and an Italian who has seen many attempts by "centre-left" governments fail, I am aware that a similar "program" (I am aware that this an exaggeration) has almost insurmountable problems. According to Unger, perhaps and unfortunately, only a very serious crisis in our economy and our lifestyles (exhaustion of energy resources, climate catastrophes, for example) could push the citizens of the industrialized world out of their indifference toward the political life. Naturally I do not wish for this to happen even though I am increasingly aware that this is coming. However, in a move that was already made by Marcuse, we can try to support more earnestly those efforts of renewal on the part of what remains of the world's proletariat, on which Marx counted to transform society, in other words, the countries of the so-called third world, which, because of their different traditions (I have in mind the Andean culture) among other things, can create and show us models of human society that are no longer obsessed by the ideal of development and competition. Unger's reference to the crisis that is supposed to shake us is what I would call, citing a poem by Kavafis, waiting for the "barbarians," the hope of "external" help – not a mythical *deus ex machina* exactly but perhaps a sort of pressure that at long last awakens our sense of belonging to a single humanity, in the knowledge that the only "*machina*" that can save us is the rediscovery of those shared roots that modernization (economic, imperialist, blindly competitive) have made us forget.

13

Concerning Politics and Love

Can we say, as does Martha Nussbaum in her recent book *Political Emotions*, that "love is important for justice" (as the subtitle, *Why Love Matters for Justice*, indicates)? Nussbaum is currently one of the most well-known political philosophers in the United States, which gives this book and its subtitle a meaning that could be defined as "epochal." It is not often (I would say it is rare) that studies of political theory (I do not mean sociology or social psychology) are dedicated to such a theme. Nussbaum recognizes that her position owes much to John Rawls's theory of justice, which pays little attention to emotions and appears, instead, to be a sort of moderate form of utilitarianism called liberalism, in the traditional Anglo-Saxon sense of behaviour that respects fundamental human rights and the attainment of justice, as Nussbaum thinks after all, in the Aristotelian sense: just distribution of goods and social responsibilities, and an egalitarian democracy. It is difficult to see how, in this tradition, love, and more generally feelings, could count. It is precisely with respect to this lacuna that Nussbaum makes a contribution in her desire to offer a kind of completion of Rawls's theory in terms of what is necessary for a just society from the standpoint of emotions. First of all, we need to know that Nussbaum's book does not deal with the importance of emotions as they relate to the political struggle or, let us say, the establishment of a liberal state; it is concerned only with the issue of which feelings should be promoted and activated in the liberal society of the type visualized by Rawls. Let us consider a contrary example, namely what Walter Benjamin writes in his brief essay on the philosophy of history, where he describes the emotional attitude of revolutionaries who are inspired in their struggle not so much by the image of the future society they plan to bring about, as by the memory of the injustices and suffering endured by their ancestors. Whatever we may think, in Nietzschean terms, of the negativity of this "resentment," here we find a very meaningful statement. We might even see in it an example of the impossibility of separating theory from praxis. A revolution does not need a specific and detailed image made in advance, a program that can be assessed rationally; what puts it in motion is precisely the intolerable present condition, whose features can be plainly seen, but without saying exactly how one thinks about building something afterwards. (Let us keep in mind the verses of Eugenio Montale in a poem from the fascist era, namely "Non chiederci la parola" ["Don't ask me for words"]: "Codesto solo oggi possiamo dirti / ciò che *non* siamo, ciò che *non* vogliamo" ["All I can tell you now is this: / what we are *not*, what we do *not* want"].) In Nussbaum's text, there is no mention of what can inspire the actions that bring about social transformation; love and other emotions matter for her in that they are the indispensable content of society; you cannot have a just, liberal society without certain feelings, which she describes and analyzes, among the citizens. We have before us, then, a program, but I would say, of the "reformist" or "complementary" type for action within a liberal society. It is a program that does not go beyond a sort of emotional *welfare state*, the models for which are taken from literature or music (*The Marriage of Figaro*); as well, it makes use of more "classical" authors from the political philosophy tradition, such as Rousseau, Comte, and Stuart Mill, or poets, like Tagore. Despite the many literally fascinating pages, what is paradoxically missing in Nussbaum's book is precisely love or emotion. This is not a literary observation. Rather, it is the fact that, in liberal political literature ("progressive," in the best sense of the word) what dominates is the description of an ideal order in which we cannot ask ourselves what the "conditions of possibility" are (to use a Kantian expression). This same type of problem arises in the theory of communicative action proposed by Habermas, who basically limits himself to describing a public communication society that is not manipulated or distorted. Certainly, in the description of the ideal conditions for a communicative society of this kind, there is also a revolutionary program (which, moreover, for a long time has made Habermas a philosopher or rather *the* philosopher of the Left), but what is missing is precisely a theory of transformation. When we set out to describe something, it is precisely the passions and emotions that are lost; this also constitutes the limits of Nussbaum's book, which aims to be a "scientific" text in the Rawls–Aristotle tradition – but which, ultimately, does not disturb the liberal order in which Nussbaum and Habermas believe they are living.

All this could remain within the confines to a simple critical academic discussion of the book. But the very fact that, as I noted at the outset, we are dealing with the work of a philosopher who is already almost a "classic" of liberal thinking, it goes beyond these limits and, at least in my view, opens up the perspective on the fate of "alternative" politics in "Western" societies. From this perspective, what we find in this book becomes somewhat emblematic of what is lacking in current liberalism and of the inability of liberal thought to fill this gap. First and foremost, it is significant that a topic like the emotions should be the point of a discussion that is not marginal with respect to political theory. Why now? In my opinion, the topicality of this issue indicates clearly the crisis of democracy in the so-called "democratic" world. Nussbaum notes and raises the question of the lack of emotions that characterizes the contemporary political climate. Everything is happening as if no one "believed" any longer. The same old electoral campaigns in many European countries no longer arouse intense public debates. In any case, there is indeed talk of a low-intensity democracy in our societies.

In many respects, we could say that what happens in a liberal society Marx already saw as the future of capitalism: it harbours within itself those who would kill it. What is more liberal or Rawlsian than a political debate centred on the economy, resources, and administration? Only rarely is there talk of general projects or worldviews in this kind of politics; this would mean falling back on ideology, the sworn enemy of any serious and realist political discussion. Fortunately for some countries (like Italy), there are homosexuals and the issue of same-sex marriage, which compel us to talk about family, real-life matters, and worldviews. What concerns the dominant classes most, instead, are the budget and the imperative of "stability." Who is ever emotional about "stability"?

Even the great ongoing war against terrorism, whether real or invented by the media and governments, is part of this picture, which is characterized by a lack of emotions: it [the war] tries to compensate for this lack with graphic descriptions that invade our television sets in prime time, but we know that excess anesthetizes our emotional response. Indifference is pervasive. The futurist slogan "war, the world's only hygiene" sadly appears to be realized in the stories of urban violence, which is usually explained as an effect of a one-dimensional world.

Could Martha Nussbaum's "liberal" emotions have therapeutic value in such a disastrous scenario? It is not by chance that she takes her positive examples from eighteenth-century opera, i.e. the music of Mozart rather than from the passionate novels of the nineteenth century or "Dostoevskian" novels. The love she speaks of as a factor that contributes to the life of a just society seems to be a socially accepted love, full of irony, worldly, and nonviolent. Still less is it "the love that dare not speak its name" (as Oscar Wilde called homosexuality) because the "good" emotions that liberal society promotes include a feeling of tolerance, which helps us to suppress the disgust experienced by some people when they are confronted by behaviours that they find detestable, outright unnatural, or "monstrous."

I am exaggerating here but not too much. The fact is that Nussbaum's book appears to be dominated by a sort of "ironical theology" that corresponds very well to the social climate of the "advanced" democracies in which we believe we are living. If it is true that modern democracy is a child of the age of Enlightenment – on the other hand it represents one of the most important legacies of the eighteenth century – we can easily find these moderate and controlled emotions discussed by Nussbaum to be an apologia for a "rational" and reasonable society, one that avoids excesses of all kinds as it lives the democratic process itself (elections, alternation of power, etc.) as something that excludes violence and, above all, change (violent, of course) in the established order. All this leads us to rethink the very idea of a well-regulated society, such as Kant's ideal cosmopolitanism. Let us always be mindful of the fact that one of the philosophers who defended the United Nations and its organs of international conflict resolution is the Kantian Jürgen Habermas who, in this regard, is evidently in agreement with Nussbaum and Rawls as well as with "Western" reformist thought as a whole.

For me, it is not a question of stigmatizing the conservative character of this reformist thought, whose institutional content, among other things, we cannot fail to appreciate. We all want to bring about a Kantian cosmopolitan republic. What we cannot accept too readily, however, is the lack of reflection on the present situation, wherein the cosmopolitan republic and its institutions of international justice, which are now already an authoritarian caricature dominated by NATO, in its role as policeman revolving around the Pentagon, in spite of recent changes. In this situation, "to describe," which is to say to theorize, liberal society means to admit that this society, in fact, exists and that it, at most, needs a "supplement of the heart" – the "positive" emotions that are at the core of Nussbaum's book.

We might agree, but then what? What affective state or emotional situation do we want to promote in a society capable of transforming itself radically, instead of thinking only of safeguarding its "stability," which is no doubt loving but always within the limits expressed, for instance, by the Latin phrase *unicuique suum* (to each his own), without being curious about the origin of the qualities we are expected to respect in this way? It is precisely in this context that I reiterate the words of Benjamin on the suffering of ancestors, quoted earlier. But I could also cite a small book that has had great success recently. In Stéphane Hassel's *Indignez-vous!* (*Time for Outrage!*), the indignation being discussed is not based on "logical" reasons, on rational calculation of the sort demanded by the citizens of some European countries that are required to accept austerity measures in order to repay "their" debt to the banks. We need, first of all, to see the suffering of "others," like the ancestors Benjamin talks about or the forgotten of all kinds (third or fourth world, the marginalized and exploited, animals subjected to biomedical experiments). It is precisely this silent world – Heidegger would call it the "silence of Being," that philosophy must know how to heed – how to respond to the call of indignation. The latter is almost something irrational, which is to say that it has the features of love or passion, because it arises in us without explanation, like the fact of falling in love. The usual objections of "formal" democrats to this kind of political emotion are largely directed at the phenomenon of the charismatic "leader"; great examples in Latin America include Castro, Chávez, Lula, Morales, etc. At this point, we are touching on the problem of *Führerprinzip* (leader principle), which I do not intend to discuss here. It is, so to speak, dangerous. But we cannot ignore it, especially in a society where the candidates running for election acquire more and more the features of charismatic leaders, or have to possess qualities of this kind, which the great revolutions have always (here is a possible topic for discussion) demanded of their "heroes," of great personalities capable of mobilizing the "masses."

We are dealing with an irrational component of politics that continues to scandalize us. But we also need theory to take up this problem, if it does not want to remain at the level of good feelings and, ultimately, at the level of an apologia, albeit an implicit one, for the status quo. If we consider that one of the major problems of revolutionary parties has always been the relationship between the masses (inspired by the indignation we are talking about) and the "central committee" (consisting of "rational" directors, delegated to produce a possible program of action and, therefore, always susceptible to the corruption of calculating minds, compromises with the existing order, etc.), we come to understand how many aspects the question of love that matters in politics has.

My conclusion here is not exactly a conclusion; it is intended merely to ask questions about our present situation: calculating and reasonable capitalism imposes on us a social life that is increasingly "neutralized," where passions (as well as suffering, says Benjamin) are in some sense suspended in the name of economics. I point out that, as Marx already stated, political economy is not a natural science; therefore, the suppression of emotions in favour of calculation is not a "natural" duty. Rather, it is the imposition of one individual on another – in short, an aspect of domination. To evoke the suffering of ancestors (and of the "other," both past and present) in order to act politically is scandalous because this does not correspond at all to rational calculation, which, moreover, is only the historical expression of class domination. Martha Nussbaum's book is, therefore, valuable because it compels us to see, once again, the contradictions of capitalism (be wise and calculating by all means, but you will not really be able to do so; you also need love) within which, we can always hope, a transforming action will occur.

14

How to Become an Anti-Zionist

Despite what Giorgio Napolitano, the president of the Italian Republic, often repeats, one can be an anti-Zionist without being antisemitic. This is so not only because there are plenty of Jews in the world who take their tradition seriously without identifying it with the State of Israel, from which they continually dissociate themselves, but also because, as the non-Zionist Jews themselves teach, the richness of the Jewish culture and its distinct presence in the spirit of the West and the modern world in general did not establish itself with the creation of the State of Israel and in fact is seriously threatened by it. Today, it makes more sense to repeat what one Jewish intellectual had the courage to say – that among all the harms produced by Hitler's politics and by the Holocaust, one can also list the creation of Israel as a Jewish state in 1948.

For many European intellectuals who came of age in the middle of the twentieth century, a reflection on Zionism appears in terms rather similar to those that shape the biography of Ilan Pappé (*Out of the Frame: The Struggle for Academic Freedom in Israel*). It presents itself as the history of a sharing that turns into a progressive dissolution of a "constitutive" mythology – the very thing that continues to be valued in the self-awareness of many Jews who remain tied to this mythology. We, namely Europeans who were born around the time of the Second World War, were raised – save for rare exceptions, as rare as those who remained fascists at the end of the 1940s – on the myth of the antifascist resistance and on the painful memory of the Holocaust. Immediately after the war in Italy, but I think generally in Europe, to be an antifascist, a democrat, and to stand behind the Jews and their struggle to return to their homeland, Palestine, was one and the same thing. Whoever knows Italian history in the second half of the twentieth century knows that only in recent years have the parties that refer back to the inheritance of fascism been "cleared" or in other words readmitted to a place of honour by a political system that wanted to rebuild itself, including its right-wing components. In principle, this was done so that no one was excluded from the democratic dialogue and yet more immediately for reasons of electoral advantage. It is also noteworthy that the reemergence of "democratic" parties that no longer demonize the fascist legacy (a famous claim comes from Gianfranco Fini, then leader of the Italian Social Movement, and today president of the Chamber of Deputies,[1] who described Mussolini as the greatest statesman of the twentieth century) has not in a similar manner diminished the love for Israel in the opinion of the Italian public. Still today, even though Fini is the third in charge of the state and ex-fascists have for some time held government positions (along with the Northern League and Silvio Berlusconi), every once in a while the authoritative voices of politicians of every political stripe clamour to propose laws that punish the denial of crimes against humanity, on the basis that even with the acceptance of fascism, pro-Zionist sentiment remains largely dominant in Italian public consciousness. Moreover, with the help of many American films that tell the story of the return of the Jews to Palestine before and after 1948, the Zionist epic has for some time stood in the imagination of the Italian public as analogous to the epic of antifascist resistance and, in its more spectacular aspects, something akin to the conquering of the West by nineteenth-century Yankees. This last "cinematographic" reference appears somewhat forced, but it comes to mind for good reasons, since no viewer of Westerns, except in recent years, has ever been concerned with the fate of the Native Americans exterminated by the advance of the white settlers and their cowboys – in a way completely analogous to the absolute forgetting endured by the Palestinians in the epic of the birth of Israel.

It was precisely the discovery of the Nakba in the second year of high school – that is, of the "disaster" represented for the Palestinians by the ethnic cleansing conducted by Israel from 1948 onward (up until today, I must add) – that pushed Ilan Pappé from his initial leftist Zionism to his current, radical polemical stance against Israel – against the leaders of Israel, but also against the Jewish state itself, the state that he would like to replace, if he could, with a secular, democratic, and egalitarian state. It is here, with all its differences, that the history of Western, often also decidedly Atlantic, democratic intellectuals (or even those convinced the communist danger might still threaten Europe and, therefore, likely to approve without or with little reservation the imperialist politics of the United States), approximates that of Pappé. We started with a "Zionist" mythology – the right of Israel to have its own state, legitimized by the horror of the Shoah and by the apparent lack of democracy in the entire Middle East – and we have over time abandoned it precisely when we discovered the Nakba; that is, when we opened our eyes, or when they were opened, to the colonialist and nationalist (even racist) sin that remains like an original sin upon the foundation of the State of Israel.

As with all mythologies, this one is not dissolved by simply taking note of the "true" nature of things. It was, and is now for many of us, a complex process that involved the whole of our sociopolitical, and in the end also our ethical and religious, conceptions, such as even our long friendships, are put into crisis. Along with other aspects of our private lives (starting with a certain ostracism by the most official and mainstream mass media). Meanwhile, it is no coincidence that I recalled the Atlanticism that accompanies, well beyond the antifascist commitment, our spontaneous "Zionism" in the years after the war. The right of Israel to establish a state appeared to be directly tied to the destiny of Western democracy or what the Voice of America was apt to call "the free world." I am not writing a documentary autobiography of an ex-Zionist but only searching to reconstruct the meaning and the motives behind my (and not only mine, as I think it is widely shared) present anti-Zionism as it matures in me alongside the dissolution of my faith in the West and the "free world." On the one side, the end of the "American myth" was certainly decisive and was totally accomplished by 1968 but became crystal clear in 1989 with the fall of the Berlin Wall and the dissolution of the Soviet Union. In 1968 many of us held the conviction that Israeli Jews were constructing an authentic, rather than a Stalinist, form of socialism – that same conviction that led many Italian families on the Left (but not only) to send their children to work on *kibbutzes* so they might learn what democratic socialism is. What did we know or think then of the Palestinians who were driven out of their homes and off their land? We more or less believed the slogan: a land without people for a people without a land. In the years that followed, we began to know the Palestinians as terrorists and suicide bombers: a desperate few turned fanatics by religious hatred, animated by blind antisemitic rage (I seem to remember that, in recent years, a French-Jewish intellectual – I believe it was André Gluckmann – even spoke about them as an example of lived nihilism, a sort of pure and simple incarnation of evil).

For a long time, there was a story that in Nasser's Egypt ex-Nazi officers were all the rage as instructors who were determined to export the Shoah to the Middle East as well. Therefore, once again, one had to be a Zionist in order to be an antifascist. But with the fall of the Berlin Wall and the breakup of the Soviet Union, things began to change, even in the general picture of the "democratic" West. The "unipolar" world, freed from the Soviet threat, showed that the escalation of "international terrorism" before and after 11 September (with all the mythology shrouding this date, beginning with the unbelievable official version of the facts provided by the American government) was more dangerous than the Cold War and involved an intensification of every type of control along with the multiplication of "peripheral" wars in every part of the world where the "terrorist beast" was being pursued (preferably, if located in an oil-producing region). The fight against terrorism brought with it, perhaps naturally or more likely due to a deliberate choice by the Israeli government, an increase in tensions in the Middle East; for example, the idea that Iran's "atomic race" could be halted with ever stronger sanctions, more rigorous controls, and even preemptive war if necessary. And alongside this, there was "Operation Cast Lead" against Gaza from the end of 2008 into 2009, which was destined to stop the launching of the almost totally harmless missiles into Israeli territory. Better still, the entire Gaza affair contributed in a decisive way, more than any other aspect of Israeli politics, to the idea (I believe with great likelihood) that against the risk of a return of refugees, which would entail the end of the "Jewishness" of the State of Israel, this situation might see no other solution than the progressive extermination of Palestinian Arabs. All this comes with ever-renewed settlement construction, promoted in every way with a racially oriented politics of accommodation that, as we all know, is also creating tensions within Israel between two classes of immigrants – fundamentally a class conflict.

From Israel we hear ever more frequently the voices of the many Israelis who, beginning with the Peace Now movement, condemn the politics of their government against Palestinians. Usually, even these movements of opposition still tend to take seriously the project of "two people, two states," which by now has been revealed to be a means of prolonging infinitely (after the past twenty years or so) pseudoattempts to solve the problem. In the meantime, the settlements multiply, the construction of new residences in East Jerusalem intensifies, and, above all, the wall that divides Palestine in two and makes the lives of Palestinians, including the citizens of Israel, ever more unbearable continues to expand. The myth of "two states for two people," another aspect of the Zionist mythology, is all too clearly a way of protracting matters so that it does not appear to be an ongoing excuse by Western democracies to avoid their responsibilities, a way to give Israel the time to continue the genocide, in Gaza and elsewhere, and also to reinforce themselves militarily in every way, including the possession of atomic weapons.

Let us – we anti-Zionist supporters of Palestinians – not hide the fact that one of the reasons behind our attitude is also and above all the increasing awareness of the link between Israeli politics and the politics of American interests. Without subscribing to theories of the Jewish–Masonic conspiracy that have the sole effect of ridiculing opinions that are often not unfounded, we are in recent years – above all since the United States began the war against "international terrorism" and namely against all countries and political powers that did not submit to their domination – more aware that the Palestinian cause is also the cause of the people who rebel against imperialism. That Brazil's president Lula was among the first "Western" leaders to welcome Iran and Ahmadinejad has an emblematic value that goes far beyond the particular significance of his visit. One must also add all the old (Cuba) and new progressive governments of Latin America that took a stand. Never before was it so evident (at least it seems to me) that what is up for grabs in Palestine is the destiny of oppressed peoples who try to avoid the rule of the new colonialism – economic but often military as well – of global capital concentrated in the United States (even if it is distributed among many countries, all of them "Atlantic"). So by now anti-Zionism is synonymous with leftist world politics, no matter what the attitudes of individuals and movements that believe – as I recalled at the outset, citing the position of President Giorgio Napolitano – Israel can still be included among the states that are democratic, progressive, etc. It is also not worth recalling the usual excuse of those who invite us to distinguish the State of Israel – whose legitimacy should never be placed in doubt – from the leaders of Israel who are responsible for the recent antidemocratic politics that scandalize us, as it is a laughable excuse. But when was there ever a government in Israel that did not pursue this sort of politics of expansion, thereby diminishing the rights of Palestinians? The Nakba has been the archetype for all Israeli politics since 1948; moreover, it was understandable, given the proposal to preserve the Jewishness of the state and, therefore, to close off every possibility of return for the refugees and also to foreclose every demographic or social expansion on the part of the Arab population. Does this not mean that what makes Israel "unacceptable" as a state is its racist-colonialist antiegalitarian original sin?

One never dares – or almost never, except in the case of Islamic heads of state like Ahmadinejad – to question the very legitimacy of Israel's existence and for good reasons of international stability, starting with the fact that, if war breaks out for a brief time, it will be the "preemptory" type that Israel wants to fight and that makes the West fight due to the Iranian threat – a threat that is exactly what is contained in the bellicose speeches of the heads of state who do not have any real possibility of making it happen. Israel continually presses the West to launch a "preventive" war against Iran, a war that would surely have the character of the self-destructive nihilism that Gluckmann attributes to Islamic terrorists who have fallen prey to a desperate death cult. As for the idea of making the State of Israel "disappear" from the map – one of the usual themes of the Iranian "threat" – its sense may not be completely unreasonable; it could, and ought, according to us, mean that the State of Israel becomes a secular, democratic, nonracist state, without walls and without discrimination among its citizens. We know well that this seems like the destruction of the State of Israel, but it would mean only a transformation of the sort that Ilan Pappé would also view favourably. Neither destruction nor bombing nor violent change of geographic boundaries but finally a modernization of the sort that has occurred in many other states who are supportive of the birth of Israel and yet feel a certain embarrassment about its politics. When he invokes the end of the State of Israel, Ahmadinejad is merely expressing a demand that should be more explicitly shared by the democratic countries, which, instead, consider him an enemy.

The democratic anti-Zionism about which I speak and write – in short, an autobiography – does not really consider the destruction of Israel (but who really thinks this? not even Ahmadinejad, for sure), neither by means of Iran's atomic bombs (today about as threatening as the rockets fired from Gaza, which have done hardly any damage, even though the Palestinians have paid for them with Operation Cast Lead), nor a secular and democratic transformation that would make Palestine a modern and ultimately liveable country. And then what? We should carry Israel with us, in us, like a weight from which we will not free ourselves any time soon, almost like the inerasable memory of the Holocaust that is imposed like a penalty and for which we have yet to atone. Only Israel itself – its politicians, its citizens – could set itself free with a radical change in politics. This is unlikely to happen, let us be clear, because it would also be unbearable for the American power that supports Israel, even as it serves it as its very own Middle Eastern policeman. To speak of Israel as an "irredeemable sin" is, therefore, not so excessive: whether one thinks about how, since its birth, the Jewish State has used the Holocaust as a permanent weapon against anyone who might question its politics (see Finkelstein, *Holocaust Industry*) or one considers how the Holocaust has been experienced by much contemporary philosophy – a sort of parameter by which the accountability of philosophies is measured, a type of Nuremburg tribunal before which all thinkers are brought in order to be judged.

First of all, we are dealing with the philosophy of Heidegger, who surely was wrong to side with Hitler's regime for a time and paid rather heavily for his sin after the war's end (above all, being forbidden to teach and so on). But, for all its shamefulness, the episode remains the subject of analysis by many Nazi hunters who never seem to get enough of justice-vengeance. Many recent studies, aided by new documents brought to light after the publication of Farias's famous book in 1983 (*Heidegger and Nazism*) and especially Emmanuel Faye (*Heidegger, The Introduction of Nazism into Philosophy*) continue to pile guilt not only on the Heidegger of 1933 and later but on his entire philosophy, which has been depicted as a philosophical translation of Hitlerism. The many who have read, interpreted, and at times followed Heidegger, even on the Left, are called to order; if they are unaware that they are following a Nazi thinker, they had better take note. With this, a great deal of contemporary thought that had defined the culture of recent decades – I am thinking especially of Derrida and of hermeneutics – has been "purged," so to speak. No more deconstruction, no more hermeneutic ontology – only the mainstream thinking of the Atlantic, North

American, and Anglo-Saxon sort! Moreover, we might add that the same Farias, in writings that came after his first text, has also pointed out a dangerous proximity between Heideggerianism and Iranian Islamic thought.

When they are not explicitly called to demonstrate that the only philosophy one can practise today is the apologetic–realist form found in Anglo-Saxon universities (Searle and company), the works of those like Faye recall Zionism in its substantially vindictive significance. It remains a matter of making someone pay for their sins against the people of Israel, even those who are no longer able to constitute a real threat. The use of the Shoah as an all-encompassing justification for all the illegitimate actions of Israel (from the continual violation of United Nations resolutions to the systematic decimation of the Palestinian population) is also revealed to be a form of radical and vindictive executionism, much more than a form of simple and cynical political expediency. All this is done to evoke the suspicion, on the part of those who always believed they belonged to the Judeo-Christian tradition, that the God of Israel, who was believed to be the father of Jesus Christ, is instead only and properly the God of the hosts of a nomadic people who, from their own mythology (divine election, the Covenant, the purity of the race) draw their legitimacy and claim to exceptionality.

When I confront the question of Israel today, particularly with the bad conscience of the Christian world for the persecution the Jews have suffered over the centuries, more and more I have the impression that this history has nothing to do with me. For example, when I continue to recite, in the Latin breviary, certain psalms, like the twelfth (*Cum reducet Dominus captive Sion*), I increasingly feel its literal, more than its allegorical, meaning: this is not a song of liberation from sin but a song of jubilation for the military victory by one people over another. And what about the psalms against the Babylonians who were guilty of enslaving the Jews, with the curse on the newborns of Babylon who should be smashed against the walls and massacred in the name (the justice) of God? All in all, even the archetype of the return – from the *regiones dissimilitudinis* ("I found myself far off from You, in the region of dissimilarity," Augustine, *Confessions* VII, 10) to the house of the father, an archetype that I also feel in my spiritual life I cannot do without – is perhaps only the feeling of a nomadic people with whom, in the end, I have nothing in common … And what of Kafka, Rosenzweig,

Walter Benjamin, Bloch ...? I certainly do not want to do without all of these essential components of my and our culture. I will not do to them what Zionist Nazi hunters have done to Heidegger, when they think of dismissing him because he sided with Hitler. Once again, I cannot free myself from the problem of Israel; it is ultimately like the original sin spoken of in the Old Testament, the Hebrew Bible. Here I will take up, to conclude this "unconcludable" reflection, a summary of an article of mine that has never been published – not by my choice – in an Italian newspaper but that crystallizes much of what I have in mind when I speak of Zionism and anti-Zionism. It begins with the viewing of the Coen brothers' film *A Serious Man*, released some years ago and perhaps one that has not been discussed and understood enough.

> So is it true that, as Deleuze once said (Deleuze, Guattari, *Kafka. Toward a Minor Literature*), that Kafka's *The Trial* (and perhaps *The Castle* as well) is a grand comedic novel? This idea returned to me after having viewed the last film of the Coen brothers, *A Serious Man*. The premise, in its entirety, is as follows: Just as the corruption and thirst for money and the power of the Church (not only Ratzinger's, alas) has allowed us (ex)Catholics to discover not only all the inquisitorial and colonial depravities of the past but also the absurdity of today (from the banning of condoms in the age of AIDS, to survival at any cost with the use of tubes and wires – until the pope do you part – to the "rights" of the embryo, obviously always represented by the Holy Roman Church), so too perhaps the bloody racist politics of the State of Israel have begun to push the American Jewish community – its better parts, certainly starting with Chomsky – to note that the much-praised richness and depth of the Judaic tradition is only so much mephitic hot air from which one must free oneself in order to avoid continuing to spill blood on account of the tomb of Rachel, the Temple grounds, or the sacred rights of the Jews to the Promised Land. The empty and sententious rabbis of the Coen brothers and Woody Allen are just like our bishops and cardinals. They are nothing but giant balloons filled with "mystic" rhetoric that sweeps us up for the love of God – the God who torments Job, his family, and the animals due to an absurd bet with that other comic character, the devil (will anyone publish this elementary reflection?).

15

Transparent Totalitarianism

Who knows why, when I think of transparency, what comes to mind is the Russian word *perestroika*, the literal meaning of which, as I read in Wikipedia – that is to say, one of the main organs of our current transparency – is "reconstruction," "restructuring" but certainly not "transparency," as I see it. Is this, perhaps, because the values at the root of Gorbachev's reconstruction (of communism? the USSR?) included a new freedom of information and, therefore, a kind of transparency in power, politics, and social relations? Be that as it may, I and perhaps many others associate the term "transparency" with something from the past, an era that was once ours but is no longer, something that evokes a certain nostalgia, like the good old days of our grandparents, our aunts and uncles, and the illusions of youth. It is a fact that no one believes in transparency any more, not even those who – like me in 1989 – made it a constitutive feature, albeit filled with contradictions, of the nascent postmodern society. In effect, when I gave a successful little book the title *The Transparent Society*, I was using the term in what was already an ironic sense. Transparency seemed to me to announce a chaotic society – knowing everything about everyone ultimately means not knowing anything, at least precisely – and, therefore, a world like the one Nietzsche has in mind when he speaks of accomplished nihilism, where the end of the highest values and of the dominant convictions obliges everyone to become an *Übermensch*, an original interpreter, or perish. For me, then, it was like saying that finally, due to the fact that ultimate truths had vanished, it was possible to love one's neighbour, the person next to me, since one could no longer say *amicis Plato sed magis amica veritas* (Plato is my friend, but truth is more friend to me) because there are all around us not only so many Platos, each deserving of the highest respect, but also no metaphysical hierarchy that places them on a lower rung, which makes them dependent on the greater or lesser value of truth. In brief, a self-contradictory transparency was at the core of the postmodern dream. Meanwhile, if we want to understand why that dream today seems *ausgeträunt*, that is to say finished or dissolved, we need to remember that the war against international terrorism was invented by the United States after the events of 11 September (how much of it was invented as well?) and with it the security policies that have by now made us all so transparent that we are unable to create confusion or Babel: search engines have been creating order in the mass of data from the beginning, and any freedom born of uncertainty and confusion now seems unthinkable. Precisely in the last few weeks they uncovered in Washington what already goes by the name of "Datagate"[1] (from the famous Watergate that ruined Nixon). At the centre of this is the National Security Agency, which, as we read in the newspapers (but which are facts that will certainly be updated), monitors on average three billion phone calls per day using a secret program called Prism. For now, they tell us that the monitoring is limited to identifying the numbers that we call and that call us but without listening to or recording the conversations. But who believes that? Moreover, having worked, a number of years ago, on a European parliamentary commission charged with studying Echelon, a global megasystem of phone and electronic message surveillance created jointly by the United States, Great Britain, Australia, Canada, and New Zealand, these numbers do not surprise me, especially because, in the course of that study, I also learned of the approximate numbers related to the "official" annual expenditures of the American government on intelligence services; I do not recall the exact numbers but they are absolutely enormous, even if they relate only to the maintenance of the services and agencies that are officially known.

In its most elementary form, the postmodern dream came down to just another mistake of technological determinism. It was like taking too seriously the "Marxian" thesis that the transformations of the means of production implied, more or less necessarily, a change in the relations of production. In this instance, it was information that travelled on the web and that, in its perverseness, seemed capable of evading all surveillance, thereby frustrating even the control of the proprietors of the net, the police, and the command centres of espionage. Perhaps we should have understood that we were dealing with a typically "modern" illusion, like the one of the individual from the big city (I have in mind Simmel's essay on the metropolis and moral life, *La metropli e la vita dello spirito* [*The Metropolis and Mental Life*], 1903) who believed that he could free himself from patriarchal morality and the familism of village ethics via the metropolitan existence in which he found himself immersed. The reference to the Marxian dialectic between modes of production and relations of production is appropriate here because it evokes the *geschichtsphilosophisch* (philosophical history) of the entire issue. Up to what point can we apply that dialectic to a production that no longer has anything to do with a physical material that needs to be changed and that no longer looks anything like, let us say, factory labour or artisanal work but rather consists of collecting, organizing, and distributing "news"? This undeniable difference explains the reason for the postmodern illusion and the "naïve" determinism that inspired it: because we are in the immaterial realm of news and we also speak of a production that uses totally unusual "machines" like computers and works with "objects" like data bits, it was not unrealistic to expect that the traditional relations between property and domination could finally be changed in a radical way.

The technological innovation, however, always takes root in a historical preexisting context and has cultural, moral, and juridical structures, which do not change overnight. A postmodern expectation that we find today, for example, as a result of the nonapplicability of copyright laws to the circulation of all kinds of content on the web. Here, perhaps even more so than in the case of the image of a postmodern Babel, it is legitimate to expect that, given the newness of the apparatus that allows us to circulate copyrighted music, texts, films, and scientific formulas without paying the lending rights prescribed by laws, these laws will be changed sooner or later, thereby permitting us to take another step toward a society that is no longer dominated by the principle of proprietorship.

Such reflections as these, which would seem to be self-criticism of postmodern thought were it not for all the events that have occurred from the moment we had those expectations, show in a concrete way what could be called "the return of history," which has rendered meaningless the theories of the end of history based on the illusion that the victory of liberal democracy in much of the world (and the probability that, one way or another, the so-called "free world" would soon install it in the rest of the planet) would end wars and struggles of every kind, thereby reducing politics to a matter of simple administration. It is to be noted that this expectation of the end of history and of political conflicts is what international imperialism is always trying to achieve through various forms of integration and globalization. We see this in the actions taken by "technical" governments, like the Italian one of recent times (it came into existence in 2011 and survives under another name but with the same "neutrality" in 2013) or like those that are still formally "political" in other countries of the European Union, which are reduced to surrendering their sovereignty to banks and international monetary funds. A reflection on the destiny of "transparency" and the postmodern dream is especially relevant today precisely because, far from being a theoretical matter, it is intensely political and concerns the chances for survival of the freedom of the world. Of course, a reflection such as this does not take us very far away from what we already knew, namely, that the total transparency that the new technology promised – which allowed us to think we were really living in a world where "the meaning of history" was destined to become, at long last, immediately understandable to those who create it (which would mean the end of alienation, according to Sartre in *Critique of Dialectical Reason*) – could not establish itself without coming to terms with the existing power relations, and, therefore, with the current historical opacity. Agreed. But the newness that we found ourselves contending with was not only this paradoxical (but also ancient) heterogenesis of objectives, that is to say, the (possible) conversion of transparency into a new form of domination. In all this, there were two original elements: the apparent inevitability of the conversion (like saying that it could not be otherwise) and the emergence of the fact that the conversion is connected with the global nature of processes. In effect, the transparency promised by technology could not avoid becoming a culture of intensified control in a world where technology and the economy were being integrated to the point that no movement or transformation, even the most marginal, could be tolerated and allowed to occur randomly.

Am I perhaps only rediscovering Rousseau's idea that only small republics can really be democratic? Or closer to our time, Adorno's idea that when the "whole" – which, according to Hegel, had to be "real" – became real (in an increasingly unlimited globalization) it turned into the false? What we know for the time being (or think we know: is Descartes's evil demon deceiving us again?) is that, in fact, the transparency we hoped was at least ambiguous in nature, with the possibility of a "Babel-like" liberation, is not at all ambiguous and is organically connected to globalization; it has become an aspect of the realm of the whole, which is no longer the real but rather its opposite. Maybe not in the radical sense of Rousseau, but in a consciously an-archic, i.e. without *arche* (first principle), what we can do to defend ourselves against this totalitarianism is obstruct globalization in every way possible, a sort of "hermeneutic" politics. But how? Does to interpret not really mean to make meanings transparent? This would be a "decoding" in a Hegelian sense basically. Better to think of the freedom to interpret Scripture, out of which came countless sects, heresies, and forms of spirituality. If we can still "talk about trees," as Brecht said, we want to let "one hundred flowers bloom" (a slogan that Mao used in 1956, inviting people to criticize the communist system), outside of the transparent greenhouses of globalized capitalism.

16

The Question of Technology Today

Does a "question of technology" exist today? Heidegger often stated that the essence of technology is not necessarily technological. Leaving aside the many meanings this claim has acquired in his thought, it can still be said that it was a prophetic statement. For this reason, it is important to underscore the word "today" in the title of this essay. We can indeed say that our experience of technology has always developed in the direction of the progressive discovery of the truth value of Heidegger's argument: there is no *technical* question of technology, i.e. we cannot say that the question of technology – assuming we can define it – is solvable in technological terms, for instance, on the basis of new discoveries or new applications of what is already known. Put simply, the question of technology is either metaphysical or ontological in nature. In other words, it has to do with the meaning of technology relative to our existence and to what we call Being, truth, and value. And the ontological or existential meaning of the question of technology is exactly the way in which that problem presents itself to us today. The very notion of such a thing as technology was unthinkable in past epochs: for Aristotle, as we may recall, *techne* was a dianoetic virtue, like *phronesis* (prudence), *nous* (intellect), etc.; *techne* was the ability to produce an object, an ergon, in the material world; the work of art was a technical product. The same word "technology" is probably difficult to find in Aristotle's lexicon. In the end, what we indicate today with the expression "the question of technology" is more or less the history of the transformation of that word: how has it come to pass that we still refer to *technologies* (in the plural) but the "question" concerns *technology* (in the singular)? I am not indulging in simple wordplay. Let me put it this way: technologies became technology when Aristotelian *techne* lost its connotation of virtue, humanity's ability as such, and developed instead into a global system of production relations or what Heidegger calls *Gestell*, the network of production and consumption of resources, etc. In what way does this global "machination" constitute a problem? Again, the question cannot be reduced to a simple one as though we were merely looking for an answer. We do not ask ourselves what technology is in the sense of a definition or essence. What I am suggesting is not simply that technologies became technology when a system of technical–scientific machination manifested itself in the form of an integrated "system." More than this, I want to draw attention to the fact that the real question of technology has become urgent; indeed, it became possible when technology became an integrated system. There was no question of technology when the different technologies developed progressively by humankind were only tools capable of making some aspects of existence easier by producing objects or modifications in the material world. Medicine, for example, has always been part of technologies, but only recently has it become part of technology. The sense of this interpretation of Heidegger's argument is rather simple: what constitutes the question of technology today is not a problem connected to the fact that human beings invent and develop tools and ways of making useful objects or new life conditions; what makes technology a question for us today is its character as an integrated system. The answers that our culture usually gives to this question – technologies are neither good nor bad in themselves but in the way they are used – are generally superficial and clearly unsatisfactory. These are not real answers. Why would we pose the question of technology if it was all so straightforward? The reason is that technology as an integrated system appears to elude these very assessments and has become something of an autonomous world, so much so that it is outright difficult to find an appropriate noun: body, connection, machination … As we know, Heidegger used the word *Gestell* (framing), the root of which is *stellen*, "to put," "to set," "to place," plus the prefix *Ge-*, which indicates the totality of something (for example, *Ge-birg* or "mountain chain"). The question per se is *Ge-*: to the extent that it develops like an ensemble of totally integrated apparatuses, technology appears to us as a "world" that increasingly eludes the possibility of our controlling and understanding it. Paradoxically, due to their global integration within a system, technologies – the sum of the apparatuses created for the purpose of transforming the material world – become more powerful and effective the more they become unable to produce, as in a sort of inert state, an authentically new object. This can be seen in some of the expressions we commonly use: for example, when we say that something is *only* a technical problem and simply calls for the application of an already known rule or implement. We could say that the problem of technology is that it hides and dissolves problems.

I am emphasizing this paradox because it seems to me that one of the problematic features of technology in our culture, the real meaning of the question of technology to which the title refers, is the fact that technology appears to be a machination created for the purpose of precluding action and choice on the part of the subject engaged in a given activity. Consider Chaplin's *Modern Times* (1936) in which the worker is depicted as being completely dependent on the rhythm of the machine, to which he is enslaved with the sole task of enabling the production to continue. Naturally, this is a trivial example, but in many ways it encapsulates the elements of the question that I am trying to analyze. From the beginning of the twentieth century – I also have in mind the artistic avant-gardes, such as Futurism and the general climate of European culture around the time of the First World War – technology gave rise to a "humanistic" resistance and a radical fear not because of its capacity to make life easier, commercial trade more economical, etc. but, on the contrary, because it seemed to be a form of impersonal domination of people by the machines they should be able to control. What is frightening about technology and explains the hostile attitudes we exhibit daily is precisely the fact that it seems to be a form of domination, which is dangerous because it is apparently impersonal, among other reasons; it is impossible to wage a clear-cut battle against technology (that's technology, *bellezza*!).

I confess that this quasi identification of technology with an impersonal power that eludes all control is also inspired by my particular experience as a European citizen of our time. The growing loss of interest in politics, which today is a generalized phenomenon – not just in Italy but in most of the European countries – is closely tied to a common perception described by the expression I just used: why are you complaining – that's economics; that's capitalism; that's technology, etc. – *bellezza*! This expression has more or less the same meaning as the French *c'est la vie!*, which we use when we are resigned to the immutable laws of reality, laws that do not appear to depend on the decision of any one person. At this time[1] in Italy we have what is called a "technical government," i.e. a kind of coalition that is not composed of elected politicians but by economists and other experts appointed by the head of state and accepted with resignation by the political parties. In spite of their differences, all the parties accepted the arrangement in the hope of restoring stability to an economic situation that seemed desperate and unresolvable if they did not put aside their incompatible political agendas. There was a sort of "realistic" acceptance of the laws of the market (that's economics, *bellezza*!). More or less the way it was in ancient Rome where, in the event of war, the Senate handed power over to a dictator. I mention these examples from Italian and Roman history to underscore the fact that technology, according to the common use of the word, entails a sort of neutralization of conflicts in the name of an "overarching" interest, i.e. the functioning of a system that has its own internal logic, on which all our lives depend ("laws that the heart does not know," I would say, paraphrasing Blaise Pascal).

And so? Should we perhaps feel nostalgic about conflicting political parties, costly election campaigns, and corruption that is so often tied to the mechanisms of representative democracy? I merely want to emphasize that the neutralization effect produced by the technical government illustrates the reason why, from the start of the Industrial Revolution and especially in the twentieth century, people tend to be very suspicious of technology. We experience it like a force that is out of our control, which (I am reminded of certain pages from Max Weber) tends to acquire the features of an unseen and fear-inspiring deity. On the basis of these observations, I propose the following argument: technology appears as a threat not only, or not primarily, because it is seen as a kind of *hybris*, a power audacious enough to compete with God himself – which explains well our fear of it. As I pointed out earlier, this fear developed when technology became a global system that cannot be modified without destroying its function in the world. The American banks that were considered "too big to fail" were saved with public funds in order to avoid a global disaster that would have impacted all of us (at any rate, this was a way of justifying the government's interventions in the last financial crisis). What scares people is not the aggressiveness of technological globalization with respect to (what we call) nature and its laws but the domination and negation of freedom that is required for the smooth functioning of the system. Adorno and the Frankfurt School called this total *Verwaltung*, total administration or organization. We find an early form of this tendency in technology, which would become oppressive and authoritarian (indeed totalitarian), in the way Max Weber describes the critical importance of monotheism in the development of modern science. Only if all the elements of the material world are subordinated to a single authority and not to different deities, as occurs in polytheism, does it become possible to construct a general science of nature, with laws that are valid everywhere (the law of gravity, for example). Newton and Galileo would never have been able to make their discoveries outside of a monotheistic view of nature. In the case of technology as a global system, the importance of a consolidated "command" is even more evident than it is in the natural sciences.

Herbert Marcuse, a philosopher who is not as popular today as he was a few decades ago, interpreting Marx, claimed that the domination of nature has also implied the domination of some people by others. He was also convinced that the emergence from prehistory and the transition to civilization were a product of technology itself, which no longer required the domination of man by man. Although it was no longer strictly required by technology, this domination survives in the form of a different kind of repression: a powerful and oppressive discipline is no longer necessary as it was at certain points in history, but it continues to exist as a sort of inertial extension of the privileges that the dominant class does not want to relinquish. One reason, among many, for which Marcuse is no longer popular is the fact that his hope seems to have lost all credibility. In a sense, he lived in a society (about fifty years ago) where technology still appeared to be capable of delivering itself from complicity with domination – but it was not so, precisely because of the intensive development of technology in our lifetime.

On this basis, our question of technology today should be reformulated in the following way: to what extent can the term technology be distinguished from domination? It has often been said that technology is a sort of "second nature" of civilized humanity. This is probably true but in the worst sense possible: as a second nature, technology is a force of domination that we have to accept (*c'est la vie*, etc.). But to the extent that domination is still required for the functioning of the global technological system, technology is anything but a neutral and natural force. If anything, it implies the persistence of man's power over man, of its appearance of neutrality, and the capacity to reduce conflicts is the worst form of domination since it does not allow itself to be recognized as such. Am I suggesting that we are all victims of a sort of lobotomy performed by the "system" that keeps us sedated and more or less content by means of a social drug of sorts? I am not inventing anything; actual proposals to legalize the use of drugs have been made in order to keep the masses of unemployed peaceful, using a method that is applied in the prisons in order to avoid clashes and riots. Naturally, I assume (hope?) that things are not (still) like this. But philosophers like Heidegger, not from some science fiction scenario, have spoken of the forgetting of Being, that is to say, the loss of all ability to distinguish Being from entities as they are given. If we forget the ontological difference, the totality of Being is reduced to what there is, to the factual order of things, which eludes innovation, transformation, and, even more importantly, revolution. Technological domination, wherein everything that happens is planned and foreseen as a matter of course – this is the good functioning of *Ge-stell* – theoretically negates the future and change. The fear of technology is the fear we feel in the face of a mechanical universe that promises a sense of security to the extent that it rules out authentic historicity. All this, of course, is largely a nightmare of pessimistic conservatives, but it identifies one of the risks that the global technological order really runs: the impossibility of the event, to return to Heidegger, is synonymous with Being. In Heidegger's philosophy, because Being cannot be identified with what there is – because this, quite simply, would hamper our ability to explain and live our experiences of freedom (hope, fear, memory, etc., in a word, human existence) – it must be understood in terms of event: authentic Being *is not* but rather *happens* when something changes the context of daily experience – like a great work of art that announces a new civilization, the founding of a new political order, the appearance of a new religion … All this may seem to be an overly romantic idea of human history but in fact it is the only way we have of taking seriously our basic notions of historical epochs, changed paradigms, revolutions, restorations, etc.

The concept of the end of history, popularized in recent years by thinkers like Francis Fukuyama, has a meaning that probably Fukuyama himself did not consciously attribute to it. Technology, the system of *Ge-stell*, global, predictable, and planned machination, is the end of history to the extent that its functioning demands (requires, orders) that nothing intervene to disrupt the regular activity of the machine. We may recall that, at the start of the Industrial Revolution, rebellious workers, frightened by the prospects of losing their jobs, destroyed the machines as part of a movement that, from the name of its inventor, was called Luddism (from general, king, or captain Ned Ludd). In many respects, the current situation of work in the Western industrialized world is very similar to that reality, not (only) on account of machines but also on account of so-called "objective" laws of economics, which cause thousands of workers to lose their jobs. And this is not an essential and objective consequence of technology.

Once again, the essence of technology is not at all technological, neither in the sense that technology develops automatically by virtue of the natural progression of its inventions and creations – development requires investments, capital, decisions, etc. – nor in the sense that it would create a situation in which conflicts between people, political clashes, etc. are overcome by a purely rational–scientific, technological organization of our lives. Stated more clearly, precisely because it does not develop automatically on its own, technology does not have an innate tendency to grow, rather, it requires choices, investments, and decisions; it is, as a result, still closely linked to power and, I might add, class struggle. The presumed neutrality of technology, so often glorified as the capacity to end conflicts and to bring about social peace, wellbeing, and order, is the mask worn by those who have the power to use it for their own purposes. What is real and original in our situation is the power (technology) of the media, which has the capacity to make us forget Being, difference, and transformations: the power to make us believe that there is no possible alternative to the present state of affairs. If this process continues – not automatically but consciously controlled by the dominant classes – we have reason to expect the end of history because history, as Benedetto Croce once said, is nothing more than the history of freedom.

17

Passive or Reactive Nihilism

The Nietzschean distinction between passive, or reactive, nihilism and active nihilism has definitely not lost its meaning in the more than one hundred years since its original formulation. This is because we are still in the same situation that Nietzsche "fore-saw" in his lifetime and that Heidegger later taught us to call the "end of metaphysics": God is dead, supreme values have become devalued; we live in a world of multiple values and, therefore, impossible to judge on the basis of a definitive criterion. The historical condition that concerns and determines us is the following: if God is dead – with all that this entails in Nietzsche's thought – we cannot have recourse to the aid of a given value as we try to orient ourselves. It is in this situation that, for Nietzsche, the *Übermensch*, the man who places himself beyond, the "overman," becomes crucially important. Although Nietzsche rejects the idea of a history dominated by pure and simple physical violence, it is also true that his world of "will to power" is one of competition and struggle – which he imagines, above all, as a "conflict of interpretations." The *Übermensch* that Nietzsche foresees in the world of *Wille zur Macht* (Will to Power) is not the blond "beast" that his Nazi interpreters imagined; it is, instead, the man able to tolerate (bear) the weight of nihilism, the condition characterized by the absence of supreme values, and the way in which an individual – as human being – can survive in such a condition requires a certain super-humanity and, therefore, essentially, the ability to become a model, if only for oneself (consider the later Foucault and his image of a world where each person lives in his own original aesthetic style). Passive or reactive nihilism in which we are "thrown," Heidegger would say, becomes active when it is taken as the starting point for creating an original model of life; in other words, when we respond by affirming an identity that we present as a model for everyone.

I am obviously touching on current problems here, not only as regards the personal psychology of "postmodern" man but also and above all the very idea of social transformation and any "revolutionary" project. Only nihilism, for the first time, makes an authentic idea of revolution possible: no longer in the name of something lost that should be "recovered" but, above all, against the idea of a "return" to the *originary* condition (before the sin?). I maintain that the Nietszchean question of two types of nihilism is extremely relevant today, for the political struggle and for personal as well as collective psychology. These two aspects – the political and the psychological – are profoundly interconnected, as we can easily understand. In order to see this all we need to do is observe how in our society (apart from national differences, at least as far as the ecumenical character of the industrialized countries is concerned) the movement of progressive integration of single elements into larger organisms is, paradoxically, accompanied by the growth of a social discipline that worries the "authorities." It is not a coincidence if, in recent decades, the arms trade has seen an increase in interest in so-called "light" weapons that can be deployed in urban riots rather than in international conflicts. On the other hand, the transformation of NATO clearly illustrates this transition: it is no longer a matter of protecting the countries of the Atlantic Pact against the aggression of Russia and China but of guaranteeing a common war against "international terrorism," which means more or less war against all internal acts of defiance of authority.

If I translate all this into Nietzschean language, with which we started, I would say that there is a parallel development between passive nihilism and "reactive" nihilism. Leaving Nietzsche aside for a moment, it could be argued that the increasingly broad and pronounced proletarianization of the masses contributes to the spread of violence, at every level of social life, starting with the family itself. Why and how is it that this violence instigated by the proletarianization of the masses does not allow the creation of the *Übermenschen*, i.e. individuals or social groups capable of creating or practising an active nihilism – which is to say, capable of giving birth to a new order? We find ourselves once more in a situation that can be read in political terms: the universal discontent – which we see in our

Western world and certainly in Europe – does not produce effective and tangible political transformations, nor does it give rise to any meaningful change in the ruling classes. Rather than see this paradoxical phenomenon as a sign of the fact that the masses are (still) not sufficiently "proletarianized" to revolt or that people are still managing too well to risk losing even the little they have, we could perhaps admit that the Nietzschean idea of the overman is not entirely out of place as a question for us to consider.

Max Weber argues that in our mass societies the need for a "charismatic" authority is becoming more and more pressing. I generally take this claim to be a kind of sign of impending danger. But is it really? Experience shows that the few successful transformations in our world came about as a result of certain cosmic–historical figures, Hegel might say, such as Lenin, Mao, Castro, Chávez, and Lula.

This kind of talk is usually considered dangerous, but it merely describes an experience we have all had, at least all those of us who, fortunately, live in formal democratic regimes. I say fortunately because, up to this point, I (still) share the sense of Churchill's famous comment on democracy: it is the worst form of government, except for all those other forms. Churchill, however, was speaking from his experience of fighting against Fascism and Stalinism. After more that sixty years of democratic "freedom," is it so scandalous to wonder if he is still right? It is not at all an exaggeration to say that formal democracy today is an item to be exported. As often happens when exporting other merchandise produced by the "free" world, in the case of Iraq, democracy was exported with the massive assistance of bombings. The few revolutionary upheavals that took place in the twentieth century – from the Russian October Revolution in 1917 and Mao's long march in China in the 1940s, to Cuba in 1959, and the democratic-socialist transformations in Latin America during the last decades – have shown to what point, even in the event of electoral victory, a charismatic figure was critically important. This is an observation that I do not like to make but that came to me from my recollection of Weber and by the reference to nihilism. In short, could it be said, accepting the inevitable scandal, that nihilism requires the *Übermensch*? For its part, nihilism is not something that we can summon up or exorcise at will, arbitrarily. Rather, it is the condition that we actually live in our late-industrial, postindustrial, and by now also postcapitalist political regimes. We need only think about the political crisis created by the growing apathy among voters, the multiplication of antipolitical groups in all "Western" countries, which reveal a state of disillusionment, passive resignation, and lack of hope. Can we define it as a "physiological" phenomenon, in the sense that we enjoy too much freedom, too much abundance, too much merchandise to concern ourselves with social dilemmas? Or are we too desperate or disenchanted to believe in a program of transformation? The idea that the United States has exported, along with its lifestyle, unhappiness to the entire world – as well as the drugs necessary to sustain it (chemical surrogates of the *Übermensch*) – is not without a foundation. On the other hand, let us not forget that the First World War, with all its objective causes both immediate and long-term, broke out precisely at the end of the *belle époque*, and the favourable reception that it received, at least in the initial phases, in "public" opinion – both intellectuals and the masses – was also a clear sign of a reaction to the dominant nihilism (see Robert Musil's *The Man without Qualities* and Thomas Mann's *The Magic Mountain*).

In the past, I too studied Nietzsche long and passionately, interpreting his plea to the *Übermensch* as an invitation to a humanity no longer prisoner of the social and psychological structures produced by man's domination of man. And I am still convinced that this is the meaning of the Nietzschean doctrine of the overman; except I realize that, on this topic, I was making a mistake analogous to the one for which, with much respect, I sometimes take Habermas to task: I was limiting myself to describing an ideal order, i.e. the one that would need to be realized at the end of a process of transformation. In doing so, I was forgetting an important passage from *Thus Spake Zarathustra*, titled "On the Vision and the Enigma," where Zarathustra describes the vision he had about a young shepherd who was in danger of being suffocated by a serpent that crawled into his mouth, unless he bit off its head. It is a passage where – as we find many times in the book, paradoxically – Nietzsche speaks about the fact that we can enter into the free world of eternal returns only by means of a decision. Much of Nietzsche's popularity today is tied to the psychological import of passages like this one: we are tired of consolatory, pacifist, democratic, rationalistic, etc. ideologies, but we do not have, do not want to have, the courage to follow Nietzsche to the end (the extreme limit). This would not mean, not even for Nietzsche himself, accepting the Nazi reading of his doctrines. I have in mind philosophers like Deleuze, Foucault, and many others, who cannot be suspected of being right-wing sympathizers, starting with Jean-Paul Sartre and his theory of "groups-in-fusion" formulated in *Critique of Dialectical Reason*. This is certainly not the theory of a Nazi or Fascist leader, and it surely presupposes a formal democratic functioning. Yet, when they decapitated the king and queen in 1793, the French revolutionaries did not do so on the basis of a referendum: a constitution did not exist to provide for such an act. Furthermore, Cuba is criticized for creating voter lists through public assemblies held in neighbourhoods, zones, etc., which is a procedure that supposedly limits the "democratic" freedom that we enjoy! Lastly, the objections to the "missions" of the Chavist revolution in Venezuela are of a similar type: in effect, the "*misioneros*" are members of the president's party, not a "democratic" body, etc. In any case, all these examples (I will not expand here on the Gramscian notion of hegemony, which seems to me to pertain to these situations) illustrate the effort to go beyond the roots of passive nihilism that shadow formal democracy, which we take as our noblest criterion for judging any political regime.

It is not a matter of identifying an escape route to get out of passive nihilism by returning to a premodern authoritarianism, although one could be more open in this regard, or by idealizing the "community" as we often find in respectable and authoritative thinkers (like MacIntyre). What I am proposing is only (only!) that we emphasize the lack in the theory (and, certainly, in practice) relating to a study of the question of a radical transformation of our society for the purpose of escaping from passive nihilism, which is recognizable by other names; indeed, it is recognized as the universal condition (of the West but exported fully to the poor areas of the third and fourth worlds). The theories of emancipation have taken into consideration the occurrence of nihilism; all the philosophical sociologies of our century (I am thinking of Simmel, Adorno, and more recently Bauman) revolve around this point. But none of them dared to consider the question of the Nietzschean *Übermensch*, which is the inevitable corollary of this event. There are, of course, good reasons to be wary of this question, especially the fear of finding oneself on slippery ground, with an untenable position. The idea that for a long time we have had of a "democratized" overman – any citizen can become an autonomous, responsible "individual" capable of no longer being a slave to the domination and the spirit of powerless revenge that characterizes passive nihilism – is a dream that ended long ago. The practical institutions and apparatuses invented to this point have proven to be ineffectual in bringing about such change; in particular, they are producing macroscopic and destructive countereffects. At least from the point of view of theory – as unarmed prophets, such as we in fact are – it would be necessary that we no longer allow ourselves to be silenced in the name of a presumed "normative" truth of the "Western" model that crushes all efforts to create an existence that is finally free from domination.

18

Mutual Recognition beyond Universalism

Not only for "institutional" reasons, so to speak, insofar as it is an "academy" and not, let us say, a political party with economic objectives, the Academia de Latinidad would appear to be designed to promote dialogue, discussion, and the exchange of opinion for the purpose of achieving agreement, unification, harmony, etc. Now, from what we see every day in our world, it is this very objective that deserves to be called into question and criticized, always in an "academic" manner, of course. But up to what point, if those who increasingly speak up in favour of dialogue, and mutual understanding among cultures and civilizations, are precisely those who, from a different perspective – economic, political, social – work against these same "humanistic" ideals even as they promote them?

It seems to me, increasingly, that this is an inescapable starting point and deserves to mark an important phase in the history of institutions like ours. We are like young (old) men and women who have grown up and no longer feel comfortable in the spiritual condition that inspired them to become involved in "academia." To some extent, this is similar to what the verses of Brecht articulate in "To those born later" (1939): "What kind of times are these, when / To talk about trees is almost a crime / Because it implies silence about so many horrors?" We have never thought about talking (only) about trees (although today even talk of this kind can appear to be revolutionary or even "terroristic" in the face of the destruction of nature caused by the capitalist economy); nevertheless, we always consider ourselves to be in a "democratic" or "Western" landscape, that is to say, essentially within an "Atlantic" framework. Like many progressive intellectuals, in the broad sense of the term, I have always been well received, or at least tolerated, by the so-called "independent" press and by the establishment of the "free world." I have never sought or ever liked the "Washington consensus," but people like me have, in fact, enjoyed the benefits – university positions, academic funding of various kinds, etc. – privileges that did not require any betrayal of our principles; on the contrary, they came with the respect that the establishment, which always needs an image of social respectability, accorded us. There is no need to spend too many words to describe this condition, which many of us know well since we have lived it personally. It is not exactly like the position of court jester but something similar. I am referring to the Euro-American progressive intellectual, a figure that, in the course of the last decades, has become greatly worn out – a deterioration that deserves serious reflection – because, at least this is my argument, it does not depend on subjective factors; rather, it corresponds to "real" transformations of class relations, we might say.

Whether we are dealing with class relations in the "classical" sense of the word or not, what I think merits our attention, nonetheless, is the fact that many traditional alibis that helped the Euro-American progressive intellectual to maintain a clean conscience are disappearing. The financial crisis in the capitalist system of "production," which characterized the post-World War II years until the 1960s, has greatly reduced the "margins" within which this intellectual class survived rather comfortably. To cite one example, Italy's so-called "economic miracle" of the 1950s and 1960s, where cultural freedom was guaranteed by a sort of division of labour: the more or less democratic Right managed the economy and social discipline, while the Left was free to express itself in the media, in the newspapers (which were read by few Italians), and, in particular, in all the cultural activities supported by public funds. The first crisis of this division of labour was caused by the spread of television, as we all know, because it is a more popular medium than print news. In spite of this, today even so-called commercial television stations of Berlusconian "persuasion" allow a good deal of freedom, in their programming, for the dissemination of popular discontent, which is a clear sign that the old custom of giving ample space to the progressive intelligentsia is still operative. As I stated earlier, this sort of political–cultural "compromise" no longer seems to hold. Along with many other factors, the decline of compromise is, I believe, tied to the lost effectiveness of the paradigm of globalization. The progressive intellectual has always justified his or her outlook with a series of what might be called "Kantian" reasons. Kant foresaw the birth (with the French Revolution) of a cosmopolitan republic. Therefore, in decades past, the birth of "universalist" institutions, from the United Nations to the European Union, has represented a sort of ideological umbrella under which stood progressive and "productive" intellectuals. This very "universalist" ideology – which was used to justify globalization – has lost all credibility, especially in recent times. Today the European and North American scene is preoccupied with the Datagate scandal: increasingly astonishing revelations on "universal," in the literal sense, surveillance carried out by the CIA, NSA, and other American agencies. Keep in mind that these revelations are connected, in Europe, to the negotiations that until recently were going on to sign the transatlantic free trade agreement between the United States and the European Union, which includes a clause that would require European governments to respect terms that often conflicted with their national legislations; all this to benefit the trade of North American goods (see Wallach, "Le traité transatlantique, un typhon qui menace les Européens"). The treaty would represent a serious limitation to the sovereignty of European states, a sovereignty that is already put into doubt by all the budgetary regulations that were imposed (by the European Union itself), first on Greece and later on Italy and Spain. These "austerity" measures have in fact deeply affected the quality of life in the countries where they were imposed, removing the mask, so to speak, of universalism that legitimated globalization. Up to the present time, globalization has produced very questionable results (to use a euphemism) and is even considered to be responsible for the crisis (see Gallino, *Il colpo di Stato di banche e governi*). In particular, statistics show that, after several years of intense globalization, the disparity between the two ends of the social ladder in terms of income has become absolutely enormous: it has gone from 1:20 to 1:200. The disillusionment of the progressive intelligentsia, which had always ensured a certain harmony between "public opinion" and the capitalist order, does not depend solely on these aspects of growing social injustice; it is, rather, the fact that economic crises reduce in real terms the amount of resources available for those activities that engaged the intellectual "workforce."

As you can see, this history of the relations between the "progressive" intelligentsia and the capitalist order is rather schematic and not very analytical. But here I am merely attempting to propose a sort of examination of our conscience, our Academy, which, with all its specificity, has always been generally directed toward a cosmopolitan humanism, proposing intercultural and even interreligious dialogue. If the historical picture that I have just sketched out is acceptable, what are the implications for academia itself? I repeat, the somewhat radical character of my proposal is also conditioned, perhaps even caused, by my experience *in partibus infedelium* (in the lands of the unbelievers), which is to say, in "universalist" institutions like the European Union. It is precisely in these institutions that the loss of faith in Kantian cosmopolitanism is felt most keenly. Due to the phenomena that I have tried to describe, I realize that the idea of the integration of different states, economies, etc. that inspired our actions for many years, is no longer enough. That idea represents the umbrella ideology that ensures the survival of a capitalist system that is increasingly greedy and, essentially, suicidal in terms of destruction of the quality of life, the ecological resources, and the social fabric, in other words, of happiness, the pursuit of which was considered to be one of the indispensable human rights for the constitutional revolutionaries of the seventeenth century. In the present circumstances, we can no longer believe that the attainment of universality is the goal we should pursue, the moral ideal that should guide us. On the contrary, if there is a moral ideal that can be legitimately proposed today, it is precisely the opposite: first and foremost, the critical dismantling of all claims to universality. Let us think of the following as an interesting challenge: how could an Academy that has always promoted "humanistic" values take universalism not as a value but, rather, as a problem, that is, as an object that needs to be critically rethought?

That critical rethinking should probably start with a reflection on the origin of our ideal of universality. To what degree was the ideal of human universalism – before it became, legitimately, the principle of asserting "human rights" advanced by modern revolutions – an effort to impose a certain kind of "humanity" on others? I have in mind not only the Greek notion of "barbarians" but the humanism of early modernity as well, i.e. Pico della Mirandola's *Oratio de hominis dignitate* (*Oration on the Dignity of Man*), written not long before Christopher Columbus's discovery of America. In the light of what we are "discovering" about globalization, does this proximity of dates not have some symbolic value? At the end of the fifteenth century we not only had the "discovery" of America – which today is the primary engine of globalization – but we were also at the onset of the great global capitalist economy.

Here the critical rethinking of the universalist ideal acquires, more explicitly than ever, the characteristic of a critique of Eurocentrism and of capitalism, which was always its correlative. This implies that our ideal of dialogue, which has guided us from the start of Candido Mendes's project to create the college, can no longer be a critical opposition to Eurocentrism alone; it must also and above all be the search for an alternative to the dominant economic system in our world. I stress that the expanded horizon I am considering here has become possible, or rather necessary, not due to a simple modification of the theory but as a consequence of what globalization itself has been in recent years.

I am not proposing that we immediately adopt Karl Marx's eleventh thesis on Feuerbach, which reads, "Philosophers have hitherto interpreted the world in various ways; the point is to change it" nor am I suggesting that we set out to storm the Winter Palace. Much more "academically" I think that, at least in the name of the philosophy of hermeneutics, which has often been one of my points of reference, we need to look not for what unites us but what differentiates us. I understand full well that, even in our "universalist" perspective, what we were discussing were mostly our differences. Now is the time to assert them rather than attempt to unify them. Adopting an approach that privileges differences rather than the ideal of a universalizing dialogue would help us to combat more firmly the rhetoric that, often in good faith, merely supports the false promises of a globalization that totally serves the interests of the capitalist economy that threatens us all.

19

Reflections on the Dialectic of Development

According to official statistics, in various states in India from 1997 to today there have been 10,000 suicides by farmers who took their own lives because they could not pay their debts. Some estimates put the number as high as 40,000 for the same period. These debts were incurred in order to cover expenses related to farming activities – debts that had grown enormously from the time the International Monetary Fund prohibited the Indian government subsidies to the agriculture industry in the name of respect for the rules of fair competition, and from the time the use of genetically modified organisms (GMOs) began to spread, especially in the cultivation of cotton, since the seeds of GMOs must be purchased every year because they cannot reproduce, unlike "natural" seeds.

This news item, which I read in the *Corriere della Sera* (21 August 2006), but which originally appeared in *The Times of India*, is one of many I can cite to demonstrate that the "globalization" we are so proud of has had negative results, instead of improving living conditions in the poor areas of our planet. When we talk about the "dialectic of development," we need to understand the term dialectic in the original sense it had in the title of the book by Horkheimer and Adorno from 1947: i.e. betrayed promises, in their case those of the Enlightenment and in our case those of the globalized economy. It is a matter not only of the negative effects of what had appeared to be the promise of greater wellbeing; what is happening to us today is that the very meaning of the word "development," due to our negative experience, by now visible throughout the world, must change radically. This transformation can be summarized by emphasizing one of the meanings that even the word dialectic originally had, namely, transformation from quantity to quality. The quantitative development of the production of goods reached the point of requiring a transition to the level of quality. Furthermore, according to an observation that is often repeated when people talk about GMOs, it is not the absolute quantity of food and vital resources that is lacking in the world but their distribution in various places. It is becoming more and more evident that what is needed is not so much increased production as better distribution. The joke about socialist regimes that circulated for quite some time – that everyone was free to buy any goods but there were no goods to buy – also turns into its opposite; that is, we live in a world of overabundance of goods, which are not accessible to those who need them.

Naturally, we could discuss the point to which this dialectic is universal because it is possible that we, Western slaves of the logic of consumerism, see things in a distorted way. Perhaps different rules apply in the different "worlds" into which our world is divided. In this scenario, we would still have the effects of an imperfect globalization. But cases like the one in India are the effects of "successful" globalization, and the regulation of the markets of large geographic zones, for example, the European Union or the World Trade Organization, generally involves limiting the production of certain goods rather than increasing the quantity of any given resource. To cite an example, Italy has often been required to pay fines to the European Union for having overproduced milk or citrus fruit. There is certainly a quantitative logic in this regulation, which aims to promote the development of certain kinds of production in some areas rather than in others. But, at least to the eye of the layman (or the philosopher, which is the same thing), the paradox seems all too obvious: we throw away excess milk in Italy while African children need it desperately.

In traditional philosophical terminology, dialectic also refers to a more or less objective "law" that is independent of the good or bad intentions of humans. What we call "reality" is not, however, something natural, like hurricanes or droughts (these too are not completely independent of the actions of humankind, as we learn from the Kyoto protocols); it is merely the result of historical choices that are made by others, either individuals or communities, and that we find in front of us like "facts" not "things." The paradoxical effects of facts that now appear in all their gravity compel us to ask ourselves if it is possible to overturn the logic, the way of thinking and acting, that has led to these results. To speak of a "logic" that needs to be overturned, and not only of facts that need to be corrected, means framing the problem in global terms. And if there is a sense in which globalization can be said to be "successful," it is precisely the universal nature of these effects. And here the principal reason for which philosophers feel called upon to speak is the presupposition that they are speaking on behalf of everyone, about humankind as such, which philosophy has always advocated – and it was certainly an "ideological" presupposition. No one could guarantee that Plato or Socrates grasped the essence of man; they were talking about Greek man – today that essence has become realistic: we exist in a world where the effects of our actions touch everyone, even those who live in places far from us. Is Wall Street like Athens of the fifth century BCE? The same dialectic and paradoxes: the world in which the philosopher can finally speak in universal terms is an effect of capitalist rationalization that now blankets the planet, even though many of the people "covered" are not explicitly aware of it. (Let us not forget the lesson contained in Sartre's *Critique of Dialectical Reason*: alienation will end – should end – only when each of the actors in history, both the individual and the community, is master and conscious of the results of his or her own actions).

The reference to Sartre is not as parenthetical as it may seem. The paradox of quantitative development that, to this point, has not succeeded in becoming qualitative is today profoundly more pertinent to consciousness than it is to the "objective" functioning of things. The Indian farmers who committed suicide are a product of a culture of quantity; they believed that they had to submit to the logic of increased production or, at any rate, the laws of the market (imposed by the IMF), and today, as we learn from the sources identified above, farmers realize that it would be better to return to the traditional method of cultivating cotton. In the 1950s, a group of industry managers and "humanist" economists (I would prefer to use this adjective rather than "progressive" because they were, in fact, the opposite) established an association, Club Roma, to promote awareness of the limits of development. Their ideas were probably too advanced to be applied at the time. Today they are relevant in all their urgency, not only for us "Westerners" but also for the world we modestly call "developing." The struggle of the indigenous people of Amazonia to curb the deforestation of their habitat appears to clash with the immediate interest of increasing the gross domestic product, but the struggle is essential for the survival of that habitat and of the planet itself.

In what terms, then, do we discuss development in Amazonia, China, India, and in many parts of Africa where people still die of hunger? It is not merely a fantasy indulged in by philosophers to think that today the "coming to consciousness" on the part of individuals and communities is a crucial factor in the survival of humanity on this planet. And it is not solely a dream of professional revolutionaries – often comfortably residing in their universities and academies – to think that this acquired awareness (a real "storming of the Winter Palace" today) passes through a (re)birth of politics. While for the quantitative development of the "modern" world discipline was of crucial importance – the absolute State, colonialism, the "scientific" organization of factory work, widespread bureaucratization – a policy of explicitly limiting development (I have in mind Heidegger's *Sein zum Tode* [Being-toward-death]) can only come about in a world of mature consciousness. More than Heidegger's Being-toward-death, here, I am naturally thinking of the master–slave dialectic in Hegel's *Phenomenology*. The slave frees himself from his condition of bondage when he stops thinking of his physical survival as the most important value and accepts that he must risk his life; you may recall that the outcome of the struggle is not, for Hegel, the destruction of the slave or the master. If he simply eliminated his master or reduced him to slavery, the slave would merely recreate the existing state of domination. Leaving aside Hegel, however, it is clear to me that only a free decision by those involved – both individuals and communities – can bring about the radical transformation required to shift from thinking of quantity to thinking of quality. Another example of the capitalist tradition comes to mind here: only in the name of salvation, achieved by obeying the biblical commandments, does the Calvinist businessman decide not to spend all his earnings immediately; rather, he saves them and reinvests them in projects that demand sacrifice on his part. If an "enlightened" minority of capitalists concerned about the fate of the planet, or revolutionaries with foresight, wanted to impose on the masses of the world (which are by now totally conditioned by pervasive advertising and the fetishism of merchandise) a drastic reduction in consumption, not only would they see widespread revolts but they would also fail to achieve the desired result. Without a cultural "conversion" it is no longer possible to limit consumerism, which in its turn, is increasingly less "objective" and increasingly qualitative – consider the fact that one of the first (if not the very first) items on the export side of the commercial trade balance sheet of the United States is "cultural" merchandise: videos, films, music, and electronic games.

This kind of "conversion" is required not only on the part of developing countries; it is also important for industrialized Western democracies. Until now, these democracies have always been guided by quantitative values; political candidates who cite the need to reduce consumption in order to avert the depletion of resources or revolts by poor populations (consider the problem of the mass immigration of refugees who want to enter Europe or the United States), see their prospects of being elected decline. Paradoxically, if the world is to have sustainable development in the future, it will depend much more on the cultural maturation of "third" world populations than on the initiative and good will of the developed countries (even in Hegel's *Phenomenology* it is, at the end of the day, a rebellious slave who helps the master to escape bondage).

Here, you may note an allusion to the ideal of the revolution of the world's proletariat in the Marxist mould, which is not realistically destined to come about in the way Marx imagined, especially one resulting from the dialectic of development on which I am reflecting. The revolution of the Marxian proletariats was supposed to be unleashed by "quantitative" poverty, by the growing scarcity of resources available to the poorest, whose numbers are increasing. Certainly, the scarcity of resources is still a critical issue in the life of so many people in the world, and I do not deny it. What is more and more evident is that the war waged on poverty cannot be class warfare. The enemy today is more powerful than the tsar was in 1917, and its power is so pervasive (you may recall Foucault's *La microfisica del potere* [*Microphysics of Power*]) that there is no Winter Palace to storm any longer, even if we had the energy to carry out such an attack. The capitalist economy is structured in such a way, i.e. as the domination of consciousness and the manipulation of desires, that the revolution – if it ever were to happen – will be possible only and above all as a reappropriation of consciousness. I do not know whether this is a dream of "metaphysics," a fantasy of philosophers who, as always, assert the importance of ideas and of individual and collective consciousness.

Am I talking only about a universal "subjectivization," the promotion, on the level of the masses, of a sort of *übermenschlich* (superhuman) model, a superman, analogous to the one Nietzsche foresaw as the only path to salvation in the world of accomplished nihilism? Perhaps a reference to Sartre is helpful here as well. The reappropriation of the meaning of history he talks about in his *Critique of Dialectical Reason* occurs, not so paradoxically, in the "groups-in-fusion" when the individual coincides, or identifies, with the revolutionary community in its struggle. According to Sartre, real reappropriation occurs then because the meaning of action taken together is shared in equal measure by the participants, with no hierarchies and, therefore, no trace of "alienation" – which, instead, is reconstituted (tragically for Sartre) when the revolution is completed and roles are assigned (he calls this a "practical-inert" moment). This reference helps me to say that the "cultural revolution" (the allusion to Mao is not purely accidental) I have in mind is something that comes about more on the collective level than it does on the individual or, more clearly, on the political level. Protection against the dangers of a purely "quantitative" capitalism dominated by gross domestic product and by immediate return to stock brokers – on account of which a business shuts some of its plants, thereby causing the value of its shares to rise on the stock market – can only be achieved by political–cultural activism. It was like this even during the French Revolution, the English one of the 1600s, and the Russian one of the early 1900s. True, but those revolutions were, in large part, "bourgeois" initiatives aimed at defeating a limited zone of domination: take the Winter Palace, occupy the centre of power, and establish a new one. Today, the "microphysics" of power assigns a new and more important role to collective consciousness. Revolution is made neither by individuals nor by small groups of conspirators. And perhaps not even by self-conscious "subjects," like those who are our models in the Western humanistic tradition. The idea of a collective action similar to Sartre's "groups-in-fusion" is not modelled on political action – which always has groups, communities, etc. as its aim and means; it is also the only one we can imagine in the current situation – both in the West and in third-world countries – where it makes no sense to think of extending to infinity the number of self-conscious subjects; just as it makes no sense to think that a "knowledge" society, so-called in a program by the European Union (established at the Lisbon European Council for a Europe of innovation and knowledge, March 2000), composed of individuals like Leonardo da Vinci, the scientist, etc. It is, of course, difficult to say what kind of individuals are considered, if not these. But by now the global spread of information technology and Internet communication, with the "collective" memory that it puts at our disposal, makes me think that the subject participating in a future "qualitative" revolution is something more collective than we are until now disposed to imagine. Perhaps, just as the universality ideologically proclaimed by philosophy is becoming a reality in the "globalized" world – with all the dangers that it entails – so too consciousness raised to the level of universality, to which Hegel aspired, will be attained as an essentially collective consciousness. But we can begin to think of it in not too pessimistic terms by taking our cue from such philosophers as Teilhard de Chardin, to whose ideas, like those of other "utopians" of the past, we should have the courage to return.

20

The Boundaries of Art

Today people increasingly talk about a post-Westphalia political world order, by which is meant that, in the age of globalization, international relations can no longer be conceived of as relations among sovereign national states, each with its own territory and without outside interference. The words borders and boundaries have become unpopular, or, at the very least, they indicate something that has to be crossed in order to take a step toward some form of "progress." The term "boundary" had a completely different meaning, for example, when Kant tried to define it in relation to the territory of pure reason, practical reason, and judgment. In the domain of aesthetics, Benedetto Croce's theory of art also stressed the importance of boundaries; he proposed to reform the Hegelian dialectic by affirming, first and foremost, the dialectic of opposites or a "dialectic of the distinct," which was intended to safeguard the autonomy of the various forms of the life of the spirit, by shielding art from undue intrusions on the part of economics, philosophy, ethics, and politics. The neo-Kantianism of the first half of the twentieth century did not offer theories much different than this; in addition, the development of Viennese neopositivism in the direction of the philosophy of language games (*Sprachspieler*) of the second Wittgenstein seems to be in many respects an updated version of these arguments, according to which philosophical problems are solved by knowing the perimeters of each field or domain of human activity and applying in each only the *propria principia* (its own principles), on whose contents philosophy in the tradition of Wittgenstein is much more laconic than a Hegelian like Croce or a neo-Kantian like Cassirer would be.

I do not know if there is a strict parallel, aesthetically speaking, between a situation from the early twentieth century and that of today. In some ways, however, such an analogy is quite likely to be valid. Both then (which we clearly see in Croce's opposition to the "romantic" Giovanni Gentile) and, especially, today, the rediscovery of boundaries seems to be generally explained by the need to "return to order," which, when all is said and done, has a quite visible "political" dimension. With all the respect that I think he deserves for the "hermeneutic," in the broad sense, aspects of his philosophy, Croce was concerned with resisting the winds of Futurism (subsequently absorbed by Fascism), which characterized the Italian version of the early-twentieth-century avant-garde and which also reflected its revolutionary spirit, as captured, for instance, in a book like Ernst Bloch's *The Spirit of Utopia* (1918), which, to my knowledge, was not known to the Futurists and the Italian avant-garde of that time. As far as the situation today is concerned, the preoccupations surrounding the return to order that inspires a good portion, indeed most, of the more orthodox analytical philosophy (that is, one that still has not come to terms with history) are analogous. I clarify this theory in the following way: the artistic avant-garde of the early twentieth century, as a not insignificant part of *fin de siècle* art, presented itself as a global criticism of the Western ethical–social tradition, with expectations that went far beyond reforming the artistic languages. The pact with the devil in Thomas Mann's *Doctor Faust* (1947) aptly symbolizes art's often troubled will to go beyond its own boundaries, which, for Marxist artists and critics were simply identical to the capitalist division of labour and, therefore, functioned like accomplices to the bourgeois order. Croce battled against the romantic and aestheticizing excesses of the avant-garde (not only Filippo Tommaso Marinetti and fascist Futurism but Gabriele D'Annunzio in particular as well) in the name of "distinctions," which at the time also had a liberal, I would say politically correct and suitable, meaning. Does it still do so today? Should the avant-garde's desire to break through the boundaries of pure aesthetic experience, which culminated most recently in the arts and politics that accompanied the wave of youth protests in the 1960s and 1970s, really be labelled as dangerous romantic "holism" and an undue invasion of the various aspects of life, of the *Lebenswelt* (life world) by the aesthetic (*das Ästhetische*), that brings with it a turbid and irrational element that is very much like the totalitarian spirit of

Fascism or Stalinist communism? In other words, do we really need an aesthetics of boundaries today? I am aware that posing the question in this way can appear to be not very philosophical to someone who thinks of philosophy as a search for essential definitions that are eternally valid because they refer to stable and (only relatively) immutable structures of human experience. At least this is how Kant understood it and how many explicit or implicit neo-Kantians still think (including Habermas, even though the key idea of *Lebenswelt* for him seems to function like a limit on the absolute sovereignty of distinctions). Staying within the bounds of the discourse outlined to this point, it does not make sense to wonder if the boundaries of art "exist" or what they "are"; instead, we need to ask ourselves if we need a theory that affirms the necessity and legitimacy of boundaries and their value as criteria in order to understand – and eventually help us to "clarify" – our current experience of art.

Those who, like me, believe that the philosophy of aesthetics has everything to gain by taking seriously the *hybris* of the avant-garde and their expectation of breaking through the walls of the theatre, the gallery, and the museum, including the explicit political engagement of Brecht but also the search for beauty in the quotidian that inspired the Bauhaus, cannot avoid looking with suspicion at an aesthetics of boundaries; the questioning of boundaries is the gist of Heidegger's reflection and Gadamer's critique of "aesthetic consciousness," which resembles in many ways the arguments made by Benjamin in his essay from 1939, *The Work of Art in the Age of Its Mechanical Reproduction* (the same year as Heidegger's *Origin of the Work of Art*). To clarify, I have no intention of concluding that I am claiming the topicality of the ethical–philosophical stance of the historical avant-garde against the serious criticisms that were subsequently levelled, among other things, due to the excesses of politicization at the hands of fascist and communist regimes. It could perhaps be said – here too we have a clear parallel with politics – that, having experienced the extreme of the "aestheticization of politics" that were Fascism and, regardless of what Benjamin thought, Communism, today we are able to rethink more clearly and perhaps more reasonably the positive alternative that Benjamin called the "politicization of art" (the parallel with politics seems clear to me: only after the fall of real Socialism in the USSR are we in a position to reconsider seriously many Marxian categories with a view to the future).

We are no longer in the situation where one needed to (at least it seems so to me) defend the avant-garde and its "holistic" objectives (of social reform, revolutionary questioning of the entire Western tradition, and not just the laws of perspective) against the sober "liberal" tradition of a Croce. In that situation, moreover, the avant-garde ended up becoming a commodity in art galleries and museums, which housed Duchamp's *Fontaine* (Fountain, a bidet that Duchamp called readymade art) and Manzoni's *Merda d'artista* (Artist's Shit). At least we can no longer see an authentic alternative, as we could when it was clear that art freed (or stripped) of its aura ended up in the Nuremberg Nazi parades or in the social rituals of Stalinist socialism and defense of the aura was reduced to either the most inert traditionalism or to Beckett's knowing but unproductive silence. Are massive rock concerts and rave parties that assemble hundreds of thousands of young and not-so-young people actually dangerously fascist phenomena because they often have rallying cries (the lyrics of many songs) with a pacifist, humanitarian, or anti-communist message? It is to be noted that even a philosopher like Gadamer devoted his positive attention to phenomena of this kind – and I do not think this is merely due to senility ("*Und es neigen die Weisen / Oft am Ende zu Schonem sich*" ["And in the end the wise / Often will tend toward the beautiful"], Hölderlin, "Sokrates und Alcibiades" ["Socrates and Alcibiades"]). I want to say that Benjamin's comparison, which was already obscure in his text, no longer seems to be a useful example for dealing with concrete phenomena. Much of the "art of the masses" is anything but reactionary and tied to totalitarian political views, whereas much elite art has lost interest in challenging tradition and in renewing the social order.

In the face of this mixing of phenomena and levels, there is philosophical reflection – and aesthetic as well – that appears to seek out a refuge against the confusion of an increasingly marked professionalization. In the philosophy practised in universities, especially in Europe, today there is a distinct tendency to close ranks, precisely in the form of a growing suspicion of the "general" discourses it has imported from the Anglo-Saxon world (which it has, in the meantime, greatly reduced: I am thinking of Richard Rorty and many post-analytical thinkers ...). Concerned, even justifiably, for the professional careers of their students, European academic philosophers pursue the ideal of constructing the figure of a philosopher that is somehow suitable for the labour force. Recently in Italy, and it is not a joke, there has been an attempt to launch research in "experimental ontology" that, in the minds of its proponents, should serve (and so, first and foremost, obtain the funding of) industries interested in understanding what the objects they are working on really are. Continental philosophy, while on the one hand is becoming more popular in American universities operating under the label of comparative literature, cultural studies, gender studies, and religious studies, thinks that it can save itself, in Europe, by discarding its own tradition of ethical–political thought and critique of the *Weltanschaungen* and by adopting the model of the "scientific" work carried out in specialized disciplines, especially under the illusion that it can free itself from that aspect of poetic creativity that has always characterized it and that today is an obstacle to the prospects of presenting credible requests for funding from foundations and governments concerned only with growing the GDP. The clash, which is becoming more and more harsh in some European universities, between a philosophy that sees itself as "scientific" and an "existentialist" philosophy (from hermeneutics to the remnants of Marxism and of the Frankfurt School) cannot hide its political substratum. What is today known, in political terms, as the return to power by the Right is for philosophy the confirmation of its "professionalism," whose exponents until now have been especially historians of philosophy, who, because of their documentary and philological research, have always enjoyed more generous funding and greater prestige: no one would fund Kant for writing the *Critique of Pure Reason*; there are, instead, numerous fellowships and other forms of aid for those who want to study one of his handwritten notes, a shopping list, for instance. Today historians have been replaced, to the pleasure of governments, by foundations, a "moderate" press, scholars in the cognitive sciences, and exponents of "spurious" philosophical disciplines, which are difficult to house and, according to a design that is well known to positivists, are destined to migrate as soon as possible to the domain of the "positive" and experimental sciences.

The enemy of these "serious" philosophies is always the same: the confusion that is supposedly created by existentialist thought, whose character, however, is not so much the "unverifiable" generality of the thesis as the project as a whole. After Heidegger and hermeneutics, authentic philosophy cannot avoid noting that its work – while respecting "Hume's law," which our new empiricism violates without batting an eyelid – consists in interpreting the human condition, *oriented*, or guided, by a project that is not inscribed in facts but that can be legitimately argued by using reasonable justifications that are never apodictic but always tied to the specific historical situation, which they interpret and in which they participate.

Such a view of contemporary philosophy and of what is at play in it, even in broadly cultural and political terms, obviously implies a predilection for art and poetics that carry on, even with different tools, the avant-garde program of breaking through boundaries. This is a predilection that, as I have emphasized, is not "proven" with cogent illustrative reason but is like a, perhaps risky, choice made in response to a situation. This program is adopted, and is considered to be convincing, also and above all, because the general context in which art and philosophy operate is no longer the one schematically imagined by Benjamin. The politicization of art that he saw as an antidote to fascist (and, for me, communist as well) aestheticism is underway and not necessarily as a crypto-fascist phenomenon. An example is rock music as a social phenomenon, which is represented by big events like Woodstock and its various imitators, but also by "Saturday Night Fever" as well as many other examples of collective aesthetic experiences that are by now mass phenomena, like fashion and the adulation of film, music, and soccer icons, including mass gatherings around the pope. Rather than the politicization of art, it is perhaps better to speak of a vast aestheticization of social life. Today the philosophy of aesthetics must come to terms with these phenomena; probably, at least in my opinion, not by restoring the "boundaries" of what is truly an aesthetic field but by asking itself what meaning the new social situation has or what valid (emancipatory) possibilities it opens up. A response that we see everywhere and that we need to be wary of reaffirms the difference between what is "authentic art" and what is not, with the result being that of reserving the label of authenticity for what, perhaps with revolutionary intent (as in the *Fontaine* and the *Merda d'artista*), is suitable to be displayed in traditional sites like art galleries and museums (where we often find land art, sometimes unduly compromised). It seems to me that the new media – let us not forget that Benjamin's thinking in his essay of 1936 dealt with photography and cinema – today pose, for philosophy but more broadly for politics, the problem of the changed status of aesthetics in society. Certainly, it is not enough to take stock of the task of finding a solution, but it is, of course, necessary to define the problem. And to define it requires that we abandon the notion of "boundaries."

It is not simply a matter of acknowledging the success of the art "of the masses," like rock concerts or phenomena like pervasive fashion. Or at least, the task of philosophy and of aesthetics is to grasp the emancipatory potential of all this. And so, we will need to understand that generalized aestheticization also means greater attention to the quality of life, a more pronounced demand for "reception" on the part of the public that has become enormously expanded due to the mass production of "superfluous" merchandise that at one time was reserved for a few people. Where is it written that what this vast public appreciates and buys is merely *trash*? Here, however, we encounter perhaps one of the most complex meanings of the discussion on the aura, a meaning that Benjamin identified but that tends to be elusive. The value of a work of art is not separable, for me, from its market value, therefore the aura dissolves with the merchandise fetish. But could it not, instead, be that a certain "rarity" of the object–work is constitutive of its desirability and of the aesthetic value we ascribe to it? Even the peak of Mont Blanc or Mount Everest becomes less exciting for climbers if there are too many rope parties on the slopes. Is this "devaluation" physiological (and so the rarity is constitutive) or it is merely the expression of our distorted mercantile, bourgeois, proprietary mentality? If we do not want to resign ourselves to ignoring the historical–social component of the aura, and tying the experience of aesthetic value to its cultural–economic inaccessibility, perhaps available (only) to the "cultured" members of society, we have to solve the problem in a way that does not ignore this aspect related to the fetish of merchandise.

Here we see that aesthetics cannot (any longer) solve the problem without philosophy and politics. The experience of value as rarity is possible in mass society only as an experience of a plurality of communities, lifestyles, and models – I would say in a star system that does not respond exclusively to the canons of Hollywood but is prepared to embrace many different canons. Beauty – as Kant was already well aware (*Critique of Judgment*, paragraph 9) – is above all experience of the creation of communities around a model, whose features, however, cannot be defined "scientifically" but that appears from time to time as an unexpected novelty. In the "closed" society of Kant and of many European thinkers of the past, the community is identified as the existing and dominant society. To be a man of culture simply meant to belong to the (only) recognized culture and not to be a man of *a* culture. This is not true today. The cultures that we find in our society are many. We may think that the artistic and poetic styles existing in each of them are analyzable and understandable philosophically on the basis of traditional aesthetics, of the boundaries of the aesthetic and its specificity. This is another aspect of the problem that the historical avant-gardes already faced but left unresolved. The African masks that the *Blaue Reiter* (Blue Rider) put on display and that Picasso took as models were not "works of art" in the sense of distinction that existed, and exists, in European culture. In a very explosive way – because in the meantime colonialism and Eurocentrism came to an end – the many "artistic" styles produced by communities–cultures that coexist in our society tend not to stay within the boundaries of traditional aesthetics. What is more, great European art was for the most part tied to other areas of experience, primarily the religious. There has been talk recently, in the climate of the war against international terrorism, of plans by Islamic fundamentalists to destroy works of art that they consider to be blasphemous (most recently, a painting in a church in Bologna). Can we respond to such a fanatical position by simply pointing out the "boundaries of art"? It seems to me that, like the increasing pervasiveness of the aesthetic experiences of the masses – in the form of big musical events, fashion, as well as in political propaganda, for example – these border violations are inseparable from the multiculturalism that in fact exists in our society.

A thesis that I find interesting – only in the sense that it should inspire a discussion and a discovery of important consequences – is that all these events and sociocultural transformations bring once more to the attention of our philosophy and our aesthetics such romantic projects as the one in *Älteste Systemprogramm des deutschen Idealismus* ("The Oldest Systematic Program of German Idealism"), an essay thought to be written by Hegel, Schelling, and Hölderlin for their seminar in Tübingen. The aim there was to restore the unity of art and religion in the form of a socially accepted and unifying mythology. Today we have only become aware that such a restoration is possible, indeed, almost destined to come about but only on the condition that it cannot be a single mythology. And the fact that there cannot be only one impedes each of the many mythologies from living peacefully side by side in an essentially apartheid situation. How can one profess one's own faith in a society where the religions are many and where they are all recognized as having equal rights? It seems to me that, for the aesthetic experience, the first consequence of this plurality is the fact that the appreciation of the beautiful – of the positive, achieved, etc. aesthetic value – cannot exist except as the experience of multiple instances of a "crossing of boundaries" that allows the "defamiliarizing" aspect to prevail over the "familiarizing" – or, to use a Heideggerian term – prevalence of the "earth" over the "world" – in one's encounter with the work of art. But is this disorientation not an effect of a breaking through boundaries that, far from being resisted with a return to order, should be considered in all its radicalness?

21

European Religious Experience

The title of this chapter relates not only to my dual role as a philosopher and a member of the European Parliament. What I intend to indicate with the title is that the philosophy of religion, or reflection on religious experience, today has the task – also and primarily – of being a philosophy of the European religious experience. The reference to Europe cannot be so easily set aside, for instance, by pointing out that in doing so we risk falling into yet another form of Eurocentrism or by noting that the cultural pluralism we find in Europe has been a well-known phenomenon (for some time now) in the United States. But this is not the subject of the discussion. When I speak of the central importance that today's European religious experience must have for philosophy, I essentially mean one thing, namely, that for the philosophy of religion – not for religion in the general sense (assuming that there is a "general" sense of religion) – referring to Europe means keeping in mind what, for centuries, were European imperialism and the missionary Eurocentrism of Christianity, not only its Catholic form. It is true that it seems wrong always to focus attention on Europe, but I stress the fact that this applies especially to the *philosophy* of religion, which is certainly a European and Western "discipline." And apart from this reference to a discipline, it is true that the European religious experience, since it has for a long time intersected with the "religions" of non-European, colonial, etc. countries, has also left its mark on these religions: starting with the fact that, perhaps, it might not have been possible to call them religions without the European culture. (Here, I have in mind the so-called "arts" of primitive populations, which we called art looking at them as if they corresponded to what art is in our tradition, especially the modern tradition.) Could this have happened even with a *single* religion? I would like to point out that, when I had the opportunity to spend some time in Japan, having been invited by the Cultural Institute, and I asked to meet some philosophers, I found myself before people who had either studied philosophy in European universities or were Buddhist monks and priests, whom I would not have promptly called "philosophers." For observations such as this, too, I think that it is possible to concentrate our attention on the European religious experience without fear of imposing a foreign, Eurocentric model on other "religions."

What characterizes the religious experience of the average European are two elements: an awareness of the end of Eurocentrism and of the misdeeds of imperialism, and, along with this, an inescapable awareness of the multiplicity of cultures and "religions." These two elements represent a kind of original "essence" of the postmodern religious experience, which we find especially in Europe.

Let us try to think of a hypothetical case, while keeping in mind the frequent "ecumenical" initiatives, so often highlighted by the media, in interreligious dialogue. Let us imagine a meeting between the Catholic pope and the Dalai Lama (which actually occurred). They greet each other, embrace, pray together, each in his own manner, and then part company. Should we think that, at this point, the pope goes to pray to God (his God) for the conversion of the poor Dalai Lama who, despite having met the head of the Catholic Church (which still claims and preaches that *extra ecclesiam nulla salus* [outside the Church, there is no salvation]), has not converted and so he will necessarily go to hell? Let us remember that, while limbo has been erased from the heavenly geography, purgatory and especially hell are still entrenched in Catholic dogma, even though more and more often people say there is a hell, but it is empty. The pope will, of course, not admit to being co-responsible for the massacres of "savage pagans" perpetrated by the conquistadores in centuries past, but certainly he cannot be unaware that, when he meets the Dalai Lama and prays with him, he is living in a "pluralistic" world, which should constitute a problem for his conviction that there is no salvation outside the Church. The hypothetical case of the pope concerned about the conversion of the Dalai Lama serves to argue that a reflection on religious experience today has to take into account both pluralism and multiculturalism, specifically current phenomena, which is quite different from centuries past. This is probably because, in those times, the Christian-European idea of a single truth was incorporated into the imperialist politics of the state, or, rather, it was not a theoretical but a practical problem: military, in the case of colonial expansion, and policing, in the case of the Inquisition and its campaign against heresy.

The postmodern religious experience that, in my hypothesis, is today's specifically European one requires us to think of truth in terms other than the absolute metaphysical ones handed down by tradition. Dietrich Bonhoeffer's statement, "Ein Gott, den es gibt, gibt es nicht" ("A God that exists does not exist," *Atto e essere* [*Act and Being*], 103), apart from the meaning it had in its original context, becomes a prophetic statement whose meaning we still need to grasp fully. If the truth of Christianity is thought of according to Tarski's proposition – "It is raining" is true if and only if it is raining – that is, based on a similar notion of truth, faith should be grounded in the "objective" fact of the incarnation and resurrection of Jesus; Catholics have learned from our catechism that the Gospels are historical in the sense that they narrate events that actually occurred in time and space. This "objective" truth of the givens of faith appears to be deducible from Paul's statement, "If Christ be not raised, your faith is vain." Yet, the utterance could be read as having a different tone and meaning; if it were not true, in a non-Tarskian sense, that Christ rose from the dead, my faith would be vain. The truth of faith can only be understood according to the meaning that the same notion of truth has assumed in the culture and philosophy of our time. Also, as regards the objective "truths" of the experimental sciences, it is difficult to find people today who understand them in terms of the conformity of the proposition to the thing. The Hegelian dialectic had implications for these sciences as well, even though they are often unaware of this. To have a dialectical, experiential notion of truth is to consider the failure and misdeeds of Eurocentric universalism. Moreover, the transformation of the notion of truth in a way not modelled on the passive mirroring of objects is also tied to the crisis of Eurocentric universalism. We can no longer think that there is an objective truth that we know and that is the legacy of "our" science, while those who do not know it are primitives, not yet civilized, etc. Even if the relationship between these two events – the evolution of the concept of truth and the end of Eurocentric universalism – is not obvious at first glance, it could be demonstrated in greater detail by means of a longer explanation. Here, I would simply like to show how a consideration of the European religious experience of today – and/or postmodern – requires that we try to think of the truth of faith in terms other than those of the description of facts.

If, as I believe, we claim that one of the aspects of religious life is prayer, to whom is the prayer directed? If one recites the psalms in the Roman breviary, or any other text from the Catholic tradition (I am referring to my own experience here), who is the interlocutor? It is obvious that, if the strictly realistic perspective is excluded and we accept Bonhoeffer's "theory" cited above, the experience of prayer too must be radically rethought.

It is not only the matter of the very important case of prayer. The entire individual and collective religious life risks losing meaning if we give up – as I think cannot be done – the realistic idea of the truth of the content of faith. Moreover, for a "traditional" believer, it is already difficult to assert the "objective" truth of the articles of the Apostles' Creed, according to which Jesus is seated to the right of the Father, or of dogmas like that of the Virgin Mary's bodily ascension into heaven. A nonbeliever colleague and mathematician often asks me if I believe that it is possible to measure the distance the mother of Jesus would have travelled into the stratosphere, having set off about two thousand years ago. I do not want to make light of this blasphemy here but merely to show the extremes to which the Catholic, and essentially authoritarian, insistence on the literal meaning of Scripture can be taken. I know full well that, from the early centuries, biblical hermeneutics was familiar with the doctrine of the different levels of the meaning of Scripture: literal, moral, allegorical, and anagogic. Deciding which meaning to give to a certain passage of the Bible is always reserved by the Church hierarchy, which has always grounded this claim in the Gospel passage that requires a literal reading: "Thou art Peter … etc." Certainly, every believer knows that Jesus is seated neither to the right nor to the left of the Father and is horrified by the suggestion that we calculate the point in space where we might find the body of the Virgin Mary. If I am not mistake, even when the first astronaut, Russian Yuri Gagarin, was sent into space, Khrushchev declared that the cosmonaut did not find God, who is traditionally located in the sky, and this was taken to be an argument in favour of atheism. But, if we assume that Jesus seated on the right of the Father and Mary ascended into heaven are "poetic metaphors," could we not also think that the resurrection and the incarnation are propositions of the same type? There is no empirical proof for either. It is the Catholic Church that literally prohibits us to think this way. By not allowing it, the Church is defending its own power, which would collapse if we attributed to the statement regarding Peter and his primacy a strictly metaphoric or allegorical meaning. Using a rather scandalous simplification, but one that I feel I can defend without being arrogant, I would come to the conclusion that *God must exist (in the sense rejected by Bonhoeffer) in order to guarantee the power of the Church*. This argument is merely a specific part of a broader argument, one that is equally scandalous but equally defensible today, after the dissolution of universalism and of what Heidegger calls metaphysics: i.e. the claim that truth must be the objective reflection of objects only to guarantee power and authority. Naturally, in order to avoid a glaring contradiction, I do not attribute to these two conclusions the value of objective truth. I intend them to be acceptable only from the point of view of the need for freedom of interpretation. This also applies, for example, to Heidegger's critique of metaphysics (since, when he rejects the theory of truth as conformity, in *Being and Time*, surely he cannot appeal to a different and more "objective" description of truth) or to Nietzsche's assertion, "There are no facts, there are only interpretations. And this too is an interpretation" (*Frammenti postumi* [Posthumous Fragments] *1885–1887*, 299). Only those who hold power are really interested in truth as the objective description of things and matters of fact. This too I do not "demonstrate" apodictically. I suggest only that we ask ourselves who it is that rejects, and has always rejected as an aberration, the thesis that there is no objective truth but only interpretations, which are never unbiased. Let us remind ourselves of what Walter Benjamin says in his "Theses on the Philosophy of History," namely, that only the victors think that history is a series of events guided by an intrinsic rationality; the vanquished have never thought so. Without stretching too much the meaning of Benjamin's theory, we can think the same way with respect to the notion of truth as objective evidence. In fact, it is those who hold power that want to impose their own interpretation on everyone else while denying that they are motivated by a special interest. So, if someone says to me, "be a man," I have reason to believe that the individual wants me to do something that, from his or her point of view, pertains to my very "nature" – a term that, coincidentally, is very popular in the official

Catholic moral code. It is true that revolutionaries also often appeal to natural rights, and they are correct in doing so, if this serves to make their revolt more effective. But if they think of this as a dogma, they inevitably become Stalinists.

I will not expand on this argument concerning the truth and its "complicity" in the wielding of power. This should not come as a shock. We live in an age dominated by what has correctly been called "single thought" (in other words the "Washington consensus"), which is a system of lies supported by money and the media that disseminates those lies. Once again, I am not saying that these are lies because I believe that I have access to a "real truth." I am simply saying that those who fabricate and spread them are precisely the dominant power that controls the most powerful military and communications apparatus in the world. I reject the fabrications because I am on the side of the oppressed, who, by the way, believe less and less the *embedded* journalists. As well, since I am talking about religion, I reject those lies because I am on the side of Christ, a friend to the weak and crucified by the powerful. Does this represent yet another performative contradiction? The pope and the defenders of orthodoxy would object that I am choosing the Christ of my liking. This is true, but they too, starting with the pope himself, choose a Christ who is convenient for them, a friend of the powerful, even if they are bloodthirsty dictators (remember John Paul II, now beatified, standing next to Pinochet?). In this sense too Christ is a symbol of contradiction. He does not promise peace but war.

How, then – attempting now to arrive at a provisional conclusion – can we think of the religious experience in the framework of the end of metaphysics and the discovery of the complicity between "objective" truth and domination? Luigi Pareyson, my mentor in Turin, devoted his last works to illustrating the following argument: philosophy is nothing more than the hermeneutics of the religious experience, that is to say, myth. This is because the religious experience does not consist of objective forms of knowledge but of myths, especially in the literal Greek sense of the word *mythos* or narrative, that which concerns the meaning of existence. However, what pertains to philosophy, and not the empirical sciences, is not the object of demonstrative knowledge but the subject matter of narrative.

Demonstrative knowledge is constructed more geometrically – principles, conclusions, etc. Since they are governed by mathematics, the experimental sciences are also of this type. Essentially, as regards

Kantian questions that are the concern of philosophy – what can I know, what should I do, what can I hope for – the answers are not provided by theory but by narratives, especially those like the biblical story of creation and redemption. Pareyson grounds (philosophically or narratively?) this assertion in his lived experience of freedom. If we have to give a meaning to our experience of freedom, we cannot certainly think that it is a structural fact, that is, deducible from some eternal essence of things (as would be the case in a Spinozian type of system). Only what is structurally connected to a system can be the object of logical demonstration, of theory. Freedom is only a *factum* – the product of an occurrence that is itself free, and that can be narrated – in a word, *mythos*. Even the Big Bang theory or the theory of evolution speaks only of the laws of a development that follows a first moment about which they can say nothing. Myth, however, does not need "scientific" proof. It is narrative that lives through its transmission and is heard by individuals, generations, and cultures (*fides ex auditu* [faith comes from hearing]). There are many myths, that is, many traditions, many cultures, and many languages. Does it make sense to think that we have to decide, once and for all, which is the "best" language or the "truest" myth? Certainly, Leibniz, in one of the constitutive moments of modernity, actually envisioned a unity of this sort. Even the failure of his project and of others like it in recent centuries illustrates the fact that this is a pointless exercise, especially considering what we have come to call the end of metaphysics (Heidegger) or the "school of suspicion" (Nietzsche, Marx, Freud).

Religious experience, however, with its constitutive element, the prayer, can still be considered (perhaps by now can be considered only) in the light of the idea of myth. Not only is it not a question of "demythologizing" scriptures; indeed, we must accept them as myths and approach them without any expectation of definitiveness. Is it still possible to pray without thinking that we are addressing someone that "exists" in the sky, in the temple, in the consecrated host, or in the great beyond? I confess that this is a suggestion, a hypothesis, that I myself make with much caution and scepticism. At least, however, a religion lived like a poetic myth that I "feel" I need in order to give meaning to my life (as happens with people whom I cannot forget or music that is the very substratum of my daily existence) will never be the cause of conflicts or "religious" wars. The trend of interreligious dialogue, to which we are more or less subjected, is merely the offspring of the "missionary" spirit that we have by now learned to recognize as imperialism, and it has nothing, or almost nothing, to do with promoting a sense of brotherhood among people. For a shared ethics, all we need is a rational application of Kantian ethics, which are well known in popular culture, namely, do not do to others what you would not have done to you. For Christians, this sensible maxim is reinforced by the love of one's neighbour that Jesus preached – the Jesus that it seems to me reasonable to prefer over so much dogmatic and disciplinary orthodoxy. Sometimes, it is thought that, in order to legislate in some areas, such as bioethics, it is necessary to base oneself on an indisputable truth, that is to say, one that is valid "for everyone." As an Italian, and a citizen of a state that is almost only a colony of the Vatican, I am all too familiar with these problems, which are made unsolvable precisely by the absolutism of the Catholic Church. After his meeting with the Dalai Lama, the pope does not expect (must not expect) that this nonbeliever will be prohibited from praying in public nor does the pope force him to convert to Catholicism through torture and ultimately the stake. He resigns himself to praying with him, each in his own language, reciting the "poems" that each has learned and to which he ties the meaning of his own life, and his own hopes for the future. All this to say that religion is a "private" affair and that the state is "naturally" – in postmetaphysical modernity, not in eternity – a lay (*secular*) institution that does not have the tools needed to choose a myth, a form of art, an "official" science, or a morality, except the one that leaves the greatest space for each citizen to choose what the meaning of a "good life" is. Of course, it is difficult to rethink one's own religious experience in these mythic–poetic terms, which are so foreign to any form of hierarchy, division (division of labour!) between clergy and laity, between bishops or popes and ordinary worshippers. But the end of metaphysics – the "discovery" of the link between universalism and power, and the end of imperialism, aided as well, and paradoxically, by the spread of information – is an event in the history of Being, we might say in Heideggerian language (or myth), and it will end up overwhelming the hierarchical structures on which the Church believes it can continue to rely, a Church that is by now dominated by a kind of suicidal instinct from which perhaps only the simple believers can hope to save themselves through their purely "poetic" prayers.

22

Religion and Emancipation

The criticism most often directed at Pope Francis from the Right and conservatives, even within the Church itself, is that he is a communist. This needs to be taken seriously; conservatives are generally very realistic; they see clearly the things that imperil their power. I myself, incidentally, recently published a small book of interviews titled *Dios es comunista* (*God Is a Communist*). Especially today, when we no longer have real communism, be it Soviet, Stalinist, etc., statements like this are not at all blasphemous. The truth expressed in these kinds of judgments is what I would like to discuss in the pages that follow.

I start with the most radical and scandalous claim: if today we consider the possibility of a Communist International (Comintern), the only place we can look to find it is the Catholic Church of Pope Francis. But why would something like a Communist International be necessary today? First of all because there is globalization, what Carl Schmitt has taught us to call a "global civil war" (*Weltburgerkrieg*). The war against international terrorism, the rallying cry of today's American imperialism, is indeed a war waged by the transnational government of large corporations against the poor of the world. More than a global civil war, we can now speak of a global class war in which there still are "national" elements typical of the wars of the past but only because armies and armaments continue to depend, at least formally, on the governments of national states. But the war on terrorism is in fact a war waged by NATO, which is dominated by the United States, against the various forms that the revolt by the world's poor takes. This struggle of the poor does not have a central point of reference, no Comintern to unify and direct it.

As a result, it is essentially powerless. Globalization itself, however, is perhaps what prevents the creation of a traditional Communist International. More or less for these reasons, I think that the only International possible today is the Catholic Church. In the current state of the global class war, the only possibility of building a counterforce that offers some hope is the "religious" kind. Why, however, are we talking about the Catholic Church? Among other things, it is there that something important and "revolutionary" has happened with the election of the Argentinian pope. Despite the emergence of "new" powers – China and India, above all – I continue to think of Europe and its principal religion, Christianity, as the centre of everything. This is especially true in the sense that economic imperialism, like military supremacy, remains historically located, in particular, in the empire of world capital controlled by Western stock exchanges and markets. Incidentally, Marx saw the possibility of the global revolution as a "Western" phenomenon, first and foremost, tied to the industrial working class. For me, this is still valid in the sense that, if we have to point to the headquarters of the economic and military power that dominates us, we always immediately think of the West, the United State, etc. I think, therefore, that we should not be embarrassed to speak of the emancipatory value of religion, mainly Christianity and the Catholic Church, which in fact – with Pope Francis – represents its cutting edge, including in political and social terms. The battle against imperialism and capitalist exploitation is waged primarily in the West, where Christianity remains the central reference point.

But religion and, in my argument Catholic Christianity and not only that form, becomes emancipatory to the degree that it emancipates itself, first and foremost, by sacrificing its "traditional" conservative function of defending so-called nonnegotiable values: family, property, sexuality, etc. We also need to understand why Christianity – but probably religion in general – has almost always functioned in this way. A possible explanation is the following: it comes into existence in a theocratic society, i.e. Judaism; it establishes itself primarily in the Roman Empire and inherits the civil function of the Roman religion after it had been its enemy (martyrs, etc.). We find such an image in Wilhelm Dilthey's *Introduction to the Sciences of the Spirit* (1883): the Church assumes the functions pertaining to the defence of society in the disintegrating world of late antiquity, where bishops are the last form of viable authority (Augustine was a philosopher but a bishop and political figure as well). Such observations can be the starting point of a discussion on the conservatism of the Church and of religion generally, at least as far as it pertains to our Western culture. Moreover, the alliance between monarchies and the Church has a long history in Europe and the West, especially in the age of colonialism. For this reason, many find it strange that a project of social transformation can today be associated with the authority of the pope. It is paradoxical but not too much so. This is especially because, in the meantime, in our late modernity, the function of conserving and maintaining social order has passed almost completely to science and technology. It is here, and certainly not in an ever-weakening "ecclesiastical authority," that the capitalist order has its most effective and loyal allies. When I speak of the emancipation of the Church, I am not referring to its abdication in the face of the exclusive authority of science, as the Enlightenment tradition had accustomed us to believe. Indeed, a certain dogmatic and "antimodern" rigidity that survives makes the Church a potential agent of resistance against the domination of capitalism and its suicidal, inhuman choices. As liberation theology, above all, has taught us, it is the poor who ultimately make a difference. For this reason, I think that a Communist International can only be religious and Christian in our day and age. Today's projects of political transformation (I truly believe this since we live in a globalized world dominated by technology) are especially exposed to the risk of becoming themselves agents of domination. We cannot speak of politics without speaking of development, growth, and increasing the gross domestic product (GDP). But these same values today are the most dubious. The devastation of the planet brought about by an increasingly intense exploitation of our natural resources, which is accompanied by an increasingly intense rationalization of social relations, and which could soon lead to global militarization (we need only mention the problem of disposing radioactive waste from nuclear reactors), shows us that the "dialectic of Enlightenment" about which Adorno and Horkheimer spoke many years ago has by now such obvious manifestations that make "positive," productive – "developmental" or human I would say – planning impossible. When, in the famous interview of 1976 in *Der Spiegel*, he says that "Now only a God can save us," Heidegger is predicting what we experience today more intensely than ever: it is not possible to have an emancipation project – one that looks beyond calculation and material success – that is not essentially "religious."

But do not the poor need material goods above all? Are the poor, "who will always be with us" according to the Gospels, hungry and thirsty because goods are scarce or because goods are not distributed fairly? In this sense, if they are hungry and thirsty for food and drink, they also hunger and thirst for justice. Expressed more cogently, they hunger and thirst for politics, for "existence" and not only for "assistance," if I am permitted this play on words. The religious perspective considers these "spiritual," but more broadly existential, aspects of the revolution much more than do economic and technical projects. We all know that a revolution is indispensable for guaranteeing acceptable basic living conditions. But, on its own it is not enough nor can it be achieved on its own. "Now only a God can save us," means that even a social transformation that achieves economic progress and a more equitable distribution of goods and burdens cannot be brought about without religious engagement. I am inclined to think so on the basis of the most banal experience of the "political crisis" in our world, among other things. The public distrust of political parties, the lack of participation, and the apathy that characterize many modern societies are certainly not to be interpreted instantly in a "religious" sense. These behaviours are also explained by, besides the corruption, the domination on the part of a technology that is marked by the self-contradictions of "progress." People no longer believe in political parties because the development projects lead to dead ends. This is another aspect of the "dialectic of Enlightenment"; as social and economic progress for all, politics is not credible any longer, even and especially because the collateral effects of such "emancipation" projects are all too visible and felt by all of us. This is not so much because, once they are completed, we discover that "they are not enough," thereby giving credence to Augustine's remark, "our heart is restless, until it reposes in Thee" (*Confessions* 1, 1.1). This could be one way of interpreting the ideas of Adorno and Horkheimer, for whom the Enlightenment is contradictory the very moment it is realized. And so, we come to understand that a fully rationalized society is a prison precisely when it becomes a reality. On the other hand, even the pure and simple quest for economic emancipation can be successful only if it is motivated by something else, i.e. "religious" inspiration. I am aware that I continue to use the adjective "religious" without clarifying it sufficiently. I believe that the only way to understand the word is by reducing it to its essential meaning, what theology did for liberation: the poor, the marginalized, those who do not have access to power. I arrive at this "reduction" as well – at least this is what experience has taught many of us in these times – by taking note of the fact that the revolutions we are familiar with have always tended to relapse into what Sartre (*Critique of Dialectical Reason*) calls the "practical-inert"; or more simply, without disturbing the Winter Palace or the Bastille, what we see is that political parties, starting out from progressive and reformist positions, become "government" parties; they change fatally into (the preservation of) power groups. This is the history of many leftist parties in Europe over the last number of years. Is it a manifestation of the moral corruption of those who operate in these conditions? This is certainly not so in Sartre's text, which describes a kind of "inertia" that leads necessarily – fatally? – to bureaucratization. This is why the poor "will always be with us"; the revolution will produce other marginalized people and other hierarchies. Is it, then, not worthwhile to become engaged? It is worthwhile only if our motivation is "religious" in nature; that is to say, if what motivates the action is not (only) the idea of creating a better or perfect society but, as Walter Benjamin would say ("Theses on the Philosophy of History"), the memory of enslaved ancestors, the memory of suffering – again, the "poor."

Such a perspective leads to a fundamentally "anarchic" conclusion about religion as a factor of emancipation. But does communism turn into anarchy, then? It could be argued that a Communist International, to the extent that it is encompassed within a religious outlook that guards it against relapsing into the practical-inert (or that compels it to renew itself), cannot avoid having an anarchic spirit (I have in mind a Christian like Jacques Ellul, who should be remembered and discussed more fully precisely from this point of view) in the sense that a religious form of political engagement does not allow itself to lead back to the founding of a state. If it wants to play a role in emancipation and liberation, the Church must free itself from the notion that it is establishing a historical order. Pope Francis's words on the duty of *hacer lío* (causing trouble) are not an exhortation to build "good" state order; they are a kind of call for permanent revolution. The phrases we frequently hear in the pope's homilies sound like a litany of empty words, good proposals that are often interpreted as pure and simple "moralizing." Perhaps at other times in history it made sense to think of Christianity as a building force (nowadays Americans who are bombing Iraq talk of *nation building*!). In the present situation, where globalization is becoming more clearly "total organization," i.e. an integrated system structured in accordance with rigid control and exploitation, religious presence is the presence of the marginalized who "press" at the borders and, with the intention of entering the capitalist "order" as well, break those borders down – *hacer lío*, indeed. The "anarchic" character that does not bring about state order and that in some sense is appropriate to papal presence is, perhaps, also what could be expected today from a Communist International that is no longer modelled on a Comintern centred on the interests of the Soviet Union. Jacques Derrida titled a book from 1993 *Spectres of Marx*, which is one of his most lucid and engaged works. There is a sense in which the communism I am talking about in reference to the Church of Pope Francis has a "spectral" aspect: it does not think of itself as a party that wants to govern, for reasons of "realism" (it makes no sense today to think of revolution as a violent takeover of power, since the forces of capitalist self-preservation are too strong) and because it wants to avoid relapsing into the practical-inert, which seems to be the fate of "successful" revolutions. The communism I have in mind can only take the form of a shadow that accompanies and torments (*hanter*, *hantise* is the French term to keep in mind: it pursues, hounds, disturbs ...) the established order and the prevailing power structures. It is said that Stalin once asked, "How many divisions does the pope have?" Religious "communism" does not have anything to do with this sort of thinking; those who see it in this light can really feel impatient and disillusioned in the face of its "impotence." Not only an ethics of Christian love, however, but a secular, realistic vision of the present state of the world too suggests that we take this impotence very seriously.

23

Christianity without Truth

"But didn't you tell me that if it were mathematically proved to you that the truth excludes Christ, you'd prefer to stick to Christ rather than to the truth?" We are accustomed to reading this line, spoken by a character in Dostoevsky's *The Possessed* (236), as a paradox, a hypothetical sentence. It is a bit like when we are moved by the story of Abraham who is, also paradoxically, ordered to sacrifice his son Isaac. However, from the standpoint of a philosophy that has experienced the entire history of Western Christian thought, that statement today is to be taken literally and more cogently. In order to choose Jesus Christ, I have to let go of truth, at least in the sense in which this term has been used in the philosophical language I inherited from that same tradition. We do not know if Dostoevsky based the remark on the saying, attributed to Aristotle, namely, *amicus Plato sed magis amica veritas* (Plato is my friend, but my greatest friend is truth), justifiably inverting it in the awareness of the many crimes committed, throughout the history of metaphysics, in the name of truth, when it is imposed in the absence of friendship. And, as heir and victim of this history, we can be Christians and follow the message of Christ only if we let go of truth. It is not the truth that sets us free; it is Jesus Christ and his message that, in the course of the cultural history he inspired, has freed us from the truth. He has done so not by showing us once and for all the eternal truth of no-truth but by making it impossible for us, in the historical conditions we have – for now – at the end of that metaphysical tradition, to still believe that *there is* such a thing as truth in the sense determined by metaphysics. It is the incarnation, i.e. the son of God becoming history, that frees us from truth, by creating the conditions in which we can no longer think of truth as metaphysical "given-ness," that is to say, as a faithful and therefore authoritative representation of the way things are. And are these conditions what we have before our eyes, like a real "given"? Certainly not; we must not confuse the condition of possibility, i.e. the specificity of our historical moments, with something that appears to us as a phenomenon; that would be an unusual way of forgetting Kant's teaching. The condition of possibility is our existence within a world that calls us to provide not an objective description but an interpretation, which we can do only as active and biased participants. All this can be summed up by saying that the history of Western metaphysics – in other words, the history of our Judeo-Greek-Christian culture – is the history (the dissolution) of truth. This is how the apocalyptic elements of our history acquire meaning; those elements include the Shoah and the massacres caused by religious wars but also and above all the humiliation of human beings caused by capitalist globalization, the massacre of animals, the destruction of "nature," which is reduced to a disposable resource for unlimited economic exploitation. Are we in the state of mind that Derrida was thinking of when he noted "an apocalyptic tone in contemporary philosophy" (*Di un tono apocalittico adottato di recente in filosofia*, 110)? But speculations on the fact that we are exhausting the planet's resources are not purely catastrophic fantasies, especially if we connect them with the ongoing dehumanization in the world of technological integration where total surveillance of the lives and choices of individuals will be increasingly possible – technically – and increasingly necessary – politically. But how has it come about that belief has determined our history? This is the question of metaphysics, its birth, and its possible supersedence. When he was writing *Being and Time* in 1927, Heidegger was still an "existentialist," at least if we compare him to the Heidegger we have after the *Kehre* (turn), that is, the Heidegger who abandons the centrality of *Eigentlichkeit* (authenticity) to mediate on the *Ereignis* (event), the history of Being. Somewhat paradoxically, this Heidegger who thinks about the history of Being also sets aside all discourses on the why of metaphysics. While in *Being and Time* he can still think that metaphysics is a sort of original sin of being-there – similar to the biblical original sin because we cannot rid ourselves of it, like a mistake that we have overcome, but still a "sin" committed by the being-there – after the *Kehre*, with the disappearance of the notion of authenticity, we also have the disappearance of this possible "explanation" of the why of metaphysics, which becomes for all intents and purposes a "destiny" of Being. In order to understand how this notion of truth as "given-ness" can be considered "responsible" for the affirmation of metaphysics and the triumph of technological dehumanization, it is important to evoke the question of authenticity in *Being and Time*. The "deictic" state of being-there, its always-already in the condition of one who contemplates Being, and also himself, on the basis of what is simply present, is directly connected to his tendency to abandon himself to *man*, to the intraworld interchange with his fellow human beings. By privileging mere presence and the "objectivity" of truth, therefore, metaphysics itself is a "product" of the social being appropriate to being-there. In addition, Heidegger can lead us to see more specifically the relationship between the "objectification" of oneself and the other, and the concept of truth as "given-ness." The inauthenticity of the everyday is not investigated further in *Being and Time* by Heidegger, who appears to consider it, somewhat simplistically, as a bad habit acquired "naturally" in the intraworld interchange. But, we might ask, does the idea of truth as factual "given-ness" establish itself in the intraworld interchange? A page from Nietzsche comes to mind here, if only to suggest an analogy: in *The Gay Science* (354) Nietzsche floats the idea that self-consciousness is not an innate quality indispensable for the life of the individual but a quality necessary for the relationship "between those who command and those who obey." The latter in fact are obliged to give an account of themselves to those who command. The relationship in which being-there is always-already thrown with one's fellow beings in the intraworld interchange is never neutral; it always takes the form of a hierarchy or, at any rate, a conflict. This is what Heidegger says in paragraph 37 of *Being and Time*, "Under the mask of Being-one-for-all, Being-one-against-the-Other dominates" (here we could also cite Hegel and the formation of self-consciousness described in his *Phenomenology*). The idea that there is, "out there," a given that serves to make one option or another correct resides in these relations. It is very likely, and logical, that no one would think to say "it is true that" if not in relation to others from whom they solicit acknowledgement or in relation to oneself in a different moment (Wittgenstein and the rules of language). In the idea of truth as objectivity that "imposes itself" and serves to "say who is right," there lies a seed of violence, precisely the violence that metaphysics inflicts from its deepest roots. I realize that here I appear to be "falling" into anthropology, psychologism – in other words, into an area that seems remote from Heidegger's ontological interest. This seems to be, however, an important "detour," especially in light of the interpretation of the, apparently distant from each other and certainly problematic, shifts in Heidegger's thinking, as is emerging, in particular recently, from our reading of the *Black Notebooks* and what they have to say about metaphysics and its connection with Judaism. It is not difficult to understand from the currently available documents, and from the initial studies of these – for example, Donatella Di Cesare's *Heidegger e gli ebrei* (*Heidegger and the Jews*) – that there is in Heidegger a close link between the "condemnation" of metaphysics (objectivism dominated by technology, calculation, etc.) and "antisemitism," an antisemitism that is never pursued by the author to the point of approving of the extermination of the Jews planned and carried out by Hitler. At any rate it requires, from those who do not wish to burn all of Heidegger's works as the product of a bloodthirsty fanatic, that they revise the concept of metaphysics itself. A rethinking of the question of authenticity and its "ethical" implications would be useful in such a revision. In the definition of Jews as a "metaphysical people" that have a sort of historical–ontological destiny to encapsulate the worst vices of modernity (from cosmopolitanism to the predominance of economic interests), we find echoes of the Heidegger of the "history of Being," which has "forgotten" the origin – human, all too human – of metaphysics and of objectivizing alienation. This should be the starting point for a rethinking of the Heideggerian concept of metaphysics, made necessary precisely by the publication of the *Black Notebooks*. Heidegger's antisemitism, to the extent that it is antisemitism without being confused with Nazi destructive racism, is based on the idea that the Jews are the metaphysical people *par excellence* because they do not have a homeland and are uprooted from "ontological historicity." This is as though the repudiation of metaphysics were motivated in Heidegger by the need, which would be essential for there-being, to have roots in the historical–natural "soil" that would make it capable of authenticity. But this is not the defect of metaphysics for Heidegger the existentialist who, in his initial analysis of existence, shares and reflects the spirit of the early-twentieth-century avant-garde, who rebelled against the existing order, especially because they saw it as a threat to freedom, as the monstrous onset of the society of total organization. The metaphysical alienation in objectivity, calculation, and the reduction of nature and humans to sheer resources to be exploited has little to do with the notion of rootedness. The antitechnological and "antimodern" Heidegger is not a fundamentalist naturalist. There is in him an "anarchic" vein that is well noted by scholars like Reiner Schürmann (see *Dai principi all'anarchia. Essere e agire in Heidegger* [From Principles to Anarchy: Being and Acting in Heidegger] and see Alberto Martinengo, *Introduzione a Reiner Schürmann* [Introduction to Reiner Schürmann]), and his insistence, against Sartre, on the history of Being (in the *Letter on Humanism* he writes, "We are at a level where there is primarily Being"), is not to be separated from the awareness that Being, for him, does not give itself except in the opening created by there-being. To forget this is a "metaphysical" error and Heidegger's self-misunderstanding, when he chooses to side with the Nazis, is the most glaring and scandalous manifestation of that.

If we are trying to find a justification for the "apocalyptic tone" that our philosophical discussion is taking, the publication of the *Black Notebooks*, but much more so the "general condition of the world" – Hegel would call it – into where we are thrown, amply provides us with one. The apparent exaggeration of taking the destiny of the present world back to metaphysics and its alienated concept of truth no longer seems to be so if we do not consider it only as an "objective" destiny of Being but rather as an "original sin" that never exists without being accompanied by a "present sin," according to the language of the catechism (and that could also be found in Kant's *Religion within the Limits of Reason Alone*). We are not responsible for the first (sin), but because of it we are always predisposed to sin again. For this reason, "first and mostly" (*zuerst und zumeist*), there-being must always be understood as inauthentic. To consider this merely as a tendency acquired from the habit of seeing oneself with others and similar to them would, I agree, be lapsing into psychologism of the most banal kind. To return to the problem of the Nazi Heidegger, leaving aside his more or less explicit antisemitism, it seems quite reasonable to think that, precisely because I described metaphysics as a destiny – albeit connected in some sense with the "present sin" of there-being in a concrete historical society – he made the mistake of hoping that Nazism could establish, or restore, a society free of metaphysics. In short, Heidegger's thought would appear to be the following: we are already-always in inauthenticity, and so (or because) our world is dominated by metaphysics – i.e. objectivization, calculation, scientism, and omnivorous technology. We cannot free ourselves from metaphysics as though it were a matter of erasing an error by correcting it. Heeding Being and making preparations for a new beginning depend on the individual's decisions. Against this, the main line of his thought, Heidegger, at a certain point, decides to trust Nazism as if such an action could overcome the error by opposing the triumph of metaphysics that would result from being dominated by Americanism or Soviet communism, and definitely the Jews, who are seen as the main conveyors of metaphysical poison. Apart from rejecting the obvious pro-Nazi choice, here Heidegger must be taken to task for a patent self-contradiction: ontological difference does not allow for the existence of a nonmetaphysical society like the one that was to be created by Nazism. The self-contradiction and, especially, the identification of Jews with the metaphysical people *par excellence* are the products of Heidegger's caving in to the opinion of the "media" of his time and his society, if not – as some of the more adversarial critics think – a totally conformist choice designed to guarantee for himself the favour of Nazi authorities. On the other hand, it could even be the case that the idea of contributing to the political construction of a non- or pre- or postmetaphysical society was motivated by the desire to avoid a purely "mystical" outcome of his thinking on Being (see *Zur Sache des Denkens* [Time and Being], 1959, 79). The emergency of the war, in particular, but also the emergency of the social crisis that he himself experienced in the years of Weimar could very well have been sufficient reason to take a position of *engagement* that entailed going beyond his previous theoretical positions. I think that now we can read in this situation the possibility – certainly contradictory in many respects or at least paradoxical – of considering a political "application" of Heideggerian ontology, which definitely avoids the mistaken interpretation of the choice of Nazism, which has become clearly untenable, on account of what we have "discovered" that is ethically repugnant following the Second World War, as well as the equally obvious reason that Nazi Germany was in the process of enacting the worst form of metaphysics – technological domination, totalitarian control of society, and the manipulation of human beings. The reason for looking in Heidegger's work specifically for the theoretical basis for conceptualizing a society that is not alienated, not metaphysical in the sense of inauthenticity, but, instead, decidedly oriented to thinking of Being as dialogical event – definitely a "communist" society (see Vattimo and Zabala, *Comunismo Ermeneutico* [Hermeneutic Communism]) – lies not in the expectation of challenging the paradox at all costs. It is, instead, realizing that we have before us a concept of Being as event and no longer as foundation ("Das Sein als den Grund des Seiden fahren zu lassen," *Zur Sache des Denkens*, 6). Here we can find a "philosophical basis" for a politics that is truly free of the Platonic legacy. This can also be seen all too well in the political events in which we are all involved: every effort to transform society in radically democratic terms is pitted against, not only on the part of the churches, the standards of "natural" law, whose naturalness is invoked in order to ethically – as well as legally – obligate citizens who profess religions or ethics different from those that those in power want to impose. I need only point to the questions connected with issues like euthanasia, assisted reproductive technology, and others. But we can ascribe to a foundationalist politics everything that involves the "clash of civilizations," that is to say, the religious war that today is at the root of the problem of "international terrorism" and that mirrors the difficulty of coexisting in a globalized world with its many different cultures – a difficulty that has become dramatic since it goes along with and, essentially, ideologically masks the border that, in the capitalist society, separates more and more the excluded masses from the rich, and naturally "free" democratic, world. With this "general condition of the world" in mind, the "apocalyptic tone" assumed by philosophy seems legitimate and, indeed, indispensable. Every "realistic" objection, which would have philosophy engaged above all in solving "concrete," manageable problems, is like an unacceptable apologia for the existing "order," which is like saying, let us leave aside the big questions and let each of us work in his or her own field. Whatever the intentions, good though they may be, of these appeals to realism and concreteness, their less than implicit acceptance of the "given" division of labour cannot evade an elementary objection from the standpoint of dialectic, which is for realists already an apocalyptic tendency.

In the world of late capitalism, which for Heidegger is also the culmination (and the possible decline) of metaphysics, truth understood as objective facticity, which is more and more entrusted exclusively to the experimental sciences, with all their technological implications, is only another aspect of power to which metaphysics, in its final crisis – which seems increasingly to parallel the failure of capitalism – tries to provide its traditional support. Here, we are certainly at the level of the most explicit of apocalyptic discourses, which is, however, confirmed by what in fact already occurs in daily life, starting with, above all, the radicalization of the difference between wealth and poverty; this is a difference that the capitalist system of globalized communication itself makes intolerable because, for example, public television can no longer purchase merchandise that is advertised but produced in the poorest areas of the world using child labour, while, in spite of the domesticated information in *mainstream* newspapers and television, the intensification of social control made necessary by the integration of technologies is becoming more and more visible. I have in mind the recent scandal called WikiLeaks and the growing militarization that a society like ours can avoid, given the vulnerability of many aspects of the social mechanism; for example, how will the highly hazardous waste produced by the "peaceful" generation of nuclear energy be safeguarded against potential misuse by terrorists? All these are questions that philosophy cannot avoid dealing with, thereby becoming an "ontology of actuality." But why ontology?

What does Being, or the *on he on* that Plato, Aristotle, and the metaphysical tradition talked about, have to do with all this? The answer is, the "existentialist" Heidegger, with his analysis of the inauthentic everyday into which the being-in-the-world is always-already thrown: Being does not give itself except in the epochal opening created from time to time by there-being. In this perspective, the destiny of Being itself is tied to the globalization of commerce, the production of atomic energy, and the tightening of social control. "Being (not entities) is something which 'there is' only in so far as truth is. And truth *is* only in so far as and as long as Dasein is" (*Being and Time*, 272). The truth discussed in this quote is *not* the truth-correspondence of metaphysics and positivism. That truth of metaphysics is the enemy not only of freedom and democracy in the world – because it is on the side of power and its mechanisms of self-preservation – but of all authentic religious experience as well. After centuries of identifying Christianity with imperialistic Eurocentrism, we can no longer believe "that" God "exists"; i.e. that he is the guarantor of the metaphysical – and therefore alienated and alienating – world order. We need to juxtapose Bonhoeffer's comment with the assertion from *Being and Time* cited above: "Einen

Gott, den es gibt, gibt es nicht" ("A God that exists does not exist"), *Atto ed Essere* (*Act and Being*, 103). A religious experience inspired by these statements has never existed because there has never been a nonmetaphysical world, that is to say, a world without some form of domination. The uncertainty of such a possibility, if there is one, is the apocalyptic meaning of existence.

24

What (the Hell) Is Enlightenment?

The title of Kant's short essay, in which he has the Enlightenment coincide with reason's coming of age, should be taken, in the form slightly modified by the term in parentheses, as a guide for a reading of Steven Nadler's recent book dedicated to Spinoza's *Tractatus theologico-politicus* (*A Theological-Political Treatise*) and importantly titled *A Book Forged in Hell*. Nadler is one of the most well-known scholars of Spinoza and of the history of ideas in modern times; suffice it to mention his *Spinoza: A Life*. Compared to that work, *A Book Forged in Hell* focuses exclusively and in great detail on the *Tractatus* and on the biographical and historical circumstances surrounding its writing, in particular as they relate to Spinoza's main work *Ethica ordine geometrico demonstrata* (*The Ethics*). In effect, when he decided to write the *Tractatus*, Spinoza interrupted for a short time the editing of *The Ethics*, motivated, it seems, by the need to respond to accusations of atheism directed at him, which were circulating for some time and had already caused him to be expelled from the synagogue of Amsterdam in 1656 (when the twenty-three-year-old philosopher had not yet published anything) and threatened to restrict the freedom to philosophize that he, at the time of the writing of the *Tractatus* in the mid-1600s, felt was being endangered throughout the United Provinces by the political violence of the time.

The title Nadler chose for this timely comment on the *Tractatus* aptly reflects the response of readers of Spinoza when they read it in 1670, namely, that it was a diabolical text aimed wholeheartedly at the destruction of religion in general and belief in sacred scripture in particular. It would seem, therefore, that the author's intention of shielding himself against the accusation of atheism produced, paradoxically, the opposite result, i.e. the readers' impression of finding themselves faced with an infernal book. This, however, is not the impression that the book, in Nadler's reconstruction and excellent commentary, generates today, and in this sense it can represent an important new perspective on the image of Spinoza that still prevails in our culture. That image, i.e. as the father of the Enlightenment, of rationalism, and indeed of the atheism that, in modernity, inspired and accompanied the progressive secularization of thought and the movement away from the great "Abrahamic" religions: Judaism, Christianity, and Islam. The phrase that best sums up Spinoza's philosophy, *Deus sive Natura* (God or Nature), which was the key to his popularity in all the subsequent epochs of thought, is the ideology of modern science, not only Newton's but also that of Einstein – according to whom, "God does not play dice" (letter to Bohr, 4 December 1926). If science makes sense it is because nature as a whole is a system of causes and effects rigidly governed by laws that hold always and everywhere. Scientists certainly also deal with probabilities, but even in mathematics and non-Euclidian geometry they prefer to think of these as different "languages" applicable to different aspects of reality for which they function with the rigour of Spinoza's mathematics. In such a view of nature, as a system upheld by rigorous laws, there is no room for intervention on the part of a providential, unfettered creator (out of nothing? Are you kidding?) God capable of suspending the laws of nature in order to perform what we call miracles. If there is such a thing as a supreme power from which everything proceeds (through mathematical consequentiality and not a deliberate act that causes an event), we can call it God, however, in the knowledge that it is nothing but nature. Rather than divinize nature (this is how the romantics, especially Schelling, read Spinoza), Spinoza wants to naturalize God. The divine is not an entity distinct from the world from which the world proceeds (freely created) but is only the totality of the physical causes and effects that envelop human beings as well. What we have always believed was God is nothing more than the entire universe in its countless rigorously structured interconnections. Why then do we have all these religious beliefs? It is because each of us, as a natural entity that wants to survive, tends to give in to those passions that are most closely connected with the instinct for self-preservation: like fear, hope, greed, etc. Clever priests take advantage of this inclination, making us believe the lies of traditional religions and keeping us in a state of servitude. Only *amor Dei intellectualis* (intellectual love of God) grounded in the knowledge of truth (everything is God–Nature; everything is governed by a necessary order that does not depend on us) sets us free. Our duty is simply to know better and better the laws of nature and so become increasingly free and good. These are the aspects of the Enlightenment Spinoza cited by those who turn to science in order to deny the merits of religion. As well, and especially, positivist scientism of the past was inspired by the idea of ending conflicts (ethical, political, etc.) through knowledge of the objective truth provided by science. Freud too may have thought along these lines: by shining a light on the subconscious, you become free (but recognize necessity), etc. And today: Spinoza or Scalfari, or Odifreddi, or Flores? Perhaps, but this same "diabolical" *Tractatus* that Nadler invites us to read offers a formidable weapon for blunting the forever recurring fanatical praise of "enlightened" reason. Atheists want believers to give up their faith because it contradicts the truth of science. But Spinoza himself teaches us that the question of religion has nothing, or almost nothing, to do with truth. Using arguments that we also find in Nietzsche (who may have borrowed them from Spinoza), where he speaks of an "affectation in the leave-taking" (*Human, All Too Human*, and *Posthumous Fragments 1876–1878*, aphorism 82): you do not need to pretend to have cogent reasons when you abandon a belief, since you did not have those same reasons when you embraced it. The beautiful chapter 16 of the *Tractatus*, which Nadler quotes in part, appears to be no less than an apologia for religion; in fact, he lists in seven points the beliefs that "it is most useful and even necessary" to cultivate in order to "encourage love for God and our fellow human beings" (*Un libro forgiato all'inferno*, 184) – love that is the essence of Spinoza's ethics (which he finds in both the Old and New Testament). To sum up: God exists, which is to say a supreme, just, and merciful entity. He is one and omnipresent and has the supreme right and dominion over all things. And so forth, including love for one's neighbour and the conviction that only those who obey this rule of life can be saved. Is all this political prudence on Spinoza's part, who is understandably motivated by his awareness of the risks that an atheist faced in European society, including Holland, in the 1600s? Perhaps. And certainly this list of "good beliefs" – which excludes sectarianism, intolerance, clericalism – can also be justified by a pragmatic choice:

they may all be lies, but they are useful for good moral conduct and, therefore, acceptable. Why, then, should the unbeliever become an enlightened atheist? Perhaps for the love of demonstrated, certain, scientific truth? But the *amor Dei intelletualis* is exercised only, or at east primarily, as devotion to a just and merciful God, as respect or love of one's neighbour, which is to say, religion. If it were something else, it would need to be a form of superstitious overestimation of knowledge as such. This is a superstition that is not completely absent from Spinoza's text, if we recall all the pages on the *vulgus* (common people) and its reliance on the imagination.

Spinoza's teaching deserves to be considered not only by atheist scientists, naturally, but also by not too "astute priests." Even for them, realizing that religion has nothing to do with truth (the "historical truth" of the resurrection, Mary's assumption into heaven, or the presumed truth of "biblical anthropology," which has replaced the indefensible cosmology of Scripture) would free them from taking many absurd positions, thereby making it easier for everyone to acknowledge the irrepressible (or so it seems) need for religion.

25

True and False Christian Universalism

Perhaps it is not a bad thing that, after the new wave of international terrorism that culminated in the attacks of 11 September 2001, people begin once more to talk about religious wars and the clash of civilizations. Not because such conversations reflect faithfully the true events that occurred, since it is more true that religion in such events is only marginally involved and this needs to be emphasized. Those who see 11 September as the playing out of a religious war are confusing things in a more or less explicitly partisan way. It is useful to bring in the religious factor for both those who planned the terrorist attacks and those who – like the Bush administration – want to defend themselves with an "endless war." In these cases, however, religion is used shamelessly like an "opiate of the masses," as Marx would say; in other words, to blame the suicide bombers and militant fanatics or to justify limiting the civil liberties in the United States of America and in countries that imitate it with varying degrees of conviction. In a situation like this, it is urgent that, from the point of view of religion – the religions that are most directly involved, i.e. Christianity, Islam, Judaism – we dispel all ambiguities. For this reason, we can consider providential, a *felix culpa* (happy fault), the fact that there is so much talk, albeit foolishly, of a religious war. To demonstrate the absurdity of such a viewpoint means not only to see more clearly what happened, thereby eliminating an error, it is also an opportunity to clarify the meaning of religion in our world for the benefit of religious consciousness itself, with the result, it is hoped, that the interests of the churches and religious confessions concerned are served. In other words, reflecting on the question and the outdated notion of a religious war in our time also means thinking more authentically of a universalism of the great religions of salvation on which the modern world is built and which have inseminated our Western civilization.

Of course, we must not exaggerate by saying that providence can be seen in the unfolding of history. But it is certainly important that the appearance of a clash of civilizations – involving Christians, Jews, and Muslims – manifests itself and is invoked now that – at least in the Christian world but to a different degree and in different forms in the Hebrew and Muslim worlds as well – the effects of the secularization of religious traditions and of the idea of truth itself are emerging fully. On this specific aspect of the issue, it is important to dispel many misconceptions, which are not always disinterested. It seems evident to those who talk of a war of civilizations and a religious war that the Christian Western world is anything but equipped for such a clash. The fact that many churchmen, like some Italian bishops and cardinals, exhort Catholics to defend Christian values against the spread of the influence of Islam in western Europe or that Western statesmen boast of the superiority of the Christian civilization, which must be protected from barbarous terrorists, clearly shows that, at least from the point of view of the Christian world, people can talk about anything but the issue of a war between religions. "None of us are any longer material for a society," wrote Nietzsche at one point (*The Gay Science*, §356). Of course, at least we, namely Westerners of today, are no longer a society capable of fighting a religious war – thank God, one might say. If we take note of this fact, another question immediately arises: should we, because of this, think of ourselves as authentically less religious than our ancestors who set off for the Crusades believing that they were fulfilling a sacred duty to God? Few people, in my view – except the cardinals, bishops, and heads of state mentioned above – really believe that. Without criminalizing our ancestors – knowing, however, that their religious motive was not as exclusive and prevalent as we might believe – we all realize that historical circumstances have changed, and we feel, often not in full awareness, that religion today enjoys a position and a weight in our individual and collective existence that is different from those it had in the age of the Crusades. For this reason, too, each of us is totally convinced that the 11 September attacks do not concern our conscience, confession, or lived religious experience. But are we able to imagine this as a religious fact for the "other side," that of the terrorists who – I have Palestine in mind – blow themselves up with suicide vests killing themselves and ever higher numbers of other people, defenseless civilians not directly involved in any war? It is easy and convenient to depict fanatical religious terrorism in this way; it even looks like we want to "understand" the reasons for actions that seem absurd to us. But the first result is precisely that of confirming and consolidating the idea that we are witnessing a clash of cultures; it goes without saying, a secular and rational culture (ours) pitted against a culture and a religion that are barbarous, primitive, superstitious, and definitely bloodthirsty. Once this way of representing terrorism is accepted as valid, it is difficult to avoid coming to the conclusion that we are dealing with a clash of civilizations or, rather, a clash between civilization and barbarism.

A misperception of this kind, precisely because what it suggests tends to seem obvious to us, obliges us to rethink its roots, which may be deep. These are connected with the ambiguous relationship, among truth, authority, and power, which has been a feature of the Christian world from its origins. It is not at all apparent that the missionary spirit promoted by Jesus in the Gospel – "Go therefore and make disciples all nations baptizing them in the name of the Father" (Matthew 28, 19–20) – should naturally turn into the dominant ideology of conquest in modernity, that is to say, during the time of the great voyages of discovery and the first colonization of the New World. It was not a contingent historical development that was recognized and rejected explicitly by the churches that were characterized by it – first among them the Catholic Church – but it is difficult to overcome all its many and profound implications, which continue to affect many aspects of the doctrine and practice of these churches. Naturally, the idea that the truth revealed in Scripture and entrusted to the apostles conferred upon the Christian Church the right to exercise supreme authority over all aspects of the life of the human community was not born with colonialism and the contemporaneous establishment of the absolute state in Europe. We can, however, reasonably assume that only in this epoch does it become an affirmed and professed ideology, according to the dictum *compelle intrare* (compel people to come in). The spirit of the Crusades, instead, was still inspired by the idea of liberating the Holy Land and the Holy Sepulchre from the rule of the infidels. For the most part, they were still territorial wars. As proof, it is thought that St Francis considered meeting the sultan Malek al-Kamil in

1219 in order to preach the Gospel and to convert him, and certainly not to impose on him the Christian truth through the forced Christianization of the state. We can also acknowledge, however, that the Franciscan spirit was not exactly prevalent in the Christian Middle Ages. In addition to the Crusades themselves, whose objective was to liberate the Holy Land, there were the bloody Crusades against heretics, which had a more clearly "doctrinal" objective. Nor can we ignore the fact that the dangerous aspect of the heresies, which the medieval Church opposed with cruelty, had a decidedly political dimension: these heresies were becoming the object of persecutions when, as oftentimes happened, they were seen as threats to the power of the pope, the wealth of the Church, and its claim of political ascendency.

Historians and philosophers of history (Wilhelm Dilthey, for example) have rightly highlighted the weight that the fact the Christian Church of the early centuries inherited many of the state functions from the collapsing Roman Empire had in determining the history of the Church and of European theology and philosophy. I ask myself, can a similar situation be found in the Muslim world, with more accentuated features, because the descendants of the Prophet were also the founders of "modern" political structures in a world of nomadic shepherds, etc.? If a theory such as this – Dilthey's for the Christian world and its equivalent in the Muslim world – makes sense, it could be imagined that the problem of the secularism of the state and the associated problem of religious wars, etc. are those of the West because of these contingent historical parallels. As for Dilthey's theory, which I borrow without making any pretence to giving it a faithful interpretation, the close link between the claim of truth and the claim of political authority would have been encrusted, so to speak, on the Christian Church from outside, due to its role as a substitute for Roman authority that it found itself playing. This argument circulated widely in the Catholic polemic of the nineteenth and twentieth centuries, and at times it appears as the ideal of the end of the "Constantinian era" – since the so-called "Donation of Constantine" (which never existed, to tell the truth!) was, supposedly, the origin of the temporal power of the papacy, with all its consequences. In many European nations this end coincided with the Protestant Reformation, which, however (from Luther's *cuius regio, eius religio* [whose realm, his religion] to Calvin's dogmatic absolutism), did not really free itself of the temporal prejudice; in other regions, including Italy obviously, the problem of the temporal power of the popes resolved itself only with the end of the Papal State in 1870 without, however, the expectations of ecclesiastical authority over the laws and structures of the state coming to an end (as is clearly seen in the case of Italy).

We can obviously discuss the historical circumstances that created the truth–authority link, and the theory that posits the relationship between the early Church and the Roman Empire is not comprehensive, because the question of the link between truth and political power arises for Christians well before they inherit the structures of the Roman Empire, precisely when the empire demands that they, under pain of martyrdom, obey the cult of emperor worship. In this way, the "blame" for correlating truth with power would be placed on Rome, which, however, had never practised forced conversion of the people it conquered. Rémi Brague has rightly drawn attention to the meaning of the Roman Pantheon as an example of religious tolerance and pluralism (Brague, *Il futuro dell'Occidente* [The Future of the West]).

A feature of the doctrinal absolutism that for many centuries typified the attitude of the Christian churches and that, in Dilthey's opinion, flows into the question of the inheritance of the structures of the Roman Empire, is the metaphysical legacy of Greek thought. So much so that, without expanding on this aspect of the question, it can be said that the dissolution, or the secularization, of this link became really possible only in our world, when even philosophy felt all the consequences of the dissolution (also enabled by Christianity) of classical Greek metaphysics. Moreover, the great Greek metaphysical legacy also contained the premises for correlating truth, authority, and political power: in the *Republic* Plato theorized that the supreme authority of the state would be exercised by the philosophers, i.e. those who had access to absolute truths.

What I mean to shed light on with such references is the completely, non- "natural" – as it might tend to appear – character of the link between truth and power. In our cultural tradition, which is not only Christian but classical and Greek as well, this linkage has deep roots. It is not, however, an anthropological constant found in all human civilizations, despite the fact that the link between political authority and some form of the sacred can be seen throughout the history of cultures. To think of this link as an anthropological constant is to think that democracy is impossible; at best, the link can seem to be what in the Christian religion is called "original sin." It certainly reappears regularly in the history of individuals and societies but not in sufficient quantity to prevent doctrines like Christianity from thinking of themselves as religions of redemption.

To sum up what has been said to this point, if we acknowledge that we are no longer a society capable of waging religious wars and if this does not appear to us as a symptom of decadence and immorality but rather as an element of civilization that pushes us to not take as obvious the idea that the enemy, the terrorist, the infidel is motivated by purely religious fanaticism, we may be able to understand that the link between truth and power is not a necessary one but rather a contingent one created by a cluster of historical circumstances. We, namely, Westerners – but perhaps this applies to Muslims and Jews as well – inherited traditions in which the political structures were constituted in strict relation to the affirmation of a given religious faith. The idea that the link is contingent is not a statement of fact proven as historical truth nor is it purely wishful thinking, as though we were deliberately falsifying the facts of history and anthropology in order to console ourselves or to achieve some objective. It is, instead – as happens to philosophical truths – a theory–praxis, a controversial interpretation driven by a particular project, which appears to be valid, more valid than others, in that it is more capable of reading and steering our situation toward a practical solution. To see the truth–authority–power nexus as an insurmountable anthropological constant would only mean – and many people push in this direction – preparing ourselves to wage a new religious war, repeating a "naturalistic" scenario, so naturalistic that it would not make any sense to take it as the basis of a conscious decision and an action plan. If we make plans, it is because we consider that link to be contingent and changeable. As well, in terms of historical validity, there are good reasons to think so: the secularization of the modern world is, if not proof, a sign that it is possible to get beyond equating the profession of a religious truth with support of a rigid political order.

To clear up the misperceptions, and the tragedies, of a religious war, we really need to accept the interpretation that I have proposed here and that is the ethical–political meaning of much of today's philosophy. The presumed authority of those who have, or claim to have, discovered the truth, a truth, is merely a violence to which we have become accustomed in a particular world, within a particular cultural and political tradition. Christian universalism of the modern "missionary" and imperialistic kind is an expression – or, probably, the exemplary and *originary*, at least in our world, illustration – of that claim and that violence. If we try to ask ourselves, quite simply, who among us would consider it just, natural, and human to force someone to accept our faith, we could have problematic answers: much of the educational relationship with our young children is based on a mixture of violent imposition and emotional coercion (do it out of love for me ...), and the example of the would-be suicide that I must, morally, try to stop even against his or her will could very well apply to the priest who forcibly baptized the "pagans," the primitives, and the savages. And yet, even in the case of children, the use of physical punishment and emotional blackmail is a sort of last resort, which is always preceded by the effort to make them understand, to explain, to cite an, albeit imperfect, freedom. As in the case of hypocrisy, which is the homage that vice renders to virtue, the relationship with the other is always depicted as the relationship with a freedom that, only in extreme cases, and without a theory to justify it in positive terms (self-defence and actual war are like this) resorts to violence.

If it manages to divest itself of the violent aspects that it has acquired through the political tradition of the West, Christian universalism can find (again) its authentic meaning, which is, incidentally, written in the Gospels. Nowadays such a process seems more and more called for and attainable. The churches have gradually lost much of their "temporal" power, both direct and indirect, to shape consciences in an irrevocable way. Philosophy has abandoned a rigidly objectivist conception of truth, linking it, instead, more explicitly to the consensus of the community that shares paradigms, traditions, and even prejudices but that are aware of their history, which appears to me as an effect of the "Christianization," even unawares, of today's philosophy itself, where it is possible to speak of a transformation of the concept of truth into the concept of charity, of respect for and listening to the other. It is the way one professes one's own religion and view of the world that is changing profoundly, at least in the West, and not because we have become less believing, more immoral, or less religiously engaged. The dialogue among the great religions, which many people discuss but few practise, is possible only if, within each of them, the faithful feel involved in believing in a less exclusive and less superstitious manner. If I say, as I believe it should be said, that since I believe that God became man, I can also think that, in other cultures, he became a sacred cow, an elephant, or a cat, I do not believe that I am blaspheming but rather that I am expressing a true aspect of the Christian truth.

A modern, secular, human rethinking of Christian universalism is possible on this basis, and, if not in the ecclesiastical hierarchies, certainly in the community of believers it is already well under way. By expanding this rethinking to include all its implications, we will also be able to defuse the bomb of religious wars and start to see the other not as a religious fanatic prepared to do anything in order to save his or her soul but, much more realistically, as someone who is fighting for concrete historical objectives, on which agreement can be found on the condition that faith and salvation are not involved, at all costs. What from the Christian – and in general "Western" – point of view can and must be done to eliminate the misunderstandings about religious wars is to start living our religiosity outside the schema so dear to Enlightenment rationalists, which offers only two possibilities: either the fanaticism of a blind faith (*credo quia absurdum* [I believe because it is absurd]) or the scepticism of reason without roots and without an effective grasp of the world. In concrete terms, a sense of rediscovered religiosity free from the concerns of power and, therefore, also free from the temptation to assert violence, should mean that the today's Western world takes seriously the historical reasons for the conflict with the so-called third world, instead of preparing for an endless war for the triumph of its own "faith." The historical reasons for the conflict are economic reasons of inequality and exploitation, which mask themselves as reasons of faith and culture only for ideological manipulation by those who control the wealth and power. Can we hope to find a kindred spirit among the other interlocutors of our dialogue, among our Muslim and Jewish friends? Much more than seeking the triumph of one faith over another, the task we all have before us is that of rediscovering – after the "metaphysical" era of absolutisms and the equivalence of truth and authority – a possible postmodern religious experience in which the relationship with the divine is not contaminated by fear, violence, and superstition.

26

From Aesthetics to Ontology

On the centenary of his birth (4 February 1918), it can be justifiably said that in the case of Luigi Pareyson time is a gentleman. Only a few years before a serious illness took his life, Pareyson's work enjoyed success even outside the academy, and from that time the success has grown and deepened to the extent that, in many ways, it can be said that his ideas had an anticipatory, if not outright prophetic impact. I think that today, more so than twenty years ago, we can recognize the relevance of his thought not only in terms of its specialized focus. And the title "tragic thought" that he often used in the later stages of his life to characterize his own theoretical position helps us to go beyond the limits of the academic horizon, which is increasingly problematic as even the most obstinate defenders of philosophy as a specialized science, as the guardian of a tradition of texts meant to be kept rigorously separate form current affairs and therefore from any kind of social usefulness (perhaps only to avoid being completely marginalized in the culture industry), are convinced that a less tenuous relationship with everyday existence, politics, religion, and the new ethical problems raised by science and technology needs to be found. This would be a relationship similar to the one that existed during the time of the great systematic philosophies like Idealism (when the young Schelling, Hegel, and Hölderlin, at the Tübingen seminary where they were fellow researchers at the end of the 1700s, followed with enthusiasm the events of the French Revolution) and that applied as well to the existentialist Kierkegaard (another master who always inspired Pareyson), author of a searing "topical" polemic against the Church of Denmark.

A good deal of the Italian and European philosophy of the last decades has travelled the pathways that Pareyson blazed, often with a prescient spirit. I have in mind philosophers of the "youngest" generation, such as Massimo Cacciari, whose books, especially the ambitious *Dell'Inizio* (*Concerning the Beginning*), explore the same perspective or another philosopher of the same generation (the 1940s), Reiner Schürmann (who is now studied by another Turin scholar, Alberto Martinengo), author of *From Principles to Anarchy*, one of the most important books on Heidegger of the last decades of the 1900s. In different terms and forms, names like those of Cacciari and Schürmann, but also many French philosophers of the Derridian and Heideggerian school (for example, Jean-Luc Nancy, especially his book *The Experience of Freedom*), illustrate the relevance of "tragic thought" in today's, for the most part, youth culture, that is to say, those who, in the universities and outside them, turn more and more often to Pareyson's later writings.

Pareyson formulated his thought by radicalizing, even more so than does a classic of hermeneutic philosophy like Gadamer, the relationship between the philosophy of interpretation and the concept of Being, which was at the core of Heidegger's meditation. If we recognize, along with Heidegger, that our experience of the world is always interpretation – in other words, an encounter in which, as Pareyson writes, "the object reveals itself to the extent that the subject expresses himself" (*Esistenza e persona* [Existence and Personhood], ed. 1985, 211) – and which is not a passive mirroring where the subject erases him- or herself in order to reflect the object faithfully, we must also think of Being in terms other than those of traditional metaphysics, namely, as ultimate, immutable, and wholly "given" foundation, which is outside all historical authenticity since, as theologians who have wrestled with the problem of predestination know, if Being (or God) is wholly present from eternity and for eternity, then becoming, history, and human freedom are purely inexplicable fictions. In order to make it possible to recognize that truth is always interpretation – even scientific truth, since scientific propositions are verified or falsified only within the framework of paradigms that scientists acquire from their training, culture, etc., and that they, therefore, "express" in their experimental work – Being needs to be thought as event and not as a fixed structure that is given once and for all. For Pareyson, but also for Schelling, Kierkegaard, and many Christian (or Jewish, like Lévinas) existentialists, this

Being that is not the eternal, immutable geometric order but rather the source of interpretation and freedom, is the biblical God who is, in turn, initiative, affirmation, and positivity that prevails over potential negativity. Such a God contains evil, albeit as prehistory that has prevailed. The tragedy of human experience, which is never totally free from limits, ills, suffering, and gratuitous violence, has more remote origins.

The fact that much of European philosophy today is tragicist does not necessarily mean that tragic thought is, for everyone including the followers of Pareyson, the truth of our current condition. There is another aspect of his philosophical legacy that circulates widely in the thinking of nontragicist philosophers and in the idea that philosophy is essentially a hermeneutics of religious experience – which means the interpretation of texts and sacred scripture (for Pareyson, the Hebrew and Christian sacred scriptures to a notable degree). While many of today's Christian philosophers, or at any rate those who want to safeguard the possibility of religion, perhaps in the name of Wittgenstein's distinction between different "language games," tend to separate religious discourse from philosophical discourse, each having its own criteria of validity (but who assigns the roles in the play? Who decides what the boundaries of the two discourses are?), Pareyson has taught us to see that there is continuity, as well as potential conflict, between philosophy and the religious tradition, and that these disciplines concern themselves with the same thing and both rely on "revelation" in which infinite possibilities of interpretation are concealed but also offer themselves. If we think of how important the plurality of cultures, religions, and myths on which these cultures are based is for the "global" society in which we find ourselves living more and more, it must be said that, even in this regard, Pareyson's philosophical legacy is anything but obsolete.

The two points of Pareyson's "topicality" I start out with are not at all separate, or separable, from his philosophy. He arrives at tragic thought by practising philosophy as the hermeneutics of religious experience and not by another route. This way of defining and practising philosophy is perhaps the most essential and most important of his messages. Certainly, we would need a broader discussion and a more complete rereading of all his writings in order to determine if, and the degree to which, it is already definable as hermeneutics of religious experience; take for example his proposal of aesthetics as theory of "formativity," which at first glance appears to be a phenomenology of artistic creation with no visible connections with the biblical and Christian tradition. But it is not difficult to see the continuity and the coherence of the trajectory that goes from aesthetics to the religious interests of recent times. The discovery of the "forming form" prompts the thought of a view of the real that has much greater affinity with Idealism than it does with any form of realism or empiricism. The form that comes into existence in artistic creation, which may be any event related to human initiative, is the manifestation of a presence that transcends the pure relationship between the subject and the object. In Heideggerian language, we can speak of an event of Being. For Pareyson, an existentialist and a Jaspers scholar, there is no all-encompassing rational discourse. What he reads in Schelling and develops in his hermeneutics of religious experience is nothing more than the development of this initial existentialist position. Retracing his journey toward the hermeneutics of religious experience, Pareyson insists on seeing freedom as the starting point of everything – in a certain sense, more Kierkegaard (and Barth) than Jaspers himself. What opens philosophy to the religious experience is not so much the impossibility of theoretically grasping the totality of Being, as the infinite but abyssal "newness" of the free act; that is, its origin in "nothingness," its pure and simple occurring, its absolute "positivity," which makes it possible or necessary. There is no logical "explanation" for this spontaneous happening; there is only narration, that is, myth, in the etymological sense. And with respect to the Big Bang, whatever it may mean, the conversation begins only after it has occurred; there is never an explanation of what there was before it or the reason for it.

Philosophy, which Pareyson calls "ontology of freedom" (the title of one of his posthumous books), encounters myth when it contemplates the problem of the origin of freedom. It encounters it in the literal sense of the word: myth appears before it, and the causality of everything also manifests itself in the fact that there is not just one myth; there are many, but they certainly do not make themselves available to a "rational," comparative selection. Their affinity with the domain of freedom and the event also consists in their presenting themselves as stories that, in some way, we already know and within which we already *are*. Anthropology teaches us that cultures have myths as their foundation. And the same anthropology, which teaches us how to study the myths of different cultures, knows that those who study myths have difficulty ignoring individual myths.

There is no "metaculture" that can be the absolute science of cultures and their myths. We know this not (only) from anthropology but from the concrete experience of the multiculturalism we live in the late-modern society and from the failed attempts to find (or impose) a "rational" (i.e. Eurocentric) ground that is universally valid.

The philosophy practised as a hermeneutics of myth, then, is not a rationalizing interpretation; it is not demythicization. Above all, it does not choose the myth to which it applies itself. But then, what does it do with myth? In what sense does philosophy make of it a hermeneutics, an interpretation? And, given that it is not aspiring to a clear truth expressed in logical–rational terms, in the light of what does philosophy make it valid for everyone?

The aesthetic "origins" of Pareyson's thought resurface powerfully here. Interpreting myth philosophically is not very different from reading and interpreting a work of art, and the communicability, the interpersonal validity, of the result of the interpretation is not different from what we have when we comment on a work that we try to make understandable to another person. The universality that is being discussed here is only the, always problematic, universality of aesthetic judgment. As so many of pages of Pareyson's aesthetics teach us, we are dealing with the capacity of the work of art to create its own public, its own community from those who appreciate it and "recognize" themselves in it.

There is no objective truth that we can search for and impose. It is true that Pareyson speaks of "clarifying and universalizing what it [philosophy] finds in religious experience and makes capable of interesting all men … as men" (*Ontologia della libertà*, 23). But, clarification universalizes in the sense that it "calls" us to share, by appealing to a common humanity that cannot be presumed to be an essence but that is sought like an always new result to be achieved.

It does not seem unreasonable to see Pareyson's aesthetics of myth as another way of describing what I feel I should call "ontology of actuality." Even in this ontology, thought strives to grasp the "origin," the meaning itself, of the historicodestinal horizon into which it finds itself thrown: what is for Heidegger the meaning of Being. We know that Heidegger imagines this task primarily as that of listening to the poetic word where truth "occurs." In the pages of *Origin of the Work of Art* where he speaks of the poetic word as the place where truth happens, other forms of that same happening are mentioned but none draws the attention that, in the entire mature work, Heidegger devotes to poetry, to "authorial words," such as Anaximander's saying, etc. For him, doing ontology means listening to the voice of Being where it makes itself heard in an eminent and inaugural way, i.e. in poetry. This kind of listening is not a "translation" or a rationalization of that word into utterances. For both Heidegger and Pareyson, such an act of listening is not capable of grasping an eternal, immutable "reality" like the timeless essences of metaphysics. Otherwise, a logically cogent and definitive/defining discourse would be really possible. What comes from this listening in philosophical discourse is a kind of repetition of the history that the myth recounts, a giving it form *ad homines* (basically, it is legitimate to call this "actuality"). It goes without saying that, in both Heidegger and Pareyson, it is difficult to express in systematic, or even didactically useful, terms the meaning of the hermeneutics of myth or of the act of listening to the word of Being. If anything, we need to ask ourselves why in Heidegger the hermeneutic approach did not lead to religion, as it did in Pareyson. Heidegger's abandonment of Christianity remains a mystery in many respects, especially if we keep in mind the absolute importance that sacred scripture had for him, specifically St Paul, in his lectures on the phenomenology of religion in 1919–20. During that time, the key concepts of *Being and Time*, from the idea of authentic temporality to the polemic against metaphysics, were already fully articulated. For Heidegger the rejection of traditional metaphysics, both the official philosophy of the Catholic Church and any relationship with dogma and ecclesiastical discipline, must have been a central factor in the decision to abandon the Christian faith. The question of scholastic metaphysics is only one aspect of Christianity's involvement in the history of late antiquity and modernity; the progressive distancing from metaphysics and the technological society that gave rise to it pushed Heidegger farther away from Christianity understood as an essential component of this history and this world. Pareyson's position is different because Christianity seemed to him like an alternative to modern metaphysics, especially in the path taken by Kierkegaard. As well, the contingent but important fact that Italian culture, during Pareyson's formative years, was dominated by secularist orientations (first Croce and Gentile, then Marxism and neo-Enlightenment, in the second half of the century) contributed in a powerful way to his reluctance to identify Christianity with modernism. The problem that arises here, however, is that of an alternative between the two positions, and Heidegger's definitely seems more consistent with Pareyson's own antimetaphysical presuppositions; that is, the hermeneutics of myth can be nothing but the act of listening to history – the narrative of Scripture and the history of its fortunes in the Christian world, including the history of the Catholic Church and other churches.

Seeing Christianity as profoundly involved in the history of modernity does not necessarily mean having to reject it, as happened in Heidegger's case. In fact, we find that such a radical refusal would end up, once again as it appears to happen with Pareyson, in the presupposition of a suprahistoricity of the metaphysical type: in Pareyson, Christianity's kernel of truth excludes (but how, if it is myth?) all historical events; in Heidegger, metaphysical and tendentially nihilistic modernity, of which Christianity is a part, is set against a hazy image of a homeland that was, for him and for a period of time, Nazi Germany. I will not expand on this point here, but I repeat that in both Heidegger and Pareyson there appears to be the risk of forgetting to listen to Being itself outside of history – a risk that is averted only through an integral historicism. The question is particularly delicate for Pareyson, for whom the hermeneutics of myth is the act of listening to the Christian myth. He is so aware of the problem that he dedicates many pages in his *Ontology of Freedom* to a discussion on eschatology that seems to me, however, invalidated by serious metaphysical limits – which are so because they use, to speak of ultimate things, too many elements taken from Plotinus and Schelling. It is true that an integral historicism also has to take into account the history of the reception of Christianity in authors like these, without, however, isolating them as "sources" of philosophical truths; they should be treated, instead, as symptoms – I realize that it seems to be an exaggeration – or as moments of a history that needs to be placed in its proper context.

What, then, would a Christianity understood, in the manner of Heidegger, as a moment of the history of Western metaphysics be? Only the history of an error to be erased using Enlightenment logic? Obviously not because that would imply having recourse to a supratemporal truth. Even understood in the manner of Pareyson, Christianity does not retain any features that the metaphysics tradition has attributed to it and with which it has for too long been identified. What then? Put succinctly, I would say that, on the basis of his hermeneutics of myth, Pareyson can certainly attend Mass and recite the rosary, not, however, in seminaries and in theology schools. Myth that is listened to but not translated and reduced to metaphysical–rational terms is expressed more adequately by Christian prayer, certainly not by theology. People who recite the rosary cannot really believe that they are talking to the Virgin Mary, who hears them from some place in the sky. And praying to God to ask him personally for something, a "grace," makes little sense. On the other hand, it can have this meaning because participating in the act of praying means staying in the myth without "translating" it. Here, the word myth can also be condensed to its current meaning: we are "only" performing a myth when we pray, as when we read Hölderlin and try to find meaning for our lives in his poetry. This act of listening, almost going beyond one's existential horizon with no expectation of coming to an understanding of it, is ontology of actuality. Is this not like pure and simple superstition, then? Only to the extent that to listen to myth does not become a magic ritual, such as that practised by those who repeat certain formulas in order to avert this or that misfortune or to produce this or that desired effect.

With this proviso, the view of prayer and its hermeneutic relationship with myth described above does not clash at all with "religious practice" as recommended by Christian preachers. Attending Mass, observing the sacraments, praying in the many forms that have been taught does not require any metaphysical adherence to philosophical and dogmatic truths. But at least believe that "God exists"? "Ground ourselves" in St Thomas's five ways? Reciting the Apostles' Creed at a certain point in the Mass is much more than affirming our belonging to the community of faithful; it is the profession of belief in the "reality" of something. Am I really supposed to believe, for example, that Jesus "sits on the right" of the Father?

Pareyson did not certainly go to such "secularizing" extremes; I do not want to attribute them to his work. But it is certain that his orthodoxy as a "Catholic" thinker was never, especially in the later years, as clear as the Church would have liked. In any case, even in the relationship between faith and philosophy as the hermeneutics of myth, on the one hand, and religion as a public fact, as presence of an institution like the Church in social and political life (especially in Italy), on the other hand, Pareyson's teaching has still not been fully appreciated – and it is very reasonable to think of it as an alternative to the wave of new-fundamentalism that seems to be overtaking us.

27

To Interpret the World Is to Change It

Until now philosophers thought they were only interpreting the world, yet they were truly changing it. This is how we might rephrase Marx's famous statement in his "Theses on Feuerbach," from the standpoint of philosophy as it has developed under the influence of Gadamer. It is precisely in this equating interpretation and transformation (operating in history) of the world, and especially ourselves in this operation, that probably lies one of the nubs, if not the most important nub, of Gadamerian hermeneutics. It is largely through Gadamer's work, if it is true as it appears to me, that hermeneutics was, and continues to be, the cultural *koine* of the West at the end of the twentieth century. We can gather together a great number of the main threads of the renewal of philosophy between the 1800s and the 1900s around this equation: starting with the new relationship that Marx wanted to establish between theory and praxis and, naturally, with the idea of history as the history of the spirit, which characterized classical German philosophy. Also included, obviously, are postpositivist epistemology, the spirit of the artistic avant-gardes of the early 1900s and of existentialism, which expressed that spirit in philosophical language, as well as the often implicit reemergence, in many modern philosophies, of the evangelical motto *veritatem facientes* (the Aristotelian *aletheuein*) *in caritates* (in social dialogue, in Lévinasian attention to the Other and in the increasingly generalized substitution of metaphysics with ethics ...).

More and more, with the passing of time and the maturation of the *Wirkung(sgeschichte)* or "effective history" of *Truth and Method*, it is in this sense – the identification of interpreting with changing the world – that the meaning of the last section of the book, where the author speaks of an "ontological turn" (*ontologische Wendung*) of hermeneutics, is clarified. The "philosophical hermeneutics" (*philosophische Hermeneutik*) to which the subtitle alludes reveals itself to be more and more, even beyond the intentions of the author, an ontological hermeneutics or, rather, a hermeneutic ontology. I believe that the words of Richard Bernstein should be read in this way: "If we take Gadamer seriously and press his assertions, they lead us beyond philosophical hermeneutics" (*Beyond Objectivism and Relativism*, 150). This is not only a preference for ontology on the part of some interpreters; above all, it is due to the fact that the discussions and objections that Gadamer's philosophy has generated in the decades that separate us from the publication of his original text lead us precisely in this direction.

Today, both the positive reception and the critical rejection of Gadamer's hermeneutics seem to be based largely on the same basic misunderstanding: the idea that it can be reduced to a theory of the finiteness and insurmountable historicity of understanding. From this point, then, pragmatists draw from it arguments they can use against the presumed hegemony of scientism and technology, in favour of a sacrosanct democratic vision of an ethics of common consciousness or *Lebenswelt* (worldview); on the other hand, critics find reasons to reproach Gadamer for a philosophy that eventually turns into historicist relativism or vague traditionalism. Now, this misunderstanding evaporates if we "push," as Bernstein used to say, Gadamer's thought beyond the limits that are commonly attributed to it and in the direction of the ontological turn announced in the third section of *Truth and Method*. In fact, only by reading more radically Gadamer's famous statement, "Sein, das verstanden werde kann, ist Sprache" ("Being that can be understood is language") can we remove the bases for a pragmatist "reduction" of hermeneutics to a lesson in wisdom and for a reading of it as historicist relativism and acritical traditionalism. Both of these reductive readings in effect presuppose that interpretation, to return to Max's remark, does not change the world and is limited to mirroring it in more or less imperfect and variable ways and, therefore, has an "objective" limit that the philosophy of interpretation supposedly taught us to recognize, with the result of making us accept the idea that there is no true knowledge and that, consequently, the only ethical imperative is tolerance, which is appropriate for the historically finite beings that we are.

In Gadamer's thought, however, we find the basis for going beyond these persistent metaphysical prejudices. If we ask ourselves what good, correct, fair interpretation consists of in *Truth and Method*, we could not say, in response, that it is truth as correspondence. But this is not because, as some hasty readings might suggest, Gadamer knows that finite beings are not given knowledge of things as they are; rather, it is because things are really what they are only in interpretation and language. Stated more clearly, for it to make sense, hermeneutics demands a profound revolution in ontology, namely that it give up the idea of Being as an objective given "out there" to which thought should try to adapt. Only by thinking of real Being in these terms can hermeneutics be read as a simple sermon on wisdom or a form of relativism and traditionalism.

It is, therefore, a question of reading in a more radical way the thesis according to which Being can be understood as language. Only Being that can be understood? If this were the case, Gadamer would be drastically limiting his own discourse on the sciences of the human spirit, thereby leaving intact the objectivism and metaphysical realism they imply. In Gadamer, we still have a distinction between the sciences of the human spirit and the natural sciences, but only on a methodological level, in the sense that he does not think it is possible to replace the rigorous procedures of verification and falsification of scientific–experimental with a method similar to the historical–comprehensive one. Conversely, we do not find in his work reasons to think that the experience of truth – by whatever method it is achieved – can have a meaning in the natural sciences that is different from the one that it has in the sciences of the human spirit, in which true experience, or experience of the truth, is "genuine experience," that is, one that changes dialectically the situation of the subject and of the object known. At any rate, any theory that regards the difference between natural science and science of the human spirit as definitive and final should also present itself as a scientific–natural proposition, that is to say, it should invoke the status of an "objective" description of the world. I do not believe that we can reconcile such a metaphysical perspective with Gadamerian hermeneutics.

The difficulty in taking radically seriously the identification of Being with language, however, is the risk of arbitrariness involved in proceeding this way. If there is no Being outside of language, we cannot explain the effort to find the right word, the effort on which

Gadamer often insisted. More generally, it seems that any distinction between true and false, between opinion and science, becomes impossible. Now, the ontological novelty of Gadamerian hermeneutics becomes clear if we realize that both the criterion used for searching for the right word and the distinction between true and false, between a correct interpretation and a faulty one, are for Gadamer all internal to language itself. Once again I remind the reader, the suspicion that criteria of this sort are inadequate to save us from arbitrariness and relativism depends entirely on the persistent metaphysical conviction whereby Being is the given, the object. The pages of *Truth and Method* where Gadamer asserts the positive function of prejudice, borrowing Heidegger's doctrine of precomprehension, provide us with important suggestions for solving this problem. In these pages, Gadamer refers to paragraph 63 of *Being and Time*, which deals with, among other things, "the methodological character of the existential analytic" and the "meaning of the Being of care." Here, Heidegger explicitly asks the question: "Where are ontological projects to get the evidence that their 'findings' are phenomenally appropriate?" (359). He brings the issue immediately to the distinction between authentic and inauthentic existence. In other words, the appropriateness of the project does not spring from an encounter of precomprehension and things in themselves but only from the fact that the project is more or less authentic. Here the methodological horizon seems to be completely pierced; we are taken back to the most radical aspects of the existential analytic since the possibility of authentic existence is tied to the firm anticipation of one's own death. In the pages of *Truth and Method* that relate to this passage in *Being and Time*, Gadamer, however, appears to translate Heidegger's thesis in these terms: "Understanding must not be understood so much as an action on the part of the subject as an inserting of the subject into the heart of the process of the transmission of history, where past and present continually coalesce" (*Verità e metodo*, 340). The link between the firm anticipation of one's own death and the insertion of oneself (*einrücken*) into the process of the transmission of history (*Überlieferungsgeschehen*) can be clearly understood if we consider that what the authors have in mind is the explicit assumption of one's own historicity. Better still, we cannot fail to recognize that, precisely in Gadamer's seemingly "urbanized" reading of Heidegger's Being-toward-death clarifies its meaning in a way that Heidegger himself was probably unaware. We learn what the decision to anticipate death in Heidegger means in a clearer way, even on the "existential" (*existenziell*) level, from the same pages of Gadamer's book. In *Being and Time*, as we know, the authentic decision toward death makes it possible to understand the past not as *Vergangen* (past) but as *Gewesen*, which is to say, as a still open possibility. Translated into terms derived from Gadamer, this authentic attitude means that the tradition on which we rely to "test" precomprehensions and to identify the legitimate and productive ones consists precisely in not seeing them as an eternal structure of metaphysical Being, which we should reflect faithfully or to which we should conform (and not even as the "out there" objectivity of "objects") but as pure historical legacy left by mortals for other mortals.

The ontological result – not only methodological, then, and not only pertinent to the epistemology of the sciences of the human spirit – to which the present line of reasoning leads us is contained entirely within this liquefaction of the objectivity against which the validity of precomprehension is measured. The effort to find the right word, the always-present difficulty of finding calmness in an interpretation, clashes with something that is not reducible to the action of the subject (*Haltung der Subjektivität*), that has its own normative cogency, and that is not the world out there but rather the *Überlieferungsgeschehen* (event of tradition) into which comprehension needs *einrücken* (to enter) in order to find its validity. Using an expression Gadamer prefers to avoid, it is what Heidegger calls the "history of Being" (*Seinsgeschichte*) or the "destiny of Being" (*Seinsgeschiche*). Neither Gadamer's term nor Heidegger's, however, allows for identification with a necessary history that would have more features of "tradition" and the "past" in the sense of *Tradition* and *Vergangen* than in the sense of *Überlieferung* and *Gewesen*.

I stated earlier that the validity of Gadamerian hermeneutics implies the theory that things are what they actually are only in interpretation. If we look at the dense dialogue that *Truth and Method* establishes with *Being and Time* in the crucial passages cited above, this theory too acquires a specific meaning, which clarifies – perhaps even urbanizes – Heideggerian theories that appeared to be extravagant and "poetic," such as the thing's authentic giving itself only in the *Geviert* of sky and earth, the mortal and the divine. Hermeneutics shows us convincingly that the assured objectivity of objects, even and especially those of science, exists only in the framework (paradigm, we say using Kuhn's term) of an inherited horizon in the face of which the interpreter, or the community of interpreters as is more clearly the case in scientific–experimental research, cannot avoid assuming a certain responsibility. Accepting one's own historicity responsibly, however, as Heidegger has illustrated in his review of Jaspers in 1919 (in Heidegger, *Segnavia*), does not mean mirroring the inherited past but interpreting it, applying it Gadamer would say, and so including it actively in a project. The normative cogency of the *Überlieferungsgeschehen* exists only in a purposeful project that, since it is open to the future, changes the world precisely because it interprets it. The change does not come from nothing; it responds to a call, which, however, resonates only in the response. Thus, skipping some steps, we can say that the crux of Gadamer's hermeneutic ontology is the identification of reality (*Wirklichkeit*) with the history of effects (*Wirkungsgeschichte).*

Since historicity is always also an interpreter's purposeful project, hermeneutics must answer the question regarding teleology on which it is based and that legitimates it. Above all, as a philosophical theory that presents itself in competition with other theories, it cannot claim its own validity, or preferability, with arguments that are descriptive (of the structure of Being). That the reality of things is, essentially, a history of effects is not affirmed in a descriptive proposition; it is the meaning of the project within whose horizon hermeneutics interprets the experience of the world. So, it is not risky to think that the statement "Sein, das verstanden werde kann, ist Sprache" should not be read merely as an utterance that lexically "clarifies" the meaning of *Sein* or in fact only that of *Sein*, of the Being that can be understood. Instead, it should be read as a teleological statement – which, I think, should be seen in conjunction with Heidegger's remark in *Being and Time*, where he says "there is [*gibt*] Being [not being] only insofar as truth is [*ist*]" (317) and "only as long as Dasein *is* (that is, only as long as an understanding of Being is ontically possible), 'is there' Being" (ibid., 212).

A coherent philosophy of interpretation, read as a call to change the objective reality of things "out there" into truth, that is, language and project, actually changes the world; in other words, it can present itself legitimately as thought that, inheriting the best of classical philosophy, answers the call of a history in which science and technology tend increasingly to consume "natural" reality in a lived intersubjective truth. Hermeneutics is not only the *koine* of humanistic culture and the sciences of the human spirit; it is also, I think we can say, a real "ontology of actuality": in other words, a philosophy of that late-modern world where the world dissolves effectively and more and more completely in the play of interpretations. Inasmuch as it is presumed to be a responsible historical project, hermeneutics actively responds to the call of Being, seeing it increasingly as the truth of human language rather than as entity or original objectivity (*Gegenständigkeit*), and it also finds in this main thread the basis for ethical choices, thereby offering itself as true critical theory. It is in this sense that it confers a new reality on Hölderlin's verses: "Full of merit, but poetically, / man lives on this earth"

28

Historicity and *Différance*

In the title I propose, I am well aware that the very term *historicity* may seem inappropriate or may at least sound too "Italian" to be acceptable. But this language problem may also serve to signal an approach that is external or rather "other," in the sense Derrida gives that word in his writings. This somewhat "discordant" title summarizes at least three questions: 1. Is there a history of Derrida? 2. Is there history in Derrida, in his works? 3. Is there history – as a philosophically recognizable notion – in Derrida (again, in his writings and in the theory expressed therein)?

It seems to me that these three questions sum up, first, the historical meaning of Derrida's work – that is, what it means within the philosophical culture of our time, with all the problematic aspects that his critics invite us to discover in it (therefore, I repeat, a historicity in a sense that is more general, more generic than the one to which our three questions refer) – and also his relation to Judaism, its "judeity," at least to the extent that I believe I recognize it (again, from a point of view that is external, foreign, etc.).

These three questions merely articulate one sole problem – one that is posed very clearly not in but by *Writing and Difference*, in which work we read that *différance* is not *in* history (which is a problem that since then has not, to my knowledge, been resolved in Derrida's subsequent works and remains an open question – meaning that nothing has changed ...). What I have in mind are questions that might be considered, at first blush, foreign to Derrida's problematic. He has often refused, for example, to consider the question of the "evolution" of his thought ("my 'thought' was in full evolution ... if the value of 'evolution' had not always been suspect to me

... and if, above all, I had not always been suspect of 'thought' ... Thought does not want to say anything," *Positions*, 48–9). In these pages, which are from a 1971 colloquium, Derrida states that he is also "very wary of the concept of history" (ibid., 50). And yet, in these very pages, there are also elements with which we may reduce – even eliminate completely – the strangeness of the questions I have just raised. This is what, as an interpreter, I shall concern myself with doing, namely, with discussing, and eventually criticizing, a work *iuxta propria principia* according to its "forming form," as Luigi Pareyson would say (despite the Derridean refusal of an "organicity" of the text that would be the expression of an inner law, a unifying intention). Just a few lines above the ones quoted, Derrida says that deconstruction cannot neglect the "('historical', if you will) inscription of the text read *and* of the new text this criticism itself writes " (ibid., 47) and further down, that "in a very determined field of the most current situation ... materialist insistence can function as a means of having the necessary generalization of the concept of text, its extension with no simple exterior limit ... not wind up, then, as the definition a new self-interiority, a new 'idealism', if you will, of the text" (ibid., 66).

The precautions that could be taken in that regard, it is true are never sufficient. The questions about historicity, in the many senses that I have just mentioned, are an attempt to proceed on the path of the precautions that Derrida himself considered necessary in that same colloquium. It appears to me that the historicity of Derrida's work – albeit in its significance for today's culture or in relation to judeity – becomes recognizable on the sole condition that there be a response to the questions I have just asked (and here I am alluding to later historical aspect of the question, i.e. to my history as interpreter of his texts).

I will dwell for a moment on that allusion to the history of my relationship with the history of Derrida's texts in order to deal with at least that aspect of the question. My choice of the title for these remarks is a fact of my biography, if I dare call it that. Underlying the three questions, there is the choice of a title, and that choice is a historical fact that depends on *my* decision, which, however – this is the hermeneutic circle – is not unrelated to the historicity of the Derridean text, with its *Wirkungsgeschichte* (history of impact), with the history of its *Wirkung* (effects) on *me*. The history of the choice of the title is one aspect, certainly not the only one historicity of Derrida, of what his texts "mean" in today's culture. It is really not necessary to make that argument. We already know well enough (following a move so frequent in Derrida) why the question of historicity can be a question, or *the* question, of the meaning of Derrida's work in our culture. It seems that it can all be summed up in the phrase about precautions that are never sufficient, taken in order to keep deconstruction from ending up being a kind of new idealism of the text. That is what critics of deconstruction criticize Derrida for. According to these critics, the idealism of the text shows itself in the arbitrariness (apparent or real) of deconstruction, according to which, in several senses, there is no *hors-texte* (something outside the text). One may also not share the criticism in its grossest sense (consider for example, American professor of mathematics Alan Sokal's "hoax"), but one cannot deny that it touches on a very specific aspect of Derrida's work, which has always concentrated on textuality, vindicating the importance of the text and of textual analysis. To put it more clearly, I believe that, in this crass sense, the criticism of Derrida's textualism has little meaning, but the fact that it is possible, that it circulates in our cultural world (the very world in which deconstruction seems to come about like a movement that is not contingent on the arbitrary choices or genius of one sole thinker), appears to me to be strictly tied to the question of historicity and to other questions that it leaves open. What must be read in these questions is not the scandal of the absence of something "outside the text" that functions as a criterion for deconstructive work that would guarantee its validity on the basis of a concept of truth as "correspondence." On the other hand, in the choice of the title/theme of my remarks, the determining factor for me is the problem of the *project* of deconstruction. In the dissatisfaction with the real or supposed arbitrariness of the deconstructive practices Derrida and so many of his imitators, I caught a glimpse, as authentic meaning, not reduced to a vulgar joke, of the question of the project that inspires deconstructive work. And here I claim proximity to, even agreement between, my approach and Derrida's own intentions. Without that, why take the precautions he speaks of in the colloquium referred to above? The precautions are taken for the realization of a project, a project that – if I understood correctly Derrida's refusal of the metaphysics of presence, which he shares with Heidegger (whom he even reproaches for not being sufficiently radical on this point) – cannot be only one of grasping more clearly, more adequately than metaphysics did, the difference that ferments *within* all supposed *compactness* of Being. In my personal history as a reader, friend, and student of Derrida, the question of historicity, or of the project, presents itself not as a question about the truth/validity of his method, of his theory, and so on but as the problem of "What do we do now?" If I listen to Derrida and not, say, to John Searle, Gadamer, or Habermas, what do I do in philosophy? In other words, is there a Derridean school? Or better yet: Does difference or *différance* make a difference?

Even in these somewhat peremptory, and perhaps categorical, terms, I do not think that I am a stranger to Derrida's proposals. Again, in the pages of the *Positions* colloquium where he talks about materialism (and of Lenin – a sign of the times), he denies that one can unambiguously characterize the concept of matter as metaphysical or nonmetaphysical: "That depends upon the work to which it yields" (ibid., 65). True, it will depend on the work of textual deconstruction but always on an effect, a result that is measured in relation to an end, that is, to a *project*.

Ultimately, then, why deconstruction? But then should my title not be "Historicity and Deconstruction" rather than "Historicity and *Différance*"? I might admit (another historicobiographical mark) that the title was chosen with the intention of borrowing the title of one of Derrida's best-known works. But not solely. For even if deconstruction is always an action, although its historicity – the fact of having a history, an unfolding, though with no certain goal – is obvious, what *has* no history and *is* not in history, is *différance* itself. If deconstruction is induced by *différance* – in two senses: of efficient cause and final cause but also perhaps as formal cause (since to deconstruct comes down to bringing out differences, to dilating caesuras) and material cause, at least as an instrument with which, or a given upon which, one works – it is because *différance* itself does not have movement. The risk, then, is that deconstruction may assume the role of *ipsum esse subsistens* (a self-subsistent being).

Does it suffice, in order to get out of metaphysics or simply to sojourn in it with that duplicity of the look that Heidegger would call the *Verwindung* and that Derrida himself considers to be the only way of "overcoming" it – does it suffice to work until one discovers at last a Being or an origin no longer compact or intact, but fissured, worked over, and split by the never-ending struggle between Dionysus and Apollo? What is metaphysics? Is it the thought of

Being as presence unfurled, as a reconciled unity, or is it rather the presupposition that the task of thought, and emancipation itself, consists in the contemplation of true Being, however it is conceived (even as a God not at peace with himself?

As is quite clear, the three questions I asked at the beginning in order to clarify the meaning of the title have not yet been answered. But they have given rise to other questions (this is perhaps the work that they produce?): the question about the historicity of the title itself, the question about the possible transformation into "other" (no longer *différance* but deconstruction), and the question about the very meaning of the term "metaphysics" for Derrida and its relation to Heidegger. To return for at least a moment to the three initial questions, I will say that, up to now, it seems that I have obtained, though elliptically, an answer, however provisional. Namely: Derrida's hesitation to speak of an evolution in his thought is, in the final analysis, bound up with his rejection of any kind of teleological vision of history, a mistrust of its alleged linearity qua construction of meaning, which would contradict the antimetaphysical intent of working (toward) – or of grasping, dilating, corresponding with – the *différance* that "gives itself" in a certain way to us as a call, a fact in progress, and so on. A bit paradoxically, one might answer, then, that there is no one history of Derrida, no one evolution, development, or "continuous," discursive, logical transformation of his thought because for him there is no such thing as History and that all this depends on *facts* that are in turn historical, those my second question envisaged. It seems to me that it is in fact in historico-factual terms that Derrida explains the "why" of deconstruction and primarily the "why" of grammatology. Let us recall, here, the almost *hapax legomenon* (thing said only once) of the first part of *Of Grammatology*: "For some time" (49ff.), where, as one can see, we have a sort of justification in "epochal" terms of the enterprise of deconstruction. In later writings, however, beginning with the discussions I mentioned earlier, Derrida tends to drastically reduce, almost to the point of nullification, the meaning of these epochal references, which are apparently too close to Heidegger's discourse on the "history of Being," not to arouse in him the suspicion of a relapse into metaphysics.

Thus, in a more recent dialogue (*A Taste for the Secret*, 1997), the absence of an explicit thematization of deconstructive practices he carries out yet again in his texts – in which the "choice" of the themes to be approached, in an apparently arbitrary way – is justified in terms of an "elliptical economy" (*Memoires per Paul de Man* [Memoires for Paul de Man], 31): the community of his readers already knows, shares with him the consciousness of the historical situation in which we live; it is, therefore, useless to give specific details. Nevertheless, in this dialogue, however, Derrida also says other things that seem more important to me and which make it possible to understand in what sense one can characterize the situation in which deconstruction acts as that which "goes without saying" to the point of not meriting more intense theoretical attention. What takes place does not merit an attention comparable to that of Heidegger because there is no history of Being nor any call that history can direct to us. *Of Grammatology* responds precisely to a situation in which one simply says, "something deconstructs" (*A Taste for the Secret*, 80). But we respond to that situation not because it constitutes a true vocation – nor because one has understood on the basis of some sign that it is better to deconstruct than not to do so. "We are in the process of deconstructing and we must answer for it" (ibid., 80). But why "we must"? "If deconstruction is anything but an initiative, or a method, or a technique, but *is* what *happens*, the event one takes note of, then why go in that direction? (ibid., 82). "It is here that I have no answer," says Derrida (ibid., 83).

To go in the direction of deconstruction does not mean simply to agree with what happens; on the contrary, deconstruction is the "anachronism in synchronism" (ibid., 82): "to attune to what happens" is to push it in the deconstructive direction that the event itself "reveals," contains, manifests. But, after all, "we must" do it because "it is what comes" and "it is better that there be a future [*de l'avenir*], rather than nothing" (ibid., 83). Here, to happen (*Advenir* or *à venir*) in the sense of to occur and to happen in the sense of futurity merge totally.

One might inquire: Why, in general, a coming about (*advenir*) rather than immobility? It is abundantly clear that to happen – in the sense of to occur and in the sense of futurity – takes the place of the Being of metaphysics. Does one truly get out of metaphysics? It seems to me that the reason why happening is evidently preferable to its opposite – which may constitute, I believe, the last word in Derrida's theoretical itinerary to date – is the fact that "the future is the opening in which the other occurs [*arrive*], and it is the value of the other or of alterity that, in the end, would be the justification.

Ultimately, this is my way of interpreting the messianic. The other may come, or he may not. I do not want to programme him, but rather to leave a place for him to come if he comes. It is the ethic of hospitality" (ibid., 83).

Even that attention to the other, which has never been absent from Derrida's text, but which has certainly increased in recent years, is perhaps an "external" historical mark that Derrida probably does not reject but to which he gives no particular attention, in order to continue to avoid the risk of a "history of Being." The event must be truly an event – and, therefore, also bear my signature, be witnessed by me – because the condition of salvation, of authenticity, of emancipation, in sum, of this "better" that from time to time turns up in Derrida's discourse (only in these pages?) is that the other may always be able to come because in him the messianic, if not the Messiah, is announced. (But can there be an announcing of these?)

At this point, we might again make the attempt, or give way to the temptation, to propose a point of arrival for Derrida's itinerary or for our itinerary toward him: the epochal justification in *Of Grammatology* and, therefore, the historicofactual enrootedness that appears to "found" it, is increasingly consumed in the development of Derrida's work. If there is a history of his thought, it may be the progressive obliteration of historicity, at least as the history of a meaning. Alongside this movement, the messianic orientation of his work, the idea that deconstruction is a way of responding to a certain ethical duty to give place to the other, asserts itself (or simply becomes more accentuated). Part of this same movement, in my view, is the institutional interest (politics, the university) that, according to some of his interpreters, marks the second phase of his thought (see Ferraris, *Derrida 1975–1985: Sviluppi teoretici e fortuna filosofica*). There has also been talk of an existentialist Derrida (see Ferraris in the Introduction to Derrida's *Heidegger's Hand*), who would not be in contradiction to the image of a Derrida, who is "committed" in politics and institutional critique. What I see in this, ultimately – and I know that it is a dangerous discourse to engage in from the point of view of French culture but which my status as a foreigner outside this history allows me to engage in – is the Sartrean paradigm of historical commitment, which, at least up until the time of the *Critique of Dialectical Reason*, corresponds to no teleology and, in Sartre, is even the consequence of an absolute metaphysical pessimism. The messianism of Derrida's later period may even be much more faithful to an existentialist perspective than was Sartre's Marxist destination, despite the latter's statements in *Questions of Method* (Marxist/Theory and Existentialism/Ideology, etc.).

But, if with existentialism, Derrida too seems to place himself *on the level at which there is only man* – for which Heidegger criticized Sartre, upholding the history of Being in opposition – are we not once again in metaphysics, at least in the sense of an existentialist metaphysics qua philosophy of finitude (of Being)? What is at play here is not a problem devoid of foundation, if we think of the passage in *Writing and Difference* (Vattimo, in the Introduction to Derrida, *Writing and Difference*), in which it is affirmed that *différance* "is not *in* history." Does messianism – the openness to the other who comes and thus ensures the advent, that is to say Being as event–advent – really remove the still-metaphysical character of this affirmation about *différance*? I ask this, bearing in mind a meaning of the word metaphysical with which, I believe Derrida himself could agree, as I said earlier – namely, a conception of the task of thought as the uncovering of a structure, or archistructure, before which we may stand (or which we may rediscover each time through the work of deconstruction). If *différance* has no history, the other who comes is always only the recollection and testimony of that archistructure. Since there are no truly different moments in the relationship with that origin-nonorigin, even the alterity of the other will be nothing but an alterity that I would call purely *formal*. The other is messianic, because he or she is not me, because he or she is an event in relation to what was already. I remember, though indistinctly, having heard Derrida say in the course of a discussion that "it is true that we are always in history." Precisely: we are always there, but what counts is precisely this "always" and not the determined moment of history in which we find ourselves. We always find ourselves in a determined moment, it is true, but it is for that very reason that one might say it is useless to seek its specific characteristics. And to get back to the other: if we know too much about him or her, if in a certain way we have expectations with respect to his or her physiognomy, even if they are negative, we will no longer be truly open to that alterity, that advent, which must always be *abrupto* (without preparation).

Several things come to mind here (I beg you to forgive the elliptical character of this progression), especially from texts by Derrida, such as that page where he says, "In a certain sense, thought means nothing" (*Positions*, 49), but that already suggests something else.

I have not been able to find a statement to this effect in the most recent writings of Derrida, but I assume he has not "retracted" it. Perhaps we should not take it literally, should not banalize it. Still, one wonders to what extent that statement may not confirm, if we read it as relating to the other, the presupposition that the alterity of the other is always accidental and that, to avoid falling back into metaphysics, we must think of it only in spatial, topological terms.

That fundamental "heterology" comes to us first and foremost from Derrida. It also comes to us from Emmanuel Lévinas, for whom the look of the other calls to mind in a certain way the absolute Other, the divine Infinite. Thus the latter takes a decisive "leap" toward a way of thinking that replaces the hypocrisy of the Greco-Christian tradition with a return to the biblical heritage, to what the Christians call the Old Testament. Derrida does not make this "leap" and not because there is an abstract distinction between religious and philosophical discourse – which, from his perspective, should have no justification. Does the other, any other whatsoever, really always bear within him or herself the trace of the Infinite? Lévinas has, after all, the Bible as a guide; for him, the messianic character of the other does not depend solely on his or her absolute diversity in relation to myself, which Derrida, by contrast, must emphasize, since he does not want to refer specifically to that revealed text. A Christian like Heidegger has the New Testament for his guide; thus, in the Introduction to the course *Phenomenology of Religion* (1920), conceived as a commentary on St Paul's two letters to the Thessalonians, the expectation of the *parousia* (presence), of the promised return of the Messiah, is not a pure tension toward just any alterity but an expectation "qualified" by what has already happened and the faithful already know. In Lévinas's case, the historicity of history, the specificity of events, is removed thanks to the choice of a vertical leap: the Last Judgment is at every moment; each alterity is in direct relation with God but is also measured and judged in this very relation. In the case of Heidegger, despite the changes in his attitude with respect to the Christian tradition, which in my opinion do not affect his fundamental nature as a "Christian theologian," as he already writes in the 1930s in a letter to Löwith, it is the directives that the faithful have already received by the teachings of Jesus that gauge the authenticity of the other. Directives that are, it is true, mainly negative ones: the Messiah will come "like a thief in the night"; do not allow yourselves to be fooled by the Antichrist, by the false Messiahs we see all around us every day. That, then, is what you should do above all. Although Paul does not positively define the traits of the true Messiah, to the point where Heidegger is prompted to see in the attitude he recommends to the faithful a kind of translation of the phenomenological *epoche*, the example of the life and death of Jesus is nevertheless amply sufficient for the alterity of the coming Messiah not to be totally indefinite.

It is, basically, in that Christian ascendancy often forgotten (in the course given in 1920, all the main elements of the analysis of the temporality of *Being and Time* and also of the antimetaphysical polemic of the *Kehre* are already present) that we can find the roots of the insistence with which Heidegger will always place the eventuality of Being in a concept, indeed a problematic one, of the history of Being.

The thesis I would like to advance here, by way of conclusion, could be formulated as follows. It is only on condition that we accentuate and radicalize the notion of a historicity of Being that we can remain loyal to the Heideggerian purpose – a purpose that Heidegger himself has not always respected – namely, not to confuse Being (*l'être*) with beings (*l'étant*) and therefore to seek a way of going beyond metaphysics. Similarly, for Derrida himself, desirous of furthering his antimetaphysical project, the point is to think the alterity of the other in concretely historical terms, beyond an "existentialist" perspective, which still runs the risk of an inadvertent relapse into metaphysics because within that perspective Being is conceptualized no longer as a compact presence but as (the presence of) a structure that is fissured, worked over, deferring. Either Being (the archistructure) truly falls into history, is consummated, and differred (*si differisce*: the Italian here may suggest, with the verb *differire*, the verb *ferire* as well; hence "to be wounded," "to be thrown against") in history, or all the differences and deconstructions merely bring us back to contemplating, in a kind of paradoxical *amor Dei intellectualis* (intellectual love of God), the archistructure or *originary* Being, merely place us back into its presence.

The other who is not concretely situated in a history endowed with "meaning" – even understood as progressive and indefinite consumption of presence and of its peremptory nature, which, in my view is consistent with Heidegger even beyond the letter of what he says – cannot take on a messianic form and function otherwise than on the basis of a "subjective" attitude, that is on the basis of my way of receiving him. The other's messianic character, devoid of any recognizable historical markings, is totally subjective. I can take as my starting point whatever term, concept, event, of whatever text, to get back to the *originary différance*, as long as I adopt the "double look" that Derrida wishes. Even the predilection for the written text, as opposed to the phono-logo-centrism that would still be peculiar to Heidegger or to Heideggerians such as Gadamer, appears to be transformed into its opposite. The written text assures a definitive, monumental presence but also turned over in each case to the deconstructing subject, who works on the text in the privacy of his or her study. What is important about the other is not his or her concrete historicity (which Plato identified with the ability of spoken discourse to defend itself) but the monument of the other, in which historicity is consumed in the constitutive finitude of existence, thus allowing the *originary* architructure to show through more clearly.

It seems to me that this risk of a metaphysical relapse – which is also that of Heidegger, and, here, of Derrida – comes, in the case of the latter, from his judeity. A messianism without a Messiah does not sidestep, in my view, the relapse into a structural conception of finitude and therefore into a negative theology or a metaphysical existentialism. Lévinas only succeeds in avoiding this risk by means of a deliberate "leap" into the religious tradition. This "leap" Derrida does not take. Perhaps Dilthey was right when he said that the beginning of the end of metaphysics in the history of the Western world is the advent of Christianity, which is also, if I may say so, a *form* of judeity. In Derrida we find at once these two souls, and the value of his texts consists perhaps in the fact that he allows us to discover these two souls in all their indispensable immediacy. But also in the fact of his placing us face to face with a choice that he seems, for the moment, not to have made.

29

A Friendly Pragmatism

In *Solidarity or Objectivity?*, which was published in the first volume of *Philosophical Writings*, Richard Rorty states, "There are two principal ways that, reflective human beings try, by placing their lives in a broader context, to give sense to those lives" (21). The prevalent philosophical tradition in the West is clearly characterized, at least up to the Enlightenment, by an attitude of the "realist" or objective kind. Rorty also reflects on the reasons for and origins of this prevalence; his hypothesis is that the idea of an objective knowledge shared by all humanity was born in Greece, probably on account of the awareness of the "sheer diversity of human communities" (ibid.) and, therefore, the desire to combat scepticism (I mention Nietzsche's *The Birth of Tragedy*: the Greeks invented the balanced classical form precisely because they were aware of the chaotic aspect of existence …). Plato best embodies this model of objectivity and on that foundation Western philosophy gradually constructs the idea of the philosopher, or the intellectual, as someone who raises himself from mere opinion to truth. With the Enlightenment, the Platonic philosopher is replaced by the Newtonian scientist, who, by opening the way to objective knowledge of nature, lays the foundation for a society free of the limits of local beliefs, superstitions, private interest, and the various *idola fori et ribus* (idols of the markets and of the tribes). As we know, Rorty, instead, locates himself within the opposite tradition, that of the pragmatists, who conceptualize truth as "what is for good for *us* to believe," according to William James (ibid., 169). Rorty emphasizes the "for us" because it is crucial: truth is not what is useful for humanity in general but for a specific, historically concrete community, to which the philosopher feels bound.

On the basis of these observations, which I draw from the essay cited above, we are able to understand the meaning of Rorty's reflection, his neopragmatism, which has the merit of opening up a dialogue between continental philosophy and Anglo-American philosophy along a felicitous trajectory that includes a triad of thinkers who left their mark on the twentieth century: Dewey, Wittgenstein, and Heidegger. Obviously, aligning these three figures can have a certain provocative and "scandalous" effect. Just as the distinction – also proposed by Rorty – between a Kantian line and a Hegelian line in contemporary thought is provocative. To understand this situation better, I propose to translate it in terms of the differentiation between two styles of philosophy suggested by Foucault: "analytics of truth" and "ontology of actuality" (*Foucault Archives: Papers, Colloquia, Interviews 3*). This pair of concepts, which is more interesting to me than the other pair, is not developed more fully by Foucault – even if his philosophy is, in a general sense, a reflection on the present (on actuality), on its differences relative to other historical epochs, and certainly not a Kantian study of the conditions of the possibility of "real" knowledge. The Foucauldian term "ontology" is of central importance for me, precisely because it marks the fundamental difference that separates me from Rorty (and from Foucault himself) – a gap that, nonetheless, seems to me increasingly insurmountable, even with respect to pragmatism. Having provided a complete description of the differences between the realist and the pragmatist attitude, in *Solidarity or Objectivity*? Rorty writes, "The best argument we partisans of solidarity have against the realistic partisans of objectivity is Nietzsche's argument that the traditional Western metaphysical–epistemological way of firming up our habits simply isn't working anymore. It isn't doing its job" (ibid., 179). As with Nietzsche, then, the argument against objectivist realism is the pragmatist idea that:

> a "merely" ethical foundation for our sense of community – or, better, that we think of our sense of community as having no foundation except shared hope and the trust created by such sharing – is put forward on practical grounds. It is *not* put forward as a corollary of a metaphysical claim that the objects in the world contain no intrinsically action-guiding properties, nor of an epistemological claim that we lack a faculty of moral sense, nor of a semantical claim that truth is reducible to justification.

> It is a suggestion about how we might think of ourselves in order to avoid the kind of resentful belatedness – characteristic of the bad side of Nietzsche – which now characterizes much of high culture. This resentment arises from the realization … that the Enlightenment's search for objectivity has often gone sour. (Ibid.)

In the perspective I propose, the notion of ontology, which Rorty never uses (this also goes for Derrida, who sees in it the risk of relapsing into objectivistic metaphysics), comes back into play. The reference to Nietzsche in fact allows us to hypothesize what Rorty could have suggested – that is, an experience, a way of feeling, a "fact" analogous to what Nietzsche calls "the death of God." To speak of the death of God, rather than of his nonexistence, implies that Nietzsche wants to avoid proposing another objective foundation in his philosophy – for example, the one that would result from the assertion that God "really" does not exist. But if this historical "fact" is not an objective given, what is it? It is precisely an experience that cannot be confronted as if it were a thing, an object; it is an event in which we are involved and which, therefore, we can only interpret – not describe, in the epistemological–metaphysical sense of the term. What I want to emphasize, however, is that, in a holistic perspective such as Rorty's, to interpret our historical condition also means to reconstruct it – not with the presumed neutral gaze of the scientist but rather on the basis of a specific project, in the Heideggerian sense. To interpret is to have an interest in and, therefore, grasp the "object" only to the extent that it is useful for *us*, as Rorty would put it. If, however, our interest in a situation must not – perhaps cannot – reflect only an instinctive preference (and, even if it were instinctive, would it really be ahistorical?), choosing a pragmatic attitude is, in its turn, a practical act that is not without a specific rationality that can be articulated, even in nonfoundationalist terms. In short, it is the history (here, I would say both "history" and "History") that Nietzsche summarizes (and interprets) with the affirmation "God is dead" and that Rorty, using less emphatic language, expresses as the awareness that the metaphysical–epistemological mode of thinking "does not function any more."

Without this appeal to history/History, could we ever choose between the two dispositions of thought? In other words, would Rorty have arrived at his neopragmatic position without the lengthy reconstruction of the philosophical tradition that is a central part of *Philosophy and the Mirror of Nature*? I do not think so, just as Nietzsche could not have spoken of the death of God except as the result of the history of nihilism or as Heidegger could not have written *Being and Time* using only the "Kantian" tools of phenomenology, if he did not have in mind the project of a *Destruktion* of the history of metaphysics, which is the "real justification" for his reproposal of the problem of the meaning of Being. But it is rather clear that, when he was writing his inaugural text, Heidegger could not have felt a theoretical dissatisfaction with the way in which the philosophy of his day thought the problem of Being nor could he have felt compelled simply to continue Husserl's search for a fundamental ontology. All these considerations are merely "theoretical" and, therefore, tied to an objectivist metaphysical perspective, as though the problem were simply that of knowing better, in a more adequate way, the sense of the term and the notion of Being. This adequacy, however, which is already present in *Being and Time*, was a metaphysical phantasm inspired by the idea of truth as conformity. If we want to do justice to these observations, we need to think that Heidegger, in writing *Being and Time*, was motivated by a reflection closer to Nietzsche's "God is dead" than to Husserl's obsession with fundamental ontology. Heidegger comes to understand that the meaning of Being he inherited from the tradition no longer functions due to the general situation of the world at the start of the twentieth century, which sees the first practical attainment of the "total organization" of society, which was also the controversial objective of the artistic avant-garde that Heidegger thought of as the consequence of positivism and scientism – the last phases of a metaphysics that forgets Being in favour of beings (entities).

In this sense, *Being and Time* is already an example of an "ontology of actuality," which, however, risks being confused with a form of phenomenology. I would be tempted to push these analogies even further. *Philosophy and the Mirror of Nature* is initially a philosophical "treatise" that analyzes and brings together many positions that "no longer work," but it does so on the basis of generally phenomenological reasons concerning the nature of the mind, the meaning of "reflection," etc. In its first part, *Being and Time* is a phenomenological analysis of human existence in general, in which being-in-the-world is not yet, as it would be in the 1930s, being-in-*a*-world – the use of the indefinite article with the noun "world" first appears in *The Origin of the Work of Art* (1936). Although it is largely oriented toward a "historical" justification of its own thesis, Gadamer's *Truth and Method* too remains in many ways a phenomenological analysis of human existence. Has the history of modern culture obscured the nature of our experience of truth, which pertains – essentially? – to art and history? The history of lived events, like *Bildung* (education or formation), *sensis communis* (common sense), or aesthetic consciousness, seems to be reconstructed as the history of a deviation and a forgetting of what they really mean. The question that always remains on the horizon for anyone reading *Truth and Method* can be formulated as follows: is the hermeneutic nature of our existence proven by an "analytics of (its) truth – to use the language of Foucault – or is it the result of an "ontology of actuality"? For twentieth-century philosophy, and for philosophers who come to terms with the antifoundationalism of Nietzsche, *Being and Time* functions as a model precisely because the writing of the book is interrupted after the author arrives at the awareness of its radical historicity. As Heidegger would say in the *Letter on Humanism*, the second section of the first part of *Being and Time* was never completed because of a lack of language; more profoundly, because the analytics of existence is aware of being, in its turn, involved in a history that Heidegger calls the "history of Being," which henceforth becomes the only reference available to speak of the authenticity and inauthenticity of existence. This is confirmed especially by the disappearance of the term *Eigentlichkeit* (inauthenticity) from the Heideggerian vocabulary; an etymological trace will remain only in the term *Ereignis*, which probably designates the event of Being and its equally problematic historicity.

I am discussing the "exemplary" meaning of *Being and Time* for any nonfoundationalist philosophy and, consequently, for Rorty's neopragmatism as well. Because *Being and Time* indicates the pathway to take for thought that wants to abandon metaphysics, Kantianism, and the myth of objectivity to which, by a sort of internal logic, that same thought appears to be destined to return. From my point of view, the works of Gadamer and Rorty illustrate this very point. Already before *Being and Time*, the archetype of this "pathway" can be found in Nietzsche's assertion, "There are no facts, only interpretations. And this too is an interpretation" (Nietzsche, *Frammenti postumi* [Posthumous Fragments] *1885–1887*, 299). That everything is interpretation is not an objective "given" that can be described from the outside and that proves the essentially hermeneutic nature of human existence. For the Heidegger of the later works, such assertions – from whose radicalness he tries to free himself (and will continue to think about it like someone who takes his thought beyond Nietzschean nihilism, while remaining entirely within it, and only in this way can he remain loyal to ontological difference) – translate into the thesis that our escape from metaphysical forgetting (of Being) depends solely on Being itself and that it is not possible for us to do anything but listen to its historicodestinal call (*geschichtlich-geschicklich*). Neither the evidence of consciousness discovered by the genius of the philosopher, nor the *cogito*, nor a phenomenological view of essences can help the philosopher to remember Being forgotten by metaphysics. Interpretation does not lead us to the thing itself; on the contrary, it is never anything other than grasping, in a less inauthentic manner, our historical destiny within the event of Being.

Is it possible to read Rorty's choice of neopragmatism in this ontological sense, though it might be considered scandalous? In what way do we recognize and construct what is useful for *us* and what we will call "truth," alongside our fellow citizens and people that we know? If we do not want to reduce pragmatism to a matter of immediate and "instinctive" preferences that, metaphysically and "objectively," we would express through our choices, the truth that interests me, and other human beings, must have a reasonableness grounded in *logos*, i.e. on discourse. When a philosopher, a writer, any person, proposes his or her own redescription of the world because the passive acceptance of current opinion is an, albeit weak, form of interpretation – how can that person be sure that it (the redescription) corresponds to what is useful for *us*? Still in the passages cited above, Rorty speaks of "our sense of community as lacking no foundation except shared hope and the trust created by that sharing" (*Solidarity or Objectivity?*, 179). The fact that they are created, insofar as they are shared, demonstrates that, having their roots in the community and not just in the individual, such hopes and values that constitute the "for us" are not always already given objectively. My thesis, which I believe Rorty would accept, is that by proposing redescriptions that aspire to being "true," i.e. useful to a community, each individual can only recommend them in the name of something already shared: not the shared foundation of an essence – human society as a whole, along the lines of Plato and metaphysics – but what constitutes historically – as well as geographically or as an effect of different contingencies – the community to which we are bound and that we want to preserve and support. This occurs in a context that is not completely predetermined by the past but that is not radically separate from it. At this point, pragmatism cannot avoid making reference, at least implicitly, to the pages of *Being and Time* in which the "authentic" attitude vis-à-vis the past, understood as *Gewesen* – as possibility already realized and yet always open – is different from the past as *Vergangen* – the raw given, the stone of the *es war* (it was) that weighs on the shoulders of Nietzsche's Zarathustra. When he proposes his own redescriptions of the world, Rorty does not imagine that others necessarily have to agree with them, but he is not indifferent to the fact that they may be received as "true," that is, useful for the community. He does not claim that they need to be grounded in apodictic, eternal, structural truths, but he thinks that they have a form of solidity and some "duration." In the end, thrown into history, Rorty cannot avoid constructing them as narratives that do not start at point zero but that are, instead, connected with antecedent shared narratives. I do not know if he actually wanted to do this, but in his work Rorty always put into practice this modality, starting with the vividly phenomenological (in the Hegelian sense) *incipit* of *Philosophy and the Mirror of Nature*, not to mention the title itself of *Consequences of Pragmatism*.

At this point would it suffice to mention Putnam's "internal realism"? And, moreover, internal to what? In *Solidarity or Objectivity?*, Rorty's discussion of the implications of Putnam's internalism indicates, among other things, a sort of "metahistorical nature" (ibid., 171) on the basis of which Putnam assumes that dialogue, ungrounded, contingent, etc. – among the various conceptions of reality – cannot really occur without implicating belief in an "ideal truth," understood as the conceptual limit to aim at, in the awareness that it will never be reached; nonetheless, it is necessary to postulate this belief, according to Putnam, in order to avoid falling into relativism. Rorty is right to reject this postulate, which, by the way, brings to mind that other Popperian postulate according to which, even if the falsification of a hypothesis says nothing positive about how things really are, we have to claim that, by dint of falsifications of false hypotheses, somehow we arrive at truth. Nevertheless, in my view, Putnam's suspicion of what he calls relativism – the claim that "there is only dialogue," to which should be added, according to him, that "there also that to which the dialogue converges" (ibid., 174)

– illustrates a certain limit in Rorty's pragmatism. This is what I propose to overcome by suggesting that we replace Rorty's "no longer function" phrase – which leads him to abandon scientific realism, i.e. metaphysics – with the Heideggerian (and in part Nietzschean) idea of the history of Being. Let us return to the question of how a pragmatist can support his claim – or redescription – so as to persuade a realist. As I have already said, it seems legitimate to me to argue that Rorty in fact uses "hermeneutic" or historicodestinal arguments; for example, when he reconstructs the history and crisis of the model of objective reflection in Western philosophical culture. It is true that Rorty himself explicitly recognizes the circularity of such a reconstruction, in the sense that this history takes shape with the last gleams of a crisis because we already find ourselves within a perspective than occurs inside the crisis. But here, is he not saying more, which is to say that we are able to recognize the crisis of the model of reflection because we cannot avoid "recounting to each other" that history, in a comprehensible way, and in these terms? The preference – certainly contingent – for the pragmatist attitude does not depend on a spontaneous and unmotivated decision, like a simple reaction that derives directly from the way "we are." Here it seems opportune to cite the famous title of an essay by Benedetto Croce, "Perché non possiamo non dirci cristiani" ("Why we cannot avoid calling ourselves Christians," 1942). Like Rorty, Croce, with these words, does not wish to claim that we necessarily have to be Christians by accepting St Thomas's five ways, the historical truth of the Gospels, etc. By going a bit beyond the literal sense of his words, we can emphasize the fact that the reference to Christianity is merely inevitable if we want to define ourselves in the terms of a language that is understood by those who are like us and not necessarily by humanity as a whole. But to profess that we are Christians means that we are redescribing ourselves within a narrative, discovering but also choosing an identity inside that story. Croce is known to be a "weak" Hegelian, a historicist who, inspired by Giambattista Vico, did not see any deterministic "rationality" in history and who criticized Hegel for his concept of history as the realization of absolute Spirit, which would also imply the elimination of all contingency from reality. A very similar position to Croce's is that taken by Gadamer, for whom we need to follow Hegel only up to the point of the objective Spirit. Therefore, the solidity that is in some way real, which Putnam searches for in his *Grenzbegriff* (border concept) perhaps can also be found in history, as it can for Rorty – at least in the sense that Rorty himself cannot rationally argue his preference for pragmatism except by interpreting the past of philosophy. Nothing is necessary in the history to which the pragmatist appeals. History offers itself to us as a contingency and a possibility (which we can reject, accept, or transform), like a question to which, when it is our turn, we respond in totally contingent ways that are not, nonetheless, completely independent of the question (or of history) itself.

The pragmatist will immediately ask: what use do we make of this thesis that brings together Rorty's conclusions (metaphysical realism no longer works), Nietzsche's idea of the death of God, and Heidegger's idea of the history of Being, which proclaims the end of metaphysics? The reply has many different implications that sustain one another. First and foremost, aligning Rorty, Nietzsche, and Heidegger helps us to imagine, in a more concrete way, the *we* to whom the usefulness of the truth relates and as such it already articulates more clearly this same utility. We also find the value of this *we* in Rorty's intellectual biography, which sees the thought and destiny of the democratic society as increasingly linked together (*Una sinistra per il prossimo secolo* [A Left for the Next Century] and other recent works). Furthermore, the connection I am proposing offers elements with which to respond to the requirements of "objectivity" stipulated by Putnam and by other critics (for example, McDowell). Naturally, the usefulness of returning to the history of Being is primarily rhetorical, but it is, nevertheless, more convincing than the usual reference to the question, "In what kind of society would you prefer to live?" Recognizing this purely rhetorical usefulness does not conflict with the decision to speak about it in terms of the history of Being. On the contrary, it allows us to read the antimetaphysical discourse more "faithfully." There is only dialogue, Rorty repeats, as he rejects Putnam's view according to which a *Grenzbegriff* must be postulated. In this sense, there is no Being outside of dialogue. Interpretations and historical events are not "mere interpretations," as though Being were in some way "outside of" them, free from the contingencies of the history of individuals and of society. If there is such a thing as Being, it is only (for Gadamer, Croce, and – I believe – Rorty) the objective Spirit, i.e. what is done and remains in history, becoming a "classic" but which is always susceptible to changes in aesthetic taste, ideas, and the destiny of materials (paintings that disappear, buildings that burn, manuscripts that are lost, etc.). The events of our world, of *us* to whom the "truth for *us*" refers, are not *the* history of Being but *a* history of Being. The shared faith and hope Rorty talks about, and that "are done" precisely to the extent to which they are shared, are not at all different from what Gadamer calls "classic" and that Heidegger saw poetically described by Hölderlin's verses: "*Was bleiber aber, stiften die Dichter*" ("What remains the poets provide") (see Heidegger, *La poesia di Hölderlin*, 49). And – why not? – I believe that Rorty might have agreed.

Notes: After Heidegger

The pages that follow are connected by the "diary of a crisis," which makes them something of an introduction; they are reflections and works born in the crisis climate of the *Black Notebooks*, at a time when, from the (always partial and above all impatient) reading of the text itself and from the critical responses it generated – and still generates (see *I Quaderni neri di Heidegger*, ed. Donatella Di Cesare) – it seemed to us "Heideggerians" that the time had come for a general reckoning and, in short, for the end of "Heideggerianism," whatever it meant. In this light are to be read, in particular, the chapters "Heidegger the Theologian," "Hermeneutics: Crossroads of the Criticism of Globalization," and "Religion and Emancipation," which assert the sense of global criticism of the dominant "machination" of the society of total *Verwaltung* (organization) in which we find ourselves thrown, which only Heidegger allows us to grasp in its most radical ontological sense.

30

Heidegger the Theologian

Up to what point should we take seriously Heidegger's claim that Christianity was the foundation of the entire trajectory of his thought (see *Bensinnung*) and that at the end of the day he was always a "Christian theologian," as the famous letter to Löwith from the 1930s asserts? The most eloquent, and in a way the only, documentation of this Christian inspiration is the lectures on the phenomenology of religion from 1919–20. In those texts and in the reflections on St Paul, around which the texts are constructed, we find most of the key concepts that Heidegger subsequently develops in *Being and Time*, as well as his constant polemic against metaphysics. Somewhat paradoxically, however, this Christian origin of all of Heidegger's work does not correspond to the presence of explicit reference to specific elements of the Christian doctrine and its texts. So much so that there is the suspicion that such an absence reflects the intention to "erase the traces" of a legacy that Heidegger himself felt was too cumbersome and that had to be set aside.

My hypothesis is that the unconfessed, or at any rate implicit, presence of the Christian legacy is a feature that in some way "determines" much of modern and contemporary Western philosophy as it relates to Christianity, the Christianity described in Croce's *Perché non possiamo non dirci cristiani*. We are obviously dealing with such a vast influence that it is not possible to describe it fully. Modern Western philosophy as a whole is permeated by that legacy, to the point that it is no longer a prominent feature. It can become so again, in Heidegger's case, since the *Contributions to Philosophy* and especially the *Black Notebooks* dramatically resurrect the problem of the meaning of his thought in relation to the entire Western religious tradition, in the light of the significant presence of Judaism as one of the themes of those works (see especially Donatella Di Cesare's *Heidegger & Sons*).

We probably need to start with the obvious paradox of the "absence" of references to Christianity in his writings that came after the 1919–20 lectures. If we think of the page in *Contributions to Philosophy* where the connection between the last pagan god and the Christian God is explicitly omitted, the task of looking for the Christian legacy in Heidegger, or the link between his thought and that legacy and its significance, seems hopeless, especially considering the chronological placement of the *Contributions to Philosophy* and the *Black Notebooks* in the biography of an author, who, as is known, explicitly wanted to emphasize its "conclusive" character. As regards this absence, we can also mention the apparently unjustified decision to place the Pauline letters in the middle of the second part of those lectures. It is claimed that, at the time, Heidegger took advantage of the Christmas break in the lectures to "skip" the connection between the discussions in the first lectures (what the *Phenomenology of the Religious Life* is, how it relates to other works from that period, works like Otto's *The Idea of the Holy*, etc.) and the analysis of the religious experience in the first Christian communities, which is undertaken without explicit justifications, as if it were an "obvious" reference.[1]

The question of the presence–absence of Christianity in the development of Heidegger's thought cannot be separated, as I hope to show later, from another serious "absence," that of an ethics. This absence still scandalizes critics, more so than do the antisemitism and the author's membership in the Nazi Party in the 1930s. It is definitely the professed absence of ethics that prevents Heidegger from declaring himself repentant after the war and of accepting the idea that, after the fall of Nazism, a new era opened up under the aegis of human rights and a rational world order guaranteed by the victory of the Allies, the Nuremberg trial, and the United Nations charter. The decision he makes (in his will) to have the *Black Notebooks* published at the end – therefore after a number of years – of the complete works seems more scandalous in that it gives the impression that Heidegger did not really take note of the end of Nazism, or at least that he still expected a future from his meditation on Being and against the triumph of global metaphysics. Obviously, in this sense, his thought still looks terribly dangerous, as one of the factors that can inspire a resurgence of Fascism in the Western world. Also, and especially, in the light of these fears, we need to not lose the opportunity to examine this issue more deeply, which is offered, in fact imposed, by the discussion of the *Black Notebooks*.[2]

Let us continue, then, from Heidegger's "denial" of ethics, which is expressed in no uncertain terms in the *Letter on Humanism*. Responding to a young man who asks him when he intends to write an ethics, Heidegger says, "The desire for an ethics presses ever more ardently for fulfillment as the obvious no less than the hidden perplexity of human beings soars to immeasurable heights" (*Letter on Humanism*, 268). We are obviously already no longer in the years of *Being and Time*, when we could expect – mistakenly however – an answer that evokes the problematics of inauthenticity, of Being-toward-death, of the anticipatory decision; in those contexts, it is still possible to attempt to construct an "ethics," a sort of image of a practicable individual existence, around the acceptance of his own past as *Gewesen* (what has been) and not as *Vergangen* (the past that is dead and gone); it is not implausible that, despite all the claims of being interested only in ontology and against all moralistic readings of the *Eigentlichkeit* (authenticity), *Dasein* (there-being) tries to orient itself in the world by relating to the *Uberlieferung* (handing down), or the legacy of living beings where it originates, and not seeing it as an eternal "value" but as an open legacy that is respected only for a certain *pietas* toward those who have been.[3] Moreover, Heidegger's entire meditation around the time he was composing *Being and Time*, as well as later, is centred on the concept of *Dasein* as *Au-Denken*, or memory and *Danken*, or thanksgiving. All this corresponds to the idea of the event and the given-ness of Being as an opening in history. It is not called ethics simply because it does not imply any metaphysical cogency, nothing that has something to do with a categorical imperative that provides a criterion for distinguishing good from evil. The only ethics that can come from a study of Heidegger, in this perspective, is an ethics of interpretation, or a hermeneutic ethics, even in the sense that hermeneutics is the reading and understanding of a text that is handed down, an assimilation of purely historical "values," a sort of ethical "classicism," which I find developed especially in Gadamer.

Gadamer is one of the names that Franco Volpi, in *È ancora possibile un'etica? Heidegger e la "filosofia pratica"* (Is an Ethics Still Possible? Heidegger and "Practical Philosophy"), which discusses the theme of Heidegger's ethics (or nonethics), mentions among Heidegger's many followers who, borrowing freely from their mentor's teachings, developed theories of ethics – naturally, no normative, metaphysically grounded ethics. These theories drew largely from Aristotle, the study of whose works (precisely from the perspective of ethics) Heidegger had devoted himself to in the decade preceding the publication of *Being and Time*, based on the reading, above all, of the *Nicomachean Ethics*, especially the sixth book, as the connecting thread for constructing an ontology of life, a "hermeneutics of facticity." The most representative of these Heideggerian authors of "ethics" is probably Gadamer, with his emphasis on *phronesis* (wisdom). But Volpi aligns him with the names of other important ex-disciples, such as Hannah Arendt and her "rehabilitation of praxis" (Volpi, 310), or Joachim Ritter and his "rehabilitation of 'ethos'," assigning "pre-eminence to the success of a form of life, i.e. a concrete ethics, relative to a criterion of observing universal but abstract principles" (ibid., 311). And, finally, Hans Jonas, who recovers the Aristotelian concept of *agathon* (benevolence) as the opposite of the modern concept of value. This brief overview shows that none of the disciples of Heidegger, though intensely interested in ethics, ever thought to develop what I would call a normative ethics based on metaphysics.

Although these references are purely indicative, it is clear that the lack of a substantive theory of ethics in Heiddegger has its roots in the "anti metaphysical" polemic – that is to say, in the rejection of the identification of Being with the entity – that permeates *Being and Time*. The only ethics that can be derived from that work, in my opinion (but not mine alone, if we recall the authors named by Volpi), is what I have called an ethics of interpretation. Dissatisfaction with that ethics depends on normative and universalizing expectations that generally frame the question of ethics as the search for "valid," and therefore rationally "necessary," criteria for distinguishing between good and evil. Why does Heidegger avoid this question? His reliance on Aristotle – who, especially in the context of the neoscholasticism, to which he was bound by his Catholic education, was the master of metaphysics *tout court* – is an explicit distancing of himself from modernity and its rationalistic, Kantian or neo-Kantian subjectivism.

But the point is not only the rejection of metaphysics; it is also, and above all, the preparatory nature of *Being and Time*. The incompleteness of the work also accounts for, at least it seems to do so, the fact that Heidegger did not feel capable of formulating an ethics. And this incompleteness remains; even after the *Letter on Humanism*, the "faltering" of language does not change. Except that, in his thinking of the history of Being, the same incompleteness acquires the ontological sense of an opening that is not destined to close. The impossibility of a way out of metaphysics is the same thing as the fact that the there-being is already-always deictic, thrown into inauthenticity of *man*, of the everyday intraworld interchange. Thus, as I believe Marxist critics like Lukács and Goldmann have observed, it seems that the "original sin" of there-being is sociality itself.[4] Is this another feature of the reactionary aspect of Heidegger's existentialism? It does not appear to be the case, if we think that the intraworld interchange with the other is always, and inextricably, also a hierarchical relationship (in *The Gay Science*, Nietzsche observes that self-consciousness itself is not necessary in the life of the individual, but it is useful in the relations between "who commands ... and who obeys" [§113]).

The relation in which the there-being is already-always thrown with one's fellow citizens in the intraworld interchange is never neutral and always gives rise to hierarchies or, at any rate, to conflicts. Moreover, it is what Heidegger says in paragraph 37 of *Being and Time*: "Under the mask of for-one another, an against-one-another is at play" (175).[5] Therefore, and paradoxically, Heidegger was not wrong when he dreamed (culpably) of constructing a premetaphysical epoch by means of a political act, believing that he could achieve it through Nazism. In the light of what we know today (but in his last notebooks Heidegger knew it as well), he could have (and should have, in my view) relied instead (as did Lukács and Bloch) on the communist revolution – which, however, at the time of his decision to join the Nazi movement, seemed to be only a more violent version of American capitalist industrialism. In short, the fact is that, precisely in the name of the historicity he cared so much about until he abandoned phenomenology in the period of *Being and Time*, he restricts significantly the very meaning of ontological difference, radically turning it into events and removing from it all vestiges of metaphysical stability. Can this be a betrayal of the ontological faith professed in *Letter on Humanism*: "We are precisely in a situation where principally there is being"? Or, as it seems to me, merely a step toward that philosophy of praxis with which we cannot, in the end, avoid identifying his thought. The "there is" of this assertion is, obviously, an *es gibt* (it gives), and that which *gibt* (gives) here is Being itself.

The praxis I am speaking about here, then, is inseparable from the reception of a gift, and the gift of Being never occurs as a coming from the exterior, from an other whom, in the same pages of *Letter on Humanism*, Heidegger explicitly refuses to call God. Being is, at once, the giver and the gift, according to the sense of the double genitive Heidegger used in these cases from time to time. Without going deeper into the theological implications of these theses, we can, nonetheless, consider it evident that it makes sense to speak of a philosophy of praxis in Heidegger, especially because it corresponds to the ontology of event in which Being is not the foundation, cause, or principle defined by its occurring.

This conclusion is certainly not the way to respond to the question of ethics that troubles those who expect to find criteria for distinguishing between good and evil. Or, as we see in the recent polemics over the *Black Notebooks*, to assess the error, the real political and moral fall of Heidegger the Nazi. If Being occurs and does not "stay" fixed in its metaphysical separateness, everything is justified. "If God is dead, then all is permitted," according to a Dostoevsky character (*The Brothers Karamazov*). Here we need to recall a verse from Hölderlin that Heidegger often quotes, "where the danger is, grows the saving power also." The death of God is the occurring itself of nihilism. The ontology of event is the ontology of nihilism, which nihilism itself makes possible. Let us look at this statement from the point of view of ethics: the death of God is the devaluation of the highest values, which makes ethics impossible. But such a devaluation, like nihilism, is not taking a "theoretical" position, a philosopher's profession of faith; it is an occurrence that Heidegger himself, following Nietzsche, has lived, being involved in it and taking note of it. It is like someone today saying that the highest value of the United Nations no longer makes any sense or that democracy itself, after it was used as an excuse for bombing Iraq and for imposing the will of the West on the world, does not deserve attention or is "not worth it." The situation to which Heidegger alludes in his reply to the young man who asks about ethics is precisely the following: man's disorientation has grown out of all proportion. Translating, metaphysics has by now established itself as the general condition of the world and has erased the meaning of all "values."

The *Black Notebooks* speak, in this regard, of *Machenschaft*, or universal machination. What at the time of the *Letter on Humanism* and in the years of the *Black Notebooks* was universal machination, the looming atomic war, the extermination and desertification of entire parts of the planet, is today the domain of the market and the technology that correspond to it. At least, this is the way the human condition of the present day is to be understood from Heidegger's point of view – and this is how those who dismiss his nonethical "apocalypsism" also read Heidegger. In an essay from several years ago, Derrida (*Di un tono apocalittico adottato di recente in filosofia*) describes and criticizes the "apocalyptic tone" that he saw spreading in Heidegger's thought of that period. The tone of the Heidegger of the *Black Notebooks* and of the *Contributions to Philosophy* is definitely apocalyptic. The last god perhaps announces a new world but not without labour pains.

Yet, according to Heidegger's expression in the famous interview in *Der Spiegel* published posthumously, "Now only a God can save us." This is anything but ethics; it is, instead, the search for a patrimony of principles (interculturally valid though it may be) that can help us to orient ourselves in the present condition of *Dürftigkeit* (meagreness). Here, Heidegger appears to echo Martin Luther's comment on St Paul: the law is written for our condemnation (see *Epistle to the Romans*); ethics and its values are merely the mirror of our sinfulness or he refers to Kierkegaard's Abraham, who is called by God to violate the moral law by sacrificing Isaac and who, having returned from Mount Moriah with the unharmed Isaac, returns to observing the ethical law, for the love of God (absurdly) and certainly not for respect of "values."

The most adequate parallel for Heidegger's nonethical position seems to be Kierkegaard's Abraham, though in a limited way. The radicalness of the divine call – go and sacrifice your son Isaac, despite all the moral laws you have been observing until now – in Heidegger takes the form of the historical consciousness of the *Dürftigkeit* of the time, the disorientation of human beings – along the lines of the shift from the "existentialist" *Eigentlichkeit* of Being as event, as history. The nonethical Heidegger of *Letter on Humanism* is like Kierkegaard's Abraham who is called to suspend ethics in favour of a more radical decision, except that he still has to deal with a God who is an entity; he guarantees the stability of the general moral law that Abraham goes back to obeying once the act of faith on Mount

Moriah is completed. But Heidegger's Being does not have these still metaphysical characteristics; it does not have an existence different than its occurring in the decision. Would we, therefore, be in a situation where there is only man, as Sartre suggests in *Existentialism Is a Humanism*? His too would be a sort of relapse into metaphysics; *there is* no Being, but *there is* man. Heidegger knows only that, in man's decision, something occurs that is not identified totally with him.[6]

In the same years when the *Contributions to Philosophy* and the *Black Notebooks* come to fruition, Heidegger writes *The Origin of the Work of Art* (1936), which marks the turn toward the ontology of the event. In this work, the artist is like the seat, the agent (the "shepherd" of Being) in which there occurs an epochal aperture that opens up a historical world. It should be mentioned here that, in the work, this occurring is only one way in which truth happens; the others are identified, but not analyzed, by Heidegger (the creation of the state, etc.).[7] But for me, it suffices to note that, in response to the situation of extreme poverty that blocks the possibility of speaking of ethics – as he also says when speaking of preparation and waiting (see Heidegger, *What Is Called Thinking?*) – Heidegger responds with a sort of "leap" into the event. This means, among other things, that it would be possible to speak of ethics only within the horizon of a new opening of Being, of another historicodestinal world.[8]

Thought that seeks to escape the metaphysical forgetting of Being is not called to "unconceal" some sort of truth that it did not know existed or had forgotten, nor is it called to apply some principle or other to which it has been faithful; that would be an ethical "escape" from the *Dürftigkeit*. What Heidegger is contemplating, or is able to contemplate, is only an action that changes the cards on the table without legitimizing itself with a given foundation. Abraham bets on the authenticity of the voice of God that calls him, and so he thinks of a legitimization, albeit a mysterious one, to support and guide him. What also counts for Heidegger is the fact that Abraham sets out without a predefined map, and the instructions for sacrificing the victim are obscure. The there-being is the seat, coauthor, etc. of an event that opens up and that is ontological to the extent that it is not the equivalent of the entity that has been, the entity as a given. But is it always like this, in all decisions, even the most banal, of the there-being? That does not depend on the decision of *Dasein*; it is a component of chance, a bet, or the occurrence of Being. Being also occurs only when there is a new opening; machination is total nihilism, the situation in which Being as such is no longer any part of it. Without pushing the analogy too far, it is reasonable to think that Heidegger's ethics–nonethics is a bet of ontological significance, in which at play is not only (only?) the eternal destiny of the soul, as in Pascal, but the occurrence of Being itself. "And then what?" would ask Heidegger critics who ask him to explain his choices. Anything goes, if it goes – Feyerabend would say. But is the "if it goes" not the ontological aspect of the bet? Are we not saying that what works is good and, therefore, the most unscrupulous, the most violent, etc., are right? Is there only anarchy, then, as in the title of Schürmann's book, *Heidegger on Being and Acting, From Principles to Anarchy*? Yes, on condition of interpreting anarchy in its radical sense: the "correct" decision, for Heidegger – according to the way I read him; it is above all what clears the ground. But this act of clearing is not, in its turn, inspired by principles; it is itself praxis – the re-action of one who suffers for those principles. Here, Heidegger is closer to Benjamin than he is to Kierkegaard; what inspires revolutionaries is not the luminous image of the future they want to achieve – they do not have very clear ideas of this image (theory and praxis) – but, rather, the memory of their enslaved ancestors. Despite all his disdain for onticity, anthropologism, etc., Heidegger finds himself led – certainly for his interpreters, but did he have another way out? – to replacing metaphysical principles with the suffering of oppressed there-being. His revolt against metaphysics and positivist objectivism in *Being and Time* already had a nontheoretical explanation but an ethical–political one. Is it an exaggeration to see in this, what appears to me as Heidegger's ontological trajectory, a sort of philo sophical translation of Paul of Tarsus, first *Letter to the Corinthians*, Hymn of Charity (*Corinthians* 1, 13, 1–3), in which the only virtue that remains, in the end, after faith and hope in the beatific vision, is charity? Being is only event and it occurs in the praxis of the there-being, even though it is not reducible to it. But praxis is not motivated by principles, theories, or loyalty to some view of the world that "would apply" in the acting. By what is it motivated, then, if not by the rebelliousness that Heidegger experiences when, as a young man, he rejects metaphysics?

This may seem arbitrary or excessive only to those who do not accept fully the Heideggerian notion *par excellence* of the history of Being and of the philosopher as imbedded in this history. The fact that Being is occurrence in which thought – thought of Being in two senses of the genitive – is revealed by its call also, and above all, means that the idea itself of *a* history of Being is *the* history of Being. This is not an abstract history; moreover, the problems related to Nazism in the *Black Notebooks* are a clear sign that the Being imbedded in history is very concrete. We might say that Heidegger specifies the historical belonging to his own epoch, but he never explicitly alludes to Christianity and the New Testament prophecy from which, at a certain point, he indeed distances himself.[9]

31

Notes on Heidegger

Why do we still need Heidegger, then? It is not only his work that appears to be tied to the past for reasons of chronology; after the *Black Notebooks*, his, albeit qualified, support of Nazism, and the antisemitism that went with it, seems ethically repugnant. Even a general assessment that is not as hostile as the one that has emerged from recent congresses – including the last one held at the Sapienza University of Rome in November 2015, "*I* Quaderni neri *di Heidegger 1931–1948*" – seems to take us along a *Holzweg* or path that leads nowhere, which comes to an end and then turns back on itself like a labyrinth. In short, it is as though the meaning of Heidegger's thought, at this point in his *Wirkungsgeschichte* (history of effects), were merely the philosophical acknowledgment of the desperate and inescapable condition in which humanity finds itself today. The famous statement from the *Der Spiegel* interview, "Now only a God can save us," must be taken exclusively as a desperate utterance implying that there is no salvation or, at least, that it is not something in which we can realistically hope. This Heideggerian position – which is philosophically well documented in the texts and in the *Black Notebooks* in particular – by now spawns all the apocalyptic literature found in philosophical texts that are attentive to the letter of Heidegger's writings and in journalistic comments that are not lacking in a kind of desperate aestheticism. The latter also relate to positions like the one expressed by Franco Volpi in his introduction to the Italian edition of *Contributions to Philosophy*. The history of this introduction and of the censorship it was to suffer at the hands of Heidegger's heirs[1] is recounted in the correspondence between Volpi and Armando Massarenti, published in the periodical *Il Sole 24 Ore* (19 April 2009). An excerpt follows:

> Dear Massarenti ... having returned [from Santiago, Chile], I have many things to tell you. My introduction to *Beiträge* (*Contributions*, which are being printed by Adelphi) was considered too critical by Heidegger's stepdaughter and censored. Negotiations are ongoing to try to have it both ways (therefore, I ask that you keep this matter in the strictest confidence), but I would really like to follow the example of Maurizio Ferraris and write a notebook: *Goodbye, Heidegger!* In Santiago, where I am going for the closing session of the congress on phenomenology and hermeneutics, I wanted to speak on Heidegger and Wittgenstein, but I decided to change the theme of my talk and submitted as the new title, *Goodbye, Heidegger! My Censored Introduction to the Beiträge.*

This was 11 October 2007. On 18 November, after other exchanges, Volpi sent Massarenti the most important of the censored passages, which has remained unpublished until now. It appears here for the first time. It is a paragraph from the introduction to *Contributions to Philosophy* titled "Naufrago nel mare dell'Essere" ("Shipwrecked in the sea of Being").

> *Contributions to Philosophy*? "The diary of a shipwreck survivor. Venturing beyond the sea of Being, his thought flounders"
>
> Nietzsche's experience empties Heidegger's metaphors, blunts his energy, and undermines the foundations of the construction of *Contributions to Philosophy*. Is it perhaps a coincidence that Heidegger places in the exergue of the two volumes dedicated to *Nietzsche* (1961) an epigraph taken from the *Antichrist*, which matches exactly the conclusion of the *Contributions*? These end with a "fugue" that deals with the last god; the first chapter of *Nietzsche* opens with the quote, "Almost two millennia and not a single new god."
>
> Perhaps, Heidegger was no longer able to raise himself philosophically from the *de profundis* of *Nietzsche*. In the bitter light of the exhaustion of Being – this usually fleeting guest of our thoughts – remains for Heidegger the last chimera worth the effort of dreaming. All his efforts are directed toward this single goal, Being, but the pathways have been blocked. His intermittent philosophical experimentation and his "groping around" in this dream have left him terribly vulnerable to criticism.

> Heidegger rejects modern rationality with the same humble gesture with which he acknowledges its domination, reprimands science that "does not think" of its limitations, demonizes technology pretending to accept it as destined, constructs a catastrophic worldview, dares to propose geopolitical theories that are, to say the least, risky – Europe caught between Americanism and Bolshevism – adding fuel to the Greco-Germanic myth of origins that is to be reconquered. Even his ingenious linguistic experimentations implode and increasingly assume the features of funambulism and nonsense. His use of etymology turns out to be an abuse ... the conviction that real philosophy can speak only in ancient Greek or German (or Latin?) a hyperbole; his celebration of the role of the poet, an overestimation, the hopes he places in poetic thought, a pious illusion; his anthropology of *Lichtung* (clearing or glade), in which man is a shepherd of Being, an unacceptable and impracticable proposal. The thought of the later Heidegger is not as enigmatic as the supine, and often lacking in critical spirit, admiration that has been showered on him and that has produced so much scholasticism.
>
> Certainly, ordinary mortals often deride the philosopher's proposals because they do not understand his problems. Therefore, you cannot take it for granted that these criticisms hit the mark. But if it were the case, then the *Contributions to Philosophy* would really be the logbook of a shipwreck. For venturing too far in the sea of Being, Heidegger's thought flounders. But when a large ship goes down, the spectacle offered to the eyes is sublime.

I reread these lines by Volpi and I reconvince myself that Heidegger needs to be "urbanized," even in the sense of secularizing him; not follow him into his mysticism. Return to the why of his thinking on Being. It was the struggle against total *Verwaltung* already in *Being and Time*. As well, his lectures on theology from 1919–20 were aimed at reconstructing an "authentic" experience of temporality – but this experience was the opposite of the inauthenticity of the industrialized world. As was his "Nazism" of 1933, his anti-Americanism, and his anti-Stalinism. We should, therefore, not insist too much on the dream of arriving, returning, perceiving Being (see above, Volpi). From this arises the ambiguity of the Nazi error: it is not Being that is of interest but escaping alienation; but if we are determined to "recover" Being and not merely transform society, we are then going off the track and into hazy mysticism. It is due to this lapse that a great interpreter of Heidegger's thought like Franco Volpi has exhorted us to abandon Heidegger to his destiny and to free ourselves of him the way we would an author who is no longer of use. From the standpoint I am proposing here, instead, what we need to do is not take note – with the aesthetic thrill that it entails – of the end of all hope but to not forget, because of the *Black Notebooks* and their apocalyptic *Stimmung* (mood), the Heidegger of *Being and Time*, *Phenomenology of the Religious Life*, and *Origin of the Work of Art*; in short, the Heidegger for whom the history of Being still has a future and an existence is still a project. Even in the *Black Notebooks*, albeit in an obscure manner, there is talk of a "new beginning" and a "last god" who opens up the way. This is certainly not much, but to reduce everything to the acknowledgement of the end is like choosing to believe the word of someone who, with all his good reasons, finds himself in a desperate *Stimmung*, in a sort of bad mood that his friends should help him to overcome.

As I am trying to do here, those who refuse to dismiss Heidegger in this fashion – it would be like seeing in him that same *Selbstvernichtung* (self-destruction) that he attributes to the "metaphysical" Jewish people, the *Judentum* condemned by the same technoscientific domination of the world that it itself contributed so powerfully to build – those who refuse this fundamentally aestheticizing interpretation of the product of Heideggerianism can escape this outlook only if they start to take the statement from the *Der Spiegel* interview literally, a statement that appears to express resignation. In Heidegger, there is a fundamental religious experience that we must acknowledge in order to be truly fair to him. The texts in which he himself recognizes it and points it out are not lacking, especially the lectures of 1919–20 on the phenomenology of religion, which anticipates, in the light of St Paul, all the basic themes of *Being and Time* and of the subsequent deconstruction of metaphysics. With these texts in mind, we can take seriously the desperate remark made in *Der Spiegel* and not forget that, beyond the psychological state it depicts, it has an indisputable basis in Luther's theology: only the grace of God, and not our works, can save us. It could be argued that here Heidegger interprets, along with Luther, the passage in the *Letter to the Romans*, where St Paul writes that the law is made for our condemnation and not for our salvation. The law is made to show us that, at this point, "now only a God can save us." Leaving aside all other exegetical considerations, it does not seem illogical to think that Heidegger's entire meditation of the final years, especially his insistence that there is no human solution to the problem of the desertification of the planet, etc. is a vast commentary on the text of St Paul and Luther. The reluctance of philosophers to notice this is completely understandable; Heidegger himself seems to force them not to confuse philosophy and theology (*Silete theologi in munere alieno*? ["Silence, theologian where you do not belong"] or precisely the opposite, if at this point "only a God can save us"?). Let me state it more clearly. The only non-"self-destructive" conclusion in Heidegger's meditation that we can find is a religious solution, and, given his historical context and the almost obvious fact that strikes us about the reference to Christianity (and not to any religious experience whatever) in the lectures of 1919–20, the religious result we are talking about, is a Christian one. Obviously, not because making a philosophical choice from among different religions led him to the Gospel and Jesus Christ, but only because – and it is the unjustified recourse to St Paul in those lectures – this result was destined to occur by his placement in history. With all that he borrows from the Greeks, Heidegger was a Christian *naturalitur* (*gesschichtlich*) and so he remained, or once again became, during a career in which he never abandoned that religion in a definitive way. This mode of being a Christian *naturalitur*, in the most banal sense of "naturally," is already in itself a suspension of the rationalizing pretensions of official Catholic theology.

I am not trying to describe faithfully Heidegger's positions, documenting them in a persuasive manner with one text or another. This too would appear to be an aesthetic attitude, in the sense that any philosophical study that places itself before its own theme, as though it were before an object to be described objectively, is essentially, aestheticizing. It is clear that I am doing something else here. I am trying to "save" Heidegger rather than to describe him faithfully. But, this is exactly what he would do in my place. It should suffice here to think of what he reprimands Jaspers for in his review (almost contemporaneous with the lectures on the phenomenology of religion) of *The Psychology of Worldviews*: you cannot put yourself before the different *Weltanschauungen* without putting into play your own worldview. (This would, indeed, be the aesthetic attitude.)

Here, then, is where we are: the religious and Christian Heidegger emerges from a reading that is not merely philological–textual but also from the answers to questions that are appropriate to the interpreter. My interest in recognizing, bringing to the surface, or emphasizing Heidegger's Christian roots is a response to an expectation that we interpreters have and that legitimizes our intention to "use him" in order to justify, legitimate, or enrich our own Christian faith. Speaking for myself, if I were not a Heideggerian, I would not be a Christian, and vice-versa. For me (only me?), Heidegger is not to be dismissed, because I need him in order to be a Christian. And my Christianity is defined in a peculiar way in that I listen to Heidegger's Christianity, the one documented in his writings and to which I refer, and perhaps only to these. I am not ignoring the controversial manner in which Heidegger drifted away from Christianity, as many pages of his works attest. I put these things to one side voluntarily (arbitrarily?) because it does not interest me to know what he "really" thought of Christ, his message, or his Church. I leave this "objectivizing" study to those who, especially after the *Black Notebooks*, have wanted to bring his writings before the tribunal of judgment. The process was started years ago by Farias, and recently, deploying more effective weapons, Faye and others entered the fray. For these authors, it is still a matter of determining Heidegger's "responsibility" in a sort of new Nuremburg. But at Nuremburg no Nazi was absolved; most were put to death. The intent of Faye and his companions is precisely to dismiss Heidegger, thereby blocking all further use of his thought – like the use that, in my view, it can and must still have when we follow the religious Christian thread that runs through his works.

Three questions come to mind at this point. Basically, I would ask, why does Heidegger help – confirm, make possible, explain – the choice of the Christian faith? Why does being a Christian coincide with preferring his philosophy, my Christianity? And, why and how does being a Christian orient me to profess his philosophy?

The dismissal of metaphysics, which is radically accomplished only in Heidegger, is of great importance for continuing to think as a Christian. Metaphysics, i.e. the objectivity, unfurled before the mind's eye, of structures of Being that are assumed to be given; in short, God as supreme Object that I cannot fail to recognize. A sort of violence because, among other reasons, where metaphysics leads me is never a god before whom we can sing and dance, nor a god that loves me (in *Letter on Humanism*, *möglich machen* also means to love, *mögen*). As a good ex-seminarian, Heidegger knows full well that metaphysics cannot happen to a personal god and that creation (the event of creation) is not rationally understandable.

But, what about the *Black Notebooks* and the feeling of futility that we experience when we read the text? I do not know if this is a way of justifying, ultimately, interpretations like Löwith's, but it seems to me that, in order to save Heidegger – in order not to condemn him to oblivion or leave him in the hands of purely mystical readers, on the one hand, or purely hostile and "justicialist" readers, on the other hand – we need to highlight the sense of his *originary* inspiration, which is subsequently lost in the mystical haziness of the *Black Notebooks* and the *Contributions to Philosophy*, which coincides with the period of his Nazi experience. The idea that Heidegger became a Nazi when he stopped reading St Paul and began to idolize Hölderlin, which is philologically difficult to defend, makes a certain amount of sense. His argument that Being is different from the entity had a precise meaning during the years of *Being and Time* and, up to a certain point, perhaps even during the *Kehre*. It was a matter of resisting the inauthenticity of the world of industrialized man; we could say that ontological difference was an appeal to resist the incipient total administration of the world. The introduction to the *Phenomenology of Religion* was certainly neither an apologetic text nor an exhortation to live the Christian life; it was a search for "authentic" temporality to set against the technoscientific alienation of Being as object. There is certainly continuity between Heidegger the *ante litteram* critic of mass culture and industrial domination and Heidegger who chooses Nazism in 1933. But somehow (better to say rather clearly) this choice is a "metaphysical" relapse, inspired by the idea of reconstructing a premetaphysical world, one that is removed from the logic of capitalist or communist (Stalin!) domination. Once it has fallen into the oblivion of ontological difference (which is implied in the idea of a return of Being that precedes oblivion), for Heidegger Being becomes an entity that is increasingly isolated from its "critical" aspects; it is no longer like an unseen god that needs to be mystically rediscovered. The time has come, perhaps, to declare that the *Black Notebooks* are of less interest than the publishers would like – until proven otherwise, that is to say, until a reader makes clear what we would lose by not reading them.

Why still Heidegger? Because his criticism of machination is what we need most at this time. At least as philosophers, though we do not ask the questions solely as specialists of an intellectual discipline, as academics, professional thinkers, etc. Why "still": here we have something like the mark of the entire crisis that the *Black Notebooks* created and creates. In this context, "still" means, notwithstanding, in spite of. Because the opportunity to resume the conversation of, on, or with Heidegger, after the *Black Notebooks*, presupposes, for me, the decision not to allow ourselves to be fascinated by them. To read them as philosophical writings worthy of study and interpretation is like an invasion of Heidegger's privacy, the presumption of studying extemporaneous notes and taking them as philosophical theorems. The decision to leave aside the *Black Notebooks* is a serious one in that it sets everyone against you: the enthusiasts of the Heidegger industry as well as the enemies, those who are scandalized, like Faye. The start of this conversation, especially the decision to set aside (*faren lassen*) the mind-racking ramblings of the *Black Notebooks*, is the theme of my paper for the Rome congress on the rediscovery of the Christian Heidegger, mentioned above. It is not only a way of recovering the meaning of his philosophy, restoring to it the sense that it had for him. The point is that to speak of the Christian Heidegger is also to bring his meditation on the history of Being back to this decisive intersection: machination is only another name for the West, for the modern industrialized and colonized world. This is to say that rediscovering Heidegger is a way of reconstituting the meaning of his thought beyond, or up to, the *Black Notebooks* and a way of radically placing this interpretation in the context of the history of Being, as Heidegger forced himself to think of it.

The idea of placing this rethink under the rubric of Christianity is taking seriously, above all, the statement in the *Der Spiegel* interview, "Now only a God can save us." Only a religious outcome can save the legacy of Heidegger, who thought the history of Being. This goes well beyond a biographical acknowledgment that reconstructs the coherence of his thought on the basis of his Christianity. I am not saying simply that Heidegger is a Christian thinker. The importance of his philosophy lies in the questioning of modernity and its products, such as the Westernization and Christianization of the world. The question of Judaism is to be seen from this perspective. The "antisemitic" tone of many pages of Heidegger's writings can probably be traced back, as can be easily established, to his anti-Christian stance as an aspect of his anti-Western stance. Last but not least, this reflection relates to the, relatively contingent, fact that fierce critics of Heidegger's antisemitism – like Faye and Farias before him – stigmatize him as an enemy of the democratic West. Furthermore, the "anti-Western" attitude is fully present in Heidegger, starting with his decision to support the Nazi cause as an expression of hatred for the world of democracies (moreover allied with Stalin). If there is a future for Heidegger and Heideggerianism, it certainly cannot be the one we find in so many twisted and often grotesque pages of the *Black Notebooks*.

And so, at this point: a) Even if only in negative terms, the *Black Notebooks* oblige us to rethink Heideggerianism as a philosophy of the history of the West; b) but with what "escape" in mind? What does it mean to say that a god can save us? c) A Heideggerian-Christian spirituality, *Andenken* (recollection) as a life of faith? Does it not risk being only a moralistic invitation for individuals? Or can the revolutionary inspiration of Christianity be found there? We need to press the point that Heidegger's thought was never intended to be read as "theory" but rather as a call to a different praxis (see the question of authenticity in *Being and Time*).

Do we dismiss Heidegger? This question, which has been circulating for some time in the public debate, and not just in Italy, resurfaces after the above mentioned Rome congress sponsored by the Philosophy Department of La Sapienza University, with the support of the German embassy and the Humboldt Foundation, and organized by Donatella Di Cesare, the world expert on Heidegger's *Black Notebooks*, four volumes of notes and observations of various kinds written between 1931 and 1948 by the philosopher who states in his will that they should be published at the end of his complete works. The multivolume works are printed by the publisher Klostermann, who added the *Notebooks* (vols. 94, 95, 96, 97), edited by Peter Trawny, for a total of 1,700 pages. The first of these volumes (1931–38) was recently published by Bompiani in an excellent Italian translation by Alessandra Iadiccio, and precisely on this occasion the debate on the much-discussed author of *Being and Time* was reopened. The *Notebooks*, which are black due to the colour of the manuscript covers, are not systematic treatments but mostly notes and almost diary entries. They should, therefore, be read together with the other books published during the author's lifetime as well as the posthumous works, which are now available in Klostermann's *Gesamtausgabe* (collected works).

But why speak of dismissing such an imposing philosophical legacy?[2] Authoritative scholars from around the world and a large number of intensely interested students participated in the Rome congress. However, in most of the papers presented, and especially in some of them (those of Bensoussan, Sloterdijk, and Vitiello), the question of what we can still do with Heidegger was addressed. This concerned not only the *Black Notebooks* but his entire work as well. In the *Notebooks* in fact the tragic "error" comes to light, the error that was quite apparent in the published works, which secured for Heidegger fame as a great *maitre à penser* or guru of twentieth-century philosophy, starting with *Being and Time*, 1927. In 1933 Heidegger openly supported Hitler and became, for a brief period, rector of the University of Freiburg; he remained enrolled in the Nazi Party in the years that followed, until he was "purged" by the Allies at the end of the war. With respect to what was already read in the texts published in his lifetime (above all in some pages of the *Introduction to Metaphysics*, from 1935, and in the *Contributions to Philosophy*, written in 1938 but published only recently), the *Black Notebooks* add little that is new, almost the only proof that Heidegger's political interests were not at all a marginal aspect of this thought and, therefore, that his experience with Nazism and antisemitism was quite a bit more than a purely practical "error" or a moral lapse that lacks any systematic link with his philosophy. But, even those who professed for a long time to be Heideggerians (myself included, and I continue to profess this) were profoundly shaken by the *Black Notebooks* precisely because of the explicitness of the positions they find in them. And this, not so much for the pro-Nazism stance, which is largely mitigated by harshly critical assertions directed at his "rough" version, which described the politics and figures of the regime. Nor for the antisemitism that we, along with Di Cesare, can call metaphysical antisemitism, which was also not at all connected with the political practice of the "final solution" that inspired the extermination. Adopting – whether culpably and acritically – the stereotypes and prejudices of the German culture of the early twentieth century, Heidegger thought of the Jewish people as the most symbolic image of the technological civilization that he detested; for him, the Jews were a people without a homeland (the diaspora) and, therefore, without historical roots; a people with a talent for calculation (banks) and, so, bearers of an abstract rationality that was at the base of the (capitalist but also Stalinist) rationalization of the world and the forms of oppression that came with it. When he chose Hitler in 1933, his main enemy was especially the growing total organization of industrial society (inspired by scientific rationalism). The folly, and also the philosophical self-contradiction, of this attitude are evident as far as I am concerned. Not only was Hitler's Germany a super-organized industrial power itself, but, in terms of Heidegger's philosophy, it was unimaginable to recreate in the current world that mythic preclassical Greece that Nietzsche and poets like Hölderlin dreamed of.

Today, those who would like to dismiss Heidegger, in some sense, rely especially on these aspects of the philosophy of history, in addition to the issues of Nazism and antisemitism. There is certainly also a degree of democratic–progressive ideology, a sort of "Atlantic" backdrop that is easily found in works like Faye's (*Heidegger, Introduction of Nazism into Philosophy*), which focus on stigmatizing his antisemitism; the fact that Heidegger never publicly "repented" for his Nazism is also a serious wound to the faith in the free West that brought war criminals to justice at Nuremburg and that today is protected by NATO, the liberal economy, and technological globalization. Of course, such designs to dismiss Heidegger were not shared by all the presenters at the Rome congress, but there is no question that in many of the papers one could detect a kind of taking stock, a sort of abandoning a figure that supposedly had nothing more to say to us, especially to the new generations. One reason, among others, is the fact that his view of history does not appear to see the future in any practicable way. This is particularly true in the last *Black Notebooks*, where the discourse is full of references to a mysterious "last god" and an equally mysterious "new beginning." These almost mystical aspects of his work often dominated the debate in Rome and the work of authors who wrote in some newspapers (Antonio Gnoli, "Nell'abisso dello Zibaldone maledetto di Heidegger" ["Into the Abyss of Heidegger's Cursed Notebook"] and Angelo Bolaffi, "L'equivoco del nazismo spirituale di Heidegger" ["The Ambiguity of Heidegger's Spiritual Nazism"], both appearing in *La Repubblica*, 27 November 2015). The "German people" are supposedly being called to the new beginning. As it seems with more and more frequency in the final pages of the *Black Notebooks*, however, they have little to do because such a new beginning depends solely on Being and not on any human initiative. This desperate pessimism is even more serious if we recall that, despite the interest in history and politics documented in the *Black Notebooks*, Heidegger never talks about ethics, precisely because everything is determined by Being. On the other hand, in his works, and not only those from the early years, there is the obsession with authentic existence, with the decision that individuals must make in order to avoid becoming confounded by the anonymous world of man, of the impersonal "they" who, for Heidegger, are always associated with the globalized oppression of the technological (and capitalist, we might add with some justification) world. In keeping with the best philosophical tradition, from Plato to Nietzsche or Wittgenstein, Heidegger sees his task as a call to a "true" life and not only in the form of disenchanted contemplation of the mortal destiny of Being. The famous statement from his last interview in *Der Spiegel*, "Now only a God can save us," perhaps is not an expression of desperation with no way out; it also evokes the possibility of salvation from that (this) world of total domination that Heidegger hated no less than did other philosophers, such as Adorno.

Sources

Some of the essays in this book originally appeared as:

1 "What Need, What Metaphysics?" *Parrheia* 21 (2014): 53–7.

2 "Philosophy and Contradiction." In *Contradictions: Logic, History, Actuality*, edited by Elena Ficara, 173–80. Berlin: De Gruyter, 2014.

3 "Wittgenstein *Gescichtlihkeit*." In *Ethics, Society, Politics: Proceedings of the 35th International Wittgenstein Symposium*, edited by Hajo Greif and Martin Gerhard Weiss, 115–30. Berlin: De Gruyter, 2013.

4 Unpublished.

5 "The Future of Hermeneutics." In *The Routledge Companion to Hermeneutics*, edited by Jeff Malpas and Hans-Helmut Gander, 721–8. London and New York: Routledge, 2014.

6 "The Political Outcome of Hermeneutics." In *Consequences of Hermeneutics: Fifty Years After Gadamer's Truth and Method*, edited by Jeff Malpas and Santiago Zabala, 281–7. Evanston, IL: Northwestern University Press, 2010.

7 "Herméneutique de l'indignation." In *Les nouveaux imaginaires démocratiques*, edited by Candido Mendes, 101–10. Rio de Janeiro: Educam-Editoria Universitária, Candido Mendes, 2013.

8 "Herméneutique et nihilisme." In *L'Europe et le legs de l'Occident*, edited by Candido Mendes, 351–8. Rio de Janeiro: Educam-Editoria Universitária, Candido Mendes, 2013.

9 Unpublished.

10 "Democracy and Hermeneutics" (Italian translation by Alberto Martinengo).

11 "Emergency and Event: Technique, Politics, and the Work of Art." *Philosophy Today* 4 (2015): 583–7.

12 "Fundamentalismo democratico e dialettica del pensiero." In *Democracia profunda, reinvenciones nacionales y subjectividades*, 403–10. Rio de Janeiro: Educam-Editoria Universitária, Candido Mendes, 2007.
13 "De la politique et de l'amour." In *Shared Values in a World of Cultural Pluralism*, edited by Candido Mendes, 17–26. Rio de Janeiro: Academy of Latinity Press, 2014.
14 "How to Become an Anti-Zionist." In *Deconstructing Zionism: A Critique of Political Metaphysics*, edited Gianni Vattino and Michael Marder, 15–22. London: Bloomsbury, 2013.
15 Unpublished.
16 "The Question Concerning Technology." In *Humanity and Difference in the Global Age*, edited by Candido Mendes, 93–104. Rio de Janeiro: Academy of Latinity Press, 2012.
17 "Nihilisme passif ou reactif" (Italian translation by Giuseppe Iannantuono).
18 "Kuala – Reconnaissance réciproque au-delà de l'universalisme." In *Post-Regionalism in the Global Age*, edited by Candido Mendes, 211–8. Rio de Janeiro, Brazil: Academy of Latinity Press, 2014.
19 "Reflexiones sobre la dialéctica del desarrollo."
20 Unpublished.
21 Unpublished.
22 Unpublished.
23 Unpublished.
24 Unpublished.
25 Unpublished.
26 Unpublished.
27 Unpublished.
28 "Historicity and *Différance*." In *Judeities. Questions for Jacques Derrida*, edited by Bettina Bergo, Joseph D. Cohen, and Raphael Zagury-Orly, 131–41. Translated by Bettina Bergo and Michael B. Smith. New York: Fordham University Press, 2007.
29 Unpublished.
30 "Heidegger teologo." In *I quaderni neri di Heidegger*, edited by Donatella Di Cesare, 183–92. Milan: Mimesis, 2016.
31 Unpublished.

Notes

CHAPTER ONE

1 This is a quote from Richard Rorty, which is also the title given to a volume collecting some interviews with Rorty. See Richard Rorty, *Take Care of Freedom and Truth Will Take Care of Itself.*

2 Friedrich Nietzsche, *Human All Too Human.* "On the First and Last Things," 1, Ebook Gutenberg Project.

CHAPTER THREE

1 On the same concept of *Bild* (picture or image) read in a way that is not at all "correspondence-based," see Borutti in D. Sparti, *Wittgenstein politico*, 128, no. 1.

CHAPTER FIVE

1 This ontologization of hermeneutics was recently developed by S. Zabala in *The Remains of Being: Hermeneutic Ontology after Metaphysics.*

2 With Zabala, I have illustrated this engagement in our book *Hermeneutic Communism: From Heidegger to Marx.*

3 Keiji Nishitani (of the Kyoto school): here the Zen readings of Heidegger's work are particularly important.

4 This idea was suggested to me by G. Chiurazzi in the seminar that he held at the University of Turin on 28 March 2014.

CHAPTER EIGHT

1 This essay was first published in 2013.

CHAPTER TEN

1 The occasion was the awarding of the National Humanities Medal to John Searle in 2004.
2 Frederick Taylor's *The Scientific Organization of Labour* was published in 1911 and applied in the Ford plants until 1913.

CHAPTER ELEVEN

1 This essay was first published in 2015.

CHAPTER FOURTEEN

1 Fini was president of the chamber from 2008 to 2013. This essay was probably written in 2012.

CHAPTER FIFTEEN

1 The reference is to events that occurred around 2013.

CHAPTER SIXTEEN

1 The time frame is roughly 2012.

CHAPTER THIRTY

1 The same obviousness, perhaps, explains why *Phenomenology and Theology* targets "Christian philosophy" considering the fact that, when we speak of theology, we have Christianity in mind.
2 Adorno, too, does not believe that Nazism is finished. It could be argued that Israel and the USA act as world police. There is an analogy between our current situation and that of the 1930s, in the form of the metaphysical menace of industrial totalitarianism.
3 This is how I myself have for a long time read and continue to read, and even practise in my own life, the only possible morality that I find in Heidegger and in the Heideggerian tradition.

4 See Sartre, "L'enfer c'est les autres" (*Huis Clos*).
5 Here we could also mention Hegel and the image the master–slave dialectic.
6 But in Sartre and in Hegel this is merely the deceptiveness of reason. Indeed: reason? Or Being itself?
7 I have suggested elsewhere that the exclusive emphasis that Heidegger places, in this text, on poetry and art as the place where the epochal opening up of Being unfolds can probably be explained by the Nazi misadventure: the creation of a state, which leads him to no longer talk about politics, to express it in banal terms.
8 It is interesting to point out that Heidegger speaks of the "epochality" of Being (see Anaximander) linking the term "epoch" to the idea of epochs as suspension and withdrawal. Note that we find the *epoche* in Husserl as well.
9 We need to keep in mind, however, the letter to Löwith: "I am a theologian nonetheless." The crucial weight of the reference to early Christian life (lectures 1919–20 and thereabouts) cannot be ignored when considering later developments. In his case, as, if not more so, in Nietzsche's, I believe it is really possible to speak of a kind of erasure of tracks.

CHAPTER THIRTY-ONE

1 For the complete version of the Introduction, see Volpi, *Goodbye, Heidegger!*
2 On which the two most important texts in Italy are those of Donatella Di Cesare, *Heidegger and the Jews* and *Heidegger & Sons*.

Bibliography

Bartley, William Warren. *Wittgenstein*. Philadelphia: Lippincott, 1973.

Benjamin, Walter. "Theses on the Philosophy of History." In *Illuminations*, edited and translated by Hannah Arendt. New York: Schoken Books, 1968.

Bernstein, Richard J. *Beyond Objectivism and Relativism: Science, Hermeneutics, and Praxis*. Oxford: Basil Blackwell, 1983.

Bloch, Ernst. *The Spirit of Utopia*. Translated by Anthony Nasser. Stanford, CA: Stanford University Press, 2000.

Bonhoeffer, Dietrich. *Atto ed essere: filosofia trascendentale ed ontologia nella teologia sistematica*. Brescia: Queriniana, 1993. English translation, *Act and Being: Transcendental Philosophy and Ontology in a Systematic Theology*. Translated by Hans-Richard Reuter. Minneapolis, MN: Fortress Press, 2009.

Brague, Rémi. *Il futuro dell'Occidente: Nel modello romano la salvezza dell'Europa* (The future of the West: The Roman model for the Salvation of Europe). Milan: Bompiani, 2005.

Brecht, Bertolt. "To Those Who Follow in Our Wake." *Harper's* magazine, 15 January 2008. https://harpers.org/2008/01/brecht-to-those-who-follow-in-our-wake/.

Broch, Hermann. *The Sleepwalkers*. Translated by Willa and Edwin Muir. London: M. Secker, 1932.

Cacciari, Massimo. *Dell'inizio* (Of the beginning). Milan: Adelphi, 1990.

Croce, Benedetto. *Perché non possiamo non dirci cristiani* (Why we cannot avoid calling ourselves Christians). Bari: Laterza, 1942.

Deleuze, Gilles, and Felix Guattari. *Kafka: Toward a Minor Literature*. Minneapolis, MN: University of Minnesota Press, 1986. (Original title *Kafka: pour une litérature mineur*).

Derrida, Jacques. "Di un tono apocalittico adottato di recente in filosofia" ("Concerning an apocalyptic tone recently adopted in philosophy"). Italian translation by A. Dall'Asta and P. Perrone. In *Di-segno: La giustizia nel discorso*, edited by in Gianfranco Dalmasso. Milan: Jaca Book, 1984.

– *La mano di Heidegger* (*Heidegger's Hand*). Rome-Bari: Laterza, 1991.

– *Of Grammatology*. Corrected edition. Translated by Gayatry Spivak. Baltimore and London: The Johns Hopkins University Press, 1974. (Original title *De la grammatologie*).

– *Positions*. Translated and annotated by Alan Bass. Chicago: University of Chicago Press, 1981.

– *Spectres of Marx: The State of Debt, the Work of Mourning, and the New International*. Translated by Peggy Kamuf. New York; London: Routledge, 2006. (Original title *Spectres de Marx*).

– *Writing and Difference*. Translated with an introduction by Alan Bass. London: Routledge & K. Paul, 1978. (Original title *L'Écriture et la différence*).

Derrida, Jacques, and Maurizio Ferraris. *A Taste for the Secret*. Translated from the French and the Italian by Giacomo Donis. Edited by Giacomo Donis and David Webb. Cambridge, UK: Polity Press, 2001. (Original title *Le goût du secret*).

De Waelhens, Alphonse. *Chemins et impasses de l'ontologie heidéggerienne: A propos des "Holzwege."* Louvrain: E. Nauwelaerts, 1953.

Di Cesare, Donatella. *Heidegger e gli ebrei: I "Quaderni neri"* (Heidegger and the Jews: "The Black Notebooks"). Turin: Bollati Boringhieri, 2014.

– *Heidegger & Sons. Eredità e futuro di un filosofo* (Heidegger & Sons. The Legacy and future of a philosopher). Turin: Bollati Boringhieri, 2015.

Dostoevsky, Fyodor. *The Possessed or The Devils*. 1871. https://freeditorial.com/en/books/the-possessed-or-the-devils. (Accessed 12 June 2020).

Einstein, Albert. Letter to Bohr from 4 December 1926. In *Scienza e vita. Lettere 1916–1955*, edited by Albert Einstein, Max Born, and Hedwig Born. Translated by Giuseppe Scattone. Milan: Mimesis, 2015.

Farias, Victor. *Heidegger and Nazism*. Philadelphia, PA: Temple University, 1987. (Original title *Heidegger et le nazisme*).

Faye, Emmanuel. *Heidegger, the Introduction of Nazism into Philosophy*. Translated by Michael B. Smith. New Haven, CT: Yale University Press, 2009. (Original title *Heidegger, L'introduction du nazisme dans la philosophie*).

Finkelstein, Norman G. *The Holocaust Industry: Reflection on the Exploitation of Jewish Suffering.* London–New York: VERSO, 2000.

Foucault, Michel. *Archivio Foucault: Interventi, colloqui, interviste 3: 1978–1985. Estetica dell'esistenza, etica, politica* (Foucault archive: essays, papers, interviews 3: 1978–1985. Aesthetics of existence, ethics, politics), edited by Alessandro Pandolfi. Milan: Feltrinelli, 1998.

– *Microfisica del potere: Interventi politici* (Microphysics of power: Political essays). Turin: Einaudi, 1977.

Gadamer, Hans Georg. *The Relevance of the Beautiful and Other Essays.* Translated by Nicholas Walker. Edited by Robert Bernasconi. Cambridge; New York: Cambridge University Press, 1986.

– *Truth and Method.* Translated and edited by Garrett Barden and John Cumming. London: Sheed & Ward, 1975.

Gallino, Luciano. *Il colpo di stato di banche e governi: L'attacco alla democrazia in Europa* (The coup d'état by banks and governments: The attack on democracy in Europe). Turin: Einaudi, 2013.

Glock, Hans-Johann. *What Is Analytical Philosophy*? Cambridge: Cambridge University Press, 2008.

– *A Wittgenstein Dictionary.* Oxford & Cambridge, MA: Blackwell Reference, 1996.

Heidegger, Martin. *Being and Time.* Translated by John Macquarrie and Edward Robinson. Oxford: Blackwell, 2001.

– *Besinnung (1938–1939)* Edited by F.W. von Herrmann. Frankfurt am Main: Klostermann, 1997.

– *Contributi alla filosofia dell'evento* (Contributions to philosophy). Edited by Franco Volpi, and Alessandra Iadicicco. Milan: Adelphi, 2007.

– "Hölderlin and the Essence of Poetry." In *The Heidegger Reader*, edited by Günter Figal. Translated by Jerome Veith. Bloomington: Indiana University Press, 2009.

– *Identità e differenza* (Identity and difference). Milan: Adelphi, 2009.

– *La poesia di Hölderlin* (The poetry of Hölderlin). Milan: Adelphi, 1988.

– *Letter on Humanism.* Translated by Frank A. Capuzzi. 1995. http://www2.hawaii.edu/~freeman/courses/phil360/17.%20Heidegger%27s%20Letter%20On%20Humanism.pdf (Accessed 12 June 2020).

– "Ormai solo un dio ci può salvare" ("Now only a God can save us"). In *Scritti politici, 1933–1960* (Political writings, 1933–1960), edited by Gino Zaccaria. Casale Monferrato: Piemme, 1998.

– *The Question concerning Technology and Other Essays.* Translated by William Lovitt. New York & London: Garland Publishing, Inc., 1977.

– *Segnavia*. Milan: Adelphi, 1987. (Original title *Wegmarken*).
– *What Is Called Thinking?* New York: Harper and Row, 1968.
– *Zur Sache des Denkens (1962–1964)*. Edited by F.W. von Herrmann. Frankfurt am Main: Klostermann, 2007. Italian translation of first part in *Tempo e essere*. Edited by Eugenio Mazzarella. Naples: Guidi, 1988.
Hölderlin, Friedrich. "Conciliatore, tu che non m'hai creduto" (Conciliator, you that no longer believed in me). In *Liriche* (Poems). Milan: Adelphi, 1993.
– "Pieno di merito, ma poeticamente abita l'uomo su questa terra" (Full of merit, but poetically man lives on this earth). In *Amabile azzurro* (Lovely blue), edited by Ernesto Forcellino. In *Pensieri* (*Thoughts*) 2 (2002): 85–6.
Hessel, Stéphane. *Time for Outrage!* Translated by Damion Searls with Alba Arrikha. London: Quartet Book, 2011. (Original title *Indignez-vous!*).
Jaspers, Karl. *Psicologia delle visioni del mondo* (The Psychology of Worldviews). Rome: Astrolabio, 1950. (Original title *Psychologie der Weltanschauunge*).
Mangabeira Unger, Roberto. *Democrazia ad alta energia: manifesto per la sinistra del XXI secolo* (High energy democracy: manifesto for the left of the twenty-first century). Rome: Fazi, 2007.
Martinengo, A. *Introduzione a Reiner Schürmann* (Introduction to Robert Schürmann). Rome: Meltemi, 2008.
Marx, Karl. "Theses on Feuerbach." 1972. https://www.marxists.org/archive/marx/works/1845/theses/theses.htm (Accessed 12 June 2020).
Monk, Ray. *Ludwig Wittgenstein. The Duty of the Genius*. London: Jonathan Cape, 1990.
Nadler, Steven. *Baruch Spinoza e l'Olanda del Seicento*. Turin: Einaudi, 2002. (Original title *Spinoza: a life*).
– *Un libro forgiato all'inferno*. Turin: Einaudi, 2013. (Original title *A Book Forged in Hell*).
Nancy, Jean-Luc. *The Experience of Freedom*. Translated by Bridget McDonald. Stanford, CA: Stanford University Press, 1993. (Original title *L'expérience de la liberté*).
Nietzsche, Friedrich. *Frammenti postumi 1876–1878* (Posthumous fragments 1876–1878), second part: *Il viandante e la sua ombra* (The wanderer and his shadow). In *Opere di Friedrich Nietzsche* (Complete works of Friedrich Nietzsche), vol. 4, tome 3. Milan: Adelphi, 1967.

– *Frammenti postumi 1885–1887* (Posthumous fragments 1885–1887). In *Opere di Friedrich Nietzsche* (Complete works of Friedrich Nietzsche), vol. 8, tome 1. Milan: Adelphi, 1975.
– *The Gay Science*. Translated by Monika M. Langer. New York: Palgrave Macmillan, 2010.
– *Human All Too Human*. Translated by Ruth Abbey. Edinburgh: Edinburgh University Press, 2020.
– *Thus Spake Zarathustra*. Translated by Thomas Common. Edinburgh: T.N. Foulis, 1911.
Nussbaum, Martha. *Political Emotions: Why Love Matters for Politics*. Cambridge, MA: Belknap Press of Harvard University Press, 2013.
Otto, Rudolf. *The Idea of the Holy: An Inquiry into the Non-Rational Factor in the Idea of the Divine and Its Relation to the Rational*. Translated by John W. Harvey. London: H. Milford and Oxford University Press, 1923.
Pappé, Ilan. *Out of the Frame. The Struggle for Academic Freedom in Israel*. London: Pluto Press, 2010.
Pareyson, Luigi. *Esistenza e persona* (Existence and personhood). Genoa: Il Melangolo, 1985.
– *Ontologia della libertà* (Ontology of freedom). Turin: Einaudi, 1995.
Pascal, Blaise. *Thoughts*. Selected and translated by Moritz Kaufmann. Cambridge and New York: Cambridge University Press, 2013.
Plato. *Sophist*. Translated by Nicholas P. White. Cambridge, MA: Hackett Publishing, 1993.
Quine, Willard van Orman. "Che cosa c'è" (On what there is). In *Da un punto di vista logico: Saggi logico-filosofico* (From a logical perspective: Logical-philosophical essays), 13–33. Milan: Raffaello Cortina, 2004.
Rorty, Richard. *Consequences of Pragmatism: Essays 1972–1980*. Minneapolis: University of Minnesota Press, 1986.
– *Philosophy and the Mirror of Nature*. Princeton, NJ: Princeton University Press, 1979.
– "Solidarity or Objectivity?" In *Relativism: Interpretation and Confrontation*, edited by Michael Kratz, 167–83. Notre Dame: University of Notre Dame Press, 1989.
– *Take Care of Freedom and Truth Will Take Care of Itself*. Edited by Eduardo Mendieta. Stanford, CA: Stanford University Press, 2006.
– *Una sinistra per il prossimo secolo: L'eredità dei movimenti progressisti americani del Novecento* (A left for the next century: The legacy of

American twentieth-century progressive movements). Milan: Garzanti, 1999.

– *Verità e libertà: Conversazioni con Richard Rory. Il testamento spirituale di uno dei principali filosofi americani* (Truth and freedom: Conversations with Richard Rorty. The spiritual testament of one of the principal American philosophers). Massa, Italy: Transeuropa, 2008.

Rorty, Richard, and Gianni Vattimo. *Il futuro della religione. Solidarietà, carità, ironia*. Milan: Garzanti, 2005. (Original title *The Future of Religion. Solidarity, Charity, Irony*).

Sartre, Jean-Paul. *Existentialism Is a Humanism*. Translated by Carol Macomber. New Haven: Yale University Press, 2007. (Original title *L'existentialisme est un humanisme*).

– *Huis Clos* (No exit). Paris: Gallimard, 1972.

Schürmann, Reiner. *Heidegger on Being and Acting: From Principles to Anarchy.* Translated by Christine-Marie Gros in collaboration with the author. Bloomington: Indiana University Press, 1987. (Original title *Principes d'anarchie*).

Simmel, Georg. *Le metropoli e la vita dello spirito* (The metropolis and mental life) Rome: Armando, 1996.

Sparti, Davide. *Wittgenstein politico* (The political Wittgenstein). Milan: Feltrinelli, 2000.

Spengler, Oswald. *The Decline of the West.* Authorized translation with notes by Charles Francis Atkins. New York: Knopf, 1926.

Spinoza, Baruch. *Trattato politico*. Edited by Paolo Cristofomini. Pisa: ETS, 2004. (Original title *Tractatus politico-philosophicus*).

Vattimo, Gianni. *Della realtà. Fini della filosofia* (Of reality: The purposes of philosophy). Milan: Garzanti, 2012.

– *Dios es comunista: Conversaciones con Manuel Gonzalez Magnasco y Adriana Farias (1987 y 2013)*. Caba, Argentina: Editoria FEDUN, Azcuènaga 770, n.d.

– "Gadamer and the Problem of Ontology." In *Gadamer's Century*, edited by Jeff Malpas, Ulrich von Arnswald, and Jens Kertscher, 299–306. Cambridge, MA: MIT Press, 2002.

– *La società trasparente* (The transparent society). Milan: Garzanti, 1989.

– "Pensiero debole e pensiero dei deboli" (Weak thought and the thought of the weak). In *Of Reality: The Purposes of Philosophy*, translated by Robert T. Valgente, 208–16. New York: Columbia University Press, 2012.

Vattimo, Gianni, and Pier Aldo Rovati, eds. *Il pensiero debole* (Weak thought). Milan: Feltrinelli, 1983.

Vattimo, Gianni, and Santiago Zabala. *Comunismo ermeneutico: da Heidegger a Marx.* (Hermeneutic communism: from Heidegger to Marx). Milan: Garzanti, 2014.

Volpi, Franco. "È ancora possibile un'etica? Heidegger e la filosofia pragmatica" (Is an ethics still possible? Heidegger and pragmatic philosophy). In *Acta Philosophica* 2 (2002): 291–313.

– "Goodbye, Heidegger! Mi Introducion Censurada a los 'Beiträge zur Philosophie.'" In *Fenomenología y Hermenéutica. Actas del 1 Congresso Internacionalde Fenomenología y Hermenéutica*, edited by S. Eyzaguirre Tafra, 43–63. Santiago, Chile: Universidad Andres Bello, 2008.

Wallach, Lori M. "Le traitè transatlantique, un typhon qui menace les Europèens." *Le Monde diplomatique*, November 2013, 4–5.

Wittgenstein, Ludwig. *On Certainty*. Edited by G.E.M. Anscombe and G.H. von Wright. Translated by Denis Paul, and G.E.M. Anscombe. Oxford: Basil Blackwell, 1969. (Original title *Uber Gewissheit*).

– *Pensieri diversi* (Thoughts). Milan: Adelphi, 1980.

– *Tractatus Logico-Philosophicus*. Translated by C.K. Ogden. Mineola, New York: Dover Publications, Inc. 1999.

Zabala, Santiago. *The Remains of Being: Hermeneutic Ontology after Metaphysics*. New York: Columbia University Press, 2009.

Zolo, Danilo. *Il nuovo disordine mondiale* (The new global disorder). Reggio Emilia: Diabasis, 2010.

Index